Praise for *It's OK to Go Up the Slide*

"In her thought-provoking new book, Shumaker challenges some of our assumptions as parents and teachers. She shows us clearly and candidly what kids truly need. This is a helpful and inspiring read for anyone concerned with raising the next generation of healthy children."

—Michael Gurian, author of *The Wonder of Boys* and *The Wonder of Girls*

"Heather Shumaker, the agent-provocateur of the young childhood set, is back in fine form with *It's OK to Go Up the Slide*. By refusing to accept received wisdom without questioning it, Shumaker makes the reader think about what children really need when it comes to safety, homework, technology, and interpersonal interactions. She'll provoke you to think afresh in places where you didn't even think there was a choice."

—Lawrence J. Cohen, PhD, author of *Playful Parenting*

"Anyone willing to stop and ask, 'Wait—why do we have to sign our kids' homework?' is on the right track. The fact that Heather Shumaker stops to re-examine almost all the conventional wisdom about childhood to figure out which of it is based on anything other than, 'That's just how it's done' makes her my hero."

—Lenore Skenazy, author of *Free-Range Kids: How to Raise Safe, Self-Reliant Children (Without Going Nuts with Worry)*

"Sensible and provocative. This book will turn notions about kids, families, and schools upside down. From homework to strangers to technology, Shumaker tackles all the big topics facing the preschool to the elementary set. Do your family or classroom a favor and grab this book."

—Amy McCready, author of *The "Me, Me, Me" Epidemic* and *If I Ha͞ ͞ Tell You One More Time* . . .

"Once again, Heather Shumaker chall͞   ͞   ͞stioned assumptions about child-raising with such clar͞   ͞   ͞ why her points weren't glaringly obvious to yo͞   ͞   ͞ddressing the issues of middle childhood, S͞   ͞   ͞g case on issues from 'safety first' (which pose͞   ͞   ͞hild than healthy risk) to kindergarten (your chil͞   ͞   ͞). Parents will especially love the 'cheat sheets' where S͞   ͞   ͞gested words to use to implement these renegade rules in real l͞   ͞

—Dr. Laura ͞   ͞   ͞am, author of *Peaceful Parent, Happy Kids*

"Heather Shumaker's comprehensive and courageous on-target book emanates common sense grounded in solid research. For parents desiring the best for their children, it can serve as a practical guide to responsible resistance to unsound current educational/parental dogmas."

—**Stuart Brown, M.D., founder and president of the National Institute for Play**

"The norms of parenting today—with their overconcern for safety and promotion of continuous surveillance and control—are stifling our children. In this delightful book, Heather Shumaker teaches us how to be renegade parents, willing and able to flout the norms in order to promote the long-term mental and physical health of our kids. I recommend it not just to parents but to anyone involved with the lives of young children."

—**Peter Gray, research professor of psychology at Boston College and author of** *Free to Learn*

"This book is chock full of reasons for joining the renegade army! In a gentle, yet direct fashion, Heather encourages us to remove our adult lenses and take a hard look at how some of our own actions lead to many of our family's stressors. She leaves us with supportive next steps and a powerful sense of 'I can do this!'"

—**Lisa Murphy, M.Ed., early childhood specialist and cofounder of Ooey Gooey, Inc.**

"This book frees parents from unfounded fears that limit their children's ability to climb, jump, run, and express themselves honestly, replacing that fear with a courageous style of parenting that benefits the child."

—**Vicki Hoefle, parent educator, speaker, and author of** *Duct Tape Parenting* **and** *A Straight Talk on Parenting*

"School needs a revolution. Parenting needs a revolution. Guess what? The revolution has arrived. It's time to go up the slide."

—**Anthony DeBenedet, M.D., coauthor of** *The Art of Roughhousing*

"I'm in love with Heather Shumaker's new book, *It's OK to Go Up the Slide*— it's going to rock boats, challenge thinking, and nudge adults in the right direction when it comes to early learning. The book's Renegade Rules often swim against the current of conventional thinking, but they are based on solid research, shared with warmth and humor, and come with ample ideas for implementation. This is a must-read for both parents and early learning professionals."

—**Jeff A. Johnson, coauthor of** *Let Them Play*

"Shumaker is like the wise elder we need beside us. In this day and age when recess and play have been set aside for worksheets and sitting still, we need to hear and heed her voice. Every parent, caregiver, teacher, and administrator will want to return to this book over and over again. Bravo to Shumaker for encouraging us to reclaim our children's childhoods."

—**Sara Bennett, coauthor of** *The Case Against Homework* **and founder of Stop Homework**

"More play. Less homework. More risks. Less sheltering and entertaining. What sounds contrarian is actually common sense that's great for our kids! Shumaker helps us put this into practice with tools like her 'words to say (and avoid)' and terrific 'try this' suggestions."

—**Paula Spencer Scott, content chief at Kinstantly and author of** *Momfidence*

"Heather Shumaker demystifies modern parenting in this immensely practical book, tackling tricky topics like technology and risk-taking. She advocates for a balanced and sensible approach to parenting that gives families tools to wade through the oceans of parenting advice. This book continues the revolution that her first book began—hold on!"

—**Emily Plank, author of** *Discovering the Culture of Childhood*

"This is the book I have been waiting for. Heather again has provided us with practical and respectful parenting advice for the child entering the big world of the elementary school years. This book is tender and completely engaging. You will want to keep it with you at all times."

—**Daniel Hodgins, author of** *Boys: Changing the Classroom, Not the Child* **and** *Get Over It: Relearning Guidance Practices*

HEATHER SHUMAKER

JEREMY P. TARCHER/PENGUIN   AN IMPRINT OF PENGUIN RANDOM HOUSE   NEW YORK

It's
OK
to GO
UP
the SLIDE

Renegade Rules
for Raising Confident
and Creative Kids

Jeremy P. Tarcher/Penguin
An imprint of Penguin Random House LLC
375 Hudson Street
New York, New York 10014

Most Tarcher/Penguin books are available at special quantity discounts for bulk
purchase for sales promotions, premiums, fund-raising, and educational needs.
Special books or book excerpts also can be created to fit specific needs. For
details, write: SpecialMarkets@penguinrandomhouse.com.

Library of Congress Cataloging-in-Publication Data
Names: Shumaker, Heather, author.
Title: It's ok to go up the slide : renegade rules for raising
confident and creative kids / Heather Shumaker.
Description: New York : Tarcher, 2016. | Includes index.
Identifiers: LCCN 2015046241 | ISBN 9780399172007 (paperback)
Subjects: LCSH: Child rearing. | Parenting. | Child development. |
Education-Parent participation. | Confidence in children. | Creative
ability in children. | BISAC: FAMILY & RELATIONSHIPS / Parenting /
General. | FAMILY & RELATIONSHIPS / Life Stages | School Age.
Classification: LCC HQ769 .S545333 2016 | DDC 306.874—dc23

Printed in the United States of America
1   3   5   7   9   10   8   6   4   2

Book design by Ellen Cipriano

Thanks to the Fred Rogers Company for permission to quote dialogue
from a 1968 *Mister Rogers' Neighborhood* special program.

To my mother and SYC.

And to

my teachers at

Indianola Informal Elementary School:

Ann, Sue, John, and

especially Ruth

Author's Note

I am once again grateful to the many families and teachers who shared their stories to bring these ideas to life. The age and sex of children depicted in the book have not been altered, but names and some individual details have been changed to protect family privacy. Real names were retained when referring to experts.

Contents

Introduction

This is not a typical parenting book. It's a book that intentionally selects the tricky topics. It takes the renegade approach: rethinking ideas we take for granted.

A reader summed up my first book by saying: "If you like respectful parenting, but are baffled by your child's intense emotions and behavior when she hits the preschool years, *It's OK Not to Share* is the answer." This second book takes you to the next step. Our kids are still young, but they're entering school, gaining independence, and encountering school expectations, some of which fly in the face of healthy child development.

The Golden Rule in my first book was this: "It's OK if it's not hurting people or property." For this book, the guiding principle is one of my mother's mantras: "If something's bothering you, it's time to make a change." This covers the feeling you have that something's wrong when your seven-year-old has gym class instead of recess, your kindergartener cries with stomachaches on school days, or technology use in your family is "just not right." Listen to what your gut's been telling you. As you read on, it's reassuring to realize the child development reasons why your gut might be right.

When kids hit school, we must parent at the next level: the level of community. Our children have so many outside teachers, including classroom teachers, principals, school bus peers, strangers, and the ever-present screen. What are our kids learning from all these other teachers? Is their time well spent? Parenting involves many partners now.

It's OK to Go Up the Slide is meant to be a thoughtful guide during these preschool, kindergarten, and elementary school years. "Write about girls this time," parents said. "Write about 'you can't come to my party,'" teachers suggested. Inside you'll find an array of topics that includes princess dress-up play, mean words, screen time, recess, and homework, plus heavy subjects such as talking about stranger risk and news disasters. You can find books focused on these individual topics, but we are parenting a whole child. All these topics matter to us. All of them affect our children. This book gathers together a suite of topics relevant to your family and daily life.

This book is intended as a bridge between child development research and actions in everyday life. The gap between what we *know* about kids and what we *do* about kids is ever widening. As we leap forward with new knowledge about children, we need to stay open to new ideas and be flexible. Familiar routines are comfortable and can be hard to change, but we owe it to the kids to make courageous change. Schools need to reconsider policies (kindergarten, recess) and we've-always-done-it-that-way practices (circle time, homework). Parents need to reinvent parenting (technology, risk, strangers). We all have to be ready to tip what we "know" upside down. We have to be willing to cross prevailing attitudes and go up the slide.

My first book was born from the unorthodox philosophy of the School for Young Children, a preschool in my hometown of Columbus, Ohio, where my mother taught for forty years. I've drawn on the wisdom of this unique preschool again for this book, but certainly many of the topics—including recess, screens, and signing homework papers—go beyond the scope of this preschool. Chapters dealing with elementary-aged children are based primarily on research and my own experiences as a renegade parent. I'm grateful to all the scholars and families who have helped me shape these ideas.

Some of the chapters grew out of a blog post I wrote about our family's unusual stance on elementary school homework. I've heard from hundreds of families and educators around the world, some explaining homework's virtues, others writing in tears about how homework is disrupting their family. Homework is one hot-button topic.

When I mention banning homework in elementary school, parents and teachers frequently look at me in shock. These are folks with four-year college degrees, and often law school degrees or Ph.D.'s. They know serious studying takes hard work, and remember their own childhoods, which typically included some homework. What they don't know is this: Research shows no evidence that homework has academic benefit in elementary school and shows very little impact in middle school. I'm not proposing an all-out ban on homework throughout life, but there are better things to do with a young child's time.

We can continue to do the opposite of what science says on topics of risk, recess, play, screens, school, and homework, or we can take the courageous step and begin to change the world, one class, one school, one family at a time.

We are bound to disagree at times. It's OK if you love one chapter and can't stand the next. My hope is this book will help you clarify your personal renegade convictions, spark new thinking, and inspire adults to make the world a better fit for children. Sometimes that means going up the slide.

The list of Children's Renegade Rights set out in *It's OK Not to Share* focused on early childhood and play. There's a need to expand this list. Here is a guide to young children's rights in the twenty-first century, including rights in schooling and in a screen-busy world.

MORE CHILDREN'S RIGHTS

A right to plentiful, unstructured free play
A right to experience independence
A right to take risks and make mistakes
A right to set limits on others' behavior
A right to be in charge of his own body

A right to age-appropriate learning
A right to regular, daily school recess
A right to be free from homework in elementary
  school
A right to be outside daily
A right to move her body vigorously
A right to adequate sleep

A right to engage in the world in which he's
  growing up
A right to interact with the real, non-screen world
  for the majority of her day
A right to learn and practice face-to-face social skills
A right to times of quiet
A right to learn healthy boundaries for technology
A right to receive regular, full attention from people
  around her

A right to have these rights consistently supported by adults

This book demands more courage from us. It means making changes to our parenting and it means reaching out to other adults. As M. Scott Peck says: "Our finest moments are most likely to occur when we are feeling deeply uncomfortable, unhappy or unfulfilled. For it is only in such moments, propelled by our discomfort, that we are likely to step out of our ruts and start searching for different ways or truer answers."

When my courage falters, I think of my mother and all the times she had to step beyond her mild nature to advocate for her children. If she could do it, I can do it. You will find your strength to go up the slide, too.

Section I

RISK and INDEPENDENCE

Security is mostly superstition. . . . Life is either a daring adventure or nothing.

—HELEN KELLER

RULE

1 Safety Second

E ven before my first child was born, I was drilled on his safety. Our childbirth class instructor passed out lists of poisonous houseplants along with correct car seat buckling and a host of other hazards. Suddenly dangers loomed everywhere.

It's no wonder we fixate on kids' safety. During the baby and toddler years, tots careen from one hazard to the next, from toppling into buckets to running into traffic. We learn to be ever vigilant about plastic bags, grapes, and marbles.

Toddlerhood primes parents for overprotection. But that's not what older kids need. Childhood is a time of risk—healthy risk. Preschool and elementary kids need independence from our presence so they can grow socially, emotionally, creatively, and physically.

Renegade Reason

Childhood is a time of constant risk. Safety first carries greater danger than healthy risk.

E. B. White writes in *Charlotte's Web* about the rope swing Fern played on in her uncle's barn: "Mothers for miles around worried about Zuckerman's swing. They feared some child would fall off. But no child ever did. Children almost always hang onto things tighter than their parents think they will."

Kids have always needed more risk than doting parents are comfortable with. Risk gives children critical skills, including risk assessment, dexterity, resilience, and social savvy.

At the School for Young Children, my childhood preschool, heavy, potentially toe-smashing bricks are part of the playground. Stacks of them. Children as young as three are welcome to lug five-pound bricks around, build teetering walls, and incorporate them into games, narrowly avoiding pinching their fingers. No one says, "Be careful." "We've had bricks for forty years and not one incident," says Jan Waters, a past director.

"You can't be too careful," you hear people say. Actually, you can. Focusing too heavily on safety stunts our kids.

Life is about change, challenge, risk, and growth. We can't be alive without risk. Our children can't be fully alive—and learn what they need to learn as growing humans—without the benefits of risk. Encountering risk gives children their chance to claim the world— to be who they are, in the world they find.

We are caregivers for our kids. Our job is to keep our children safe. But that's only one of our jobs.

Renegade Blessings ||||||||||||||||||||||||||||||||||||||||||||||||||||||||||||||||||||||||||||||||||||||||||||||||

A child who grows up taking healthy risks is more apt to be cautious about dangerous risks. She'll also gain confidence, independence, and a sense of joy in the world.

The world is wonderful.
I'm ready to try new things.

I know what my body can do.

I know what my limits are.

No one's forcing me. I can take new chances when
   I'm ready.

Sometimes I goof up. That's normal. I can try again.

Really bad things can happen. You have to watch out.

It's OK to get bumped or feel sad sometimes.

My parents aren't always bugging me.

Adults around me think I'm capable.

Why It Works

Childhood is full of taking risks and reaching out. For a child, every-thing's new. Making friends, talking to people outside the family, being sad, trying to draw a picture, climbing high, running fast. So is handling a hammer, a bicycle, and a sharp knife. Taking risks is how kids learn new things. Risk is not the problem. Risk is neces-sary to life. The key is to separate fear from risk and healthy risk from dangerous risk.

"Risk has become a four-letter word in the U.S.—something to protect children from at all costs," writes Joan Almon. She's the di-rector of the nonprofit Alliance for Childhood and author of the booklet *Adventure: The Value of Risk in Children's Play.* She observes that children take on as much adventure as they are ready for. Ac-cording to Almon, "The benefits of experiencing risk need to be weighed against the harm done by never learning to cope with it. The latter can be truly dangerous."

Kids become safer when they gain experience using their bodies. A child's body is constantly changing, so kids are keen to experiment with the new model and see what it can do. When children use their bodies and test their own limits they gain body awareness and a sense of those limits. They also gain dexterity, balance, and strength. Giving children a chance to take risks puts them in a position as partners in their own safety.

Physical risk with playmates—tickle fests, wrestling, roughhousing, and other rough partner play—helps kids learn trust, impulse control, body awareness, and setting limits on play partners. Stuart Brown, of the National Institute for Play, says that this kind of play is necessary for young social mammals. Besides teaching physical and social skills, it trains them to deal with unpredictability, allowing them to approach life with flexibility. Even flexibility takes practice.

Research collected from Adventure playgrounds, in Houston, found that allowing children to enjoy risky play did not bring higher accident rates, and insurance companies in Germany reported lower accident rates at Adventure playgrounds than at playgrounds designed to be safe. Gever Tulley and Julie Spiegler, coauthors of *50 Dangerous Things (You Should Let Your Children Do)*, say childhood risk helps kids become adults who are confident, resilient, and adventurous. As Tulley writes, "the best way to be safe is to learn how to judge danger." Experiencing risk helps children gain skills in recognizing, assessing, and reducing risk.

Risk is not just physical. Children need to take social and emotional risks, too. This includes getting their feelings hurt, being told no, feeling left out sometimes, and experiencing anger, frustration, jealousy, and sorrow. Social rejection gives kids practice for developing resiliency. The more often they dare to try a new friendship or social relationship, the more often they encounter a range of reactions and can adjust and try again. Learning social nuances takes practice.

Taking risk develops the frontal lobe of the brain. That's the same area needed for executive functions, including concentration, memory, flexibility, and problem solving.

A university research team in New Zealand concluded that removing risk is more dangerous to children in the long run. What's more, risk has to be experienced, not "taught." "[Children] have to learn risk on their own terms," says Grant Schofield, a professor of public health who worked on the project. "They have to get out there."

Kids of all ages seek challenges. Our job is to equip them with tools to cope and be brave enough ourselves to let go and let kids face risks and challenges. As early childhood educator Bev Bos says, "Risk propels us forward and helps us trust ourselves."

Take Off Your Adult Lenses

We equate risk with danger. But *risk* is not a bad word. Healthy risk should be our ally; it helps us raise our kids and lets them develop into competent, confident people. We long to shield our children from mishaps in life. We're not in the mood for another spill, mess, or tear-filled scene that could result from kids making mistakes and assessing risk on their own. But kids need this constant series of risks to develop judgment, skill, and confidence. If safety is always first, children can become afraid to try new things. Fear can stop children from trying. But often it's *our* fear that stops them. Overprotection can be more harmful than risk.

Welcoming Risk

My father encouraged me to run down hills, leap across streams, and fall—especially fall. He'd grown up clambering on granite rocks in New England. "The important thing is to know how to fall," he said. "Most people don't know how to fall right, and that's when they get hurt." He taught me to roll with the fall, rather than try to avoid it and put my hands out. The assumption was: Life will have plenty of falls. Know what to do. Get up. Don't be scared to try.

Welcoming risk first means acknowledging that we can't eliminate it. What if the worst happens? Caring for a living child involves both joy and terror. The child we love might get seriously hurt or die. As author Elizabeth Stone says, "Making the decision to have a child—it is momentous. It is to decide forever to have your heart go walking around outside your body." It scares us to have that piece of our heart walking around. But soon it will not only be walking, but climbing trees, crossing streets solo, and riding buses alone.

We need to stop chasing the illusion of total safety. Being alive simply means there's a chance we will meet pain, no matter how careful we are. Knowing we cannot eliminate risk frees us up to embrace life. We cannot eliminate all risk, but we cannot be paralyzed by risk either.

Dangers of Limiting Risk

"Be careful!" "Get down from there!" "You'll get hurt!" Too much of this message can cause kids to shrink back and avoid all risk, even necessary risks. Education professors Howard Gardner and Katie Davis, authors of *The App Generation*, say that today's children are becoming more averse to risk. Instead of exploring and trying things out by themselves, they wait to see what adults want them to do. We add to this by tethering our children to us. Nine-year-olds get cell phones. Seven-year-olds don't walk to the park alone.

I passed by another empty playground the other day. It could be that all the kids are indoors attached to screens, but there's another factor at work here. Many kids find modern playgrounds boring.

Legal worries, licensing, and outright fear cause adults to limit children's access to reasonable risk. A report by Kristen Copeland and colleagues in the journal *Pediatrics* found that kids are "primarily sedentary" as preschoolers in childcare settings. The main barrier to children's active movement was simply adult fear of "someone getting hurt." The new play equipment required by licensing didn't interest the children. In the same report, a teacher said, "They're walking up the slide much more than they ever did. . . . You can see they are just trying to find those challenges."

Walking up the slide is just one way children show us their need for risk.

Why Kids Go Up the Slide

If you've ever been on a public playground, you know one of the biggest controversies is this: Should kids be allowed to go up the slide?

"All kids, if left alone, want to go up the slide at some point," says Jan Waters.

Why do kids go up the slide? They are seeking risk and challenge in their play. Kids feel powerful scaling the slide. Going up the slide is fun. It's healthy adventure, often part of imaginative play. Climbing the slide helps kids test their strength, find their limits and gain balance, spatial awareness, and yes, social awareness and consideration. If a conflict comes up—another child wants to slide down—it's a prime opportunity for kids to practice problem solving in their play.

Like all play, slide play should follow the Renegade Golden Rule: It's OK if it's not hurting people or property. That could mean setting limits, such as: "Wait until the child at the bottom is out of the way before you slide"; or "The red slide is too high. You can go up the blue one"; or "It's crowded at the park today. The slide's only for going down right now."

Relax the parents around you: "It's OK with me if they go up" or "Seems as if they're doing fine."

Up or down, a slide is for play. Child-directed, sometimes risky play.

The Risks of Risk

FOR THE CHILD
Mostly bumps, bruises, and skinned knees
Being sad
Being temporarily lost or scared
Getting feelings hurt
Being frustrated when an idea doesn't work
Making a mistake

FOR THE GROWN-UP
Feeling guilty and anxious
Taking time to cope with mess, bandages, or feelings
Adjusting to a new role of not being needed

Healthy Risk

We limit four key areas for our kids: physical risk, creative risk, social risk, and emotional risk. Observe what you tend to limit in your child's life. For some of us it's primarily physical, such as running on concrete or playing with sticks. For too many of us (despite our best intentions) it's creative risk, which comes alive in free play during unstructured time. Social and emotional risk are not always recognized as the risks they are, but these risks include making mistakes, experiencing rejection, interacting in public, solving conflicts, and feeling scared, sad, and angry.

REWARDS OF HEALTHY RISK

Risk helps kids . . .
Strive and challenge themselves
Try new things
Try something slightly beyond their comfort level

Keep trying

Stay curious

Develop persistence

Gain resiliency

Practice failing and recovering

Decrease urge for inappropriate risk with chance for
appropriate risk

Experience and cope with difficult emotions
(fear, embarrassment, frustration, sadness)

Manage fear

Overcome fear

Gauge speed, distance, and slippery conditions

Learn how to fall

Develop increased body awareness, dexterity, and skill

Judge danger

Cultivate flexible thinking

Make new friends

Think up new ideas

Gain practice reading others' emotions and reactions

Deal with setbacks

Take reasonable chances

Gain pride in newfound abilities

Begin to understand who they are

Develop responsibility for their own safety

Reduce power struggles

Discover joy in independence

Physical Risk

Physical risk for kids is about trying things with their bodies: running fast (and too fast), climbing high, using sharp tools, pouring and
spilling, wrestling, crossing streets, riding bikes, balancing on walls.
It also involves experimenting with their bodies in nature: putting

sticks in a fire, climbing trees, jumping over streams, or rock hopping. The risk involved is not always bruises and bumps; sometimes it's mess. Physical risk for a child may mean climbing trees or it may mean pouring her own milk.

My six-year-old and his friend, Ava, delighted in taking the physical risk of jumping over a manure pile. It was pumpkin-patch season, and despite the attractions of the corn maze and doughnuts, their greatest thrill was the risk involved in running and straddling the giant pile of horse poo at the last minute. Risky. The only real risk involved was that they'd have to scrub their shoes under the hose. After twenty leaps, they never missed.

My childhood preschool provides a workbench with real hammers and saws for four- and five-year-olds. As former director Jan Waters explains, the school waits to give kids real tools until they're four, an age when children have more hand-eye coordination. The saws and their sharp teeth have never drawn blood. "Kids have hit their finger with the hammers," she reports. "So what? That's how they learn to pound and avoid their fingers. Kids need to try stuff."

Preschool teachers working in Montessori schools devote a section of learning to practical life skills, which may involve cutting cucumbers or apples with a sharp kitchen knife or using a hot iron. Inviting children to use real tools, with real consequences, helps put them in charge of their own risk and safety, plus it gives kids a sense of mastery and independence.

When we shout out, "You'll get hurt!" and nothing happens, it can make kids doubt our judgment. "No, I won't!" they shout back, and then think to themselves: *See? I didn't get hurt.*

Ellen Sandseter, a professor of early childhood education in Norway, noted that children's need for physically risky play commonly falls into six categories: 1) climbing high, 2) handling sharp knives or other tools that feel dangerous, 3) playing near fire or water, 4) play fighting and rough-and-tumble play, 5) going too fast, and 6) exploring without adults around. My first book, *It's OK Not to Share*, devotes a section to boxing, wrestling, and other rough-and-tumble play and describes children's needs for physical motion and power behaviors.

> ## With life comes risk and change.

Creative Risk

Creative risk is the risk of ideas. It means deviating from model-based craft projects and letting kids experiment with paint and materials in their own way. It means letting children write the stories they want, expressing the ideas inside. Creative risk is fundamentally about freedom to play. Play is the most creative expression of ideas for children. It may get messy. It may seem silly. It may not even seem risky to adults, but children explore ideas, make mistakes, and constantly challenge themselves through play.

Creative risk is dangerously limited by adults when we curtail unstructured time. It's also limited when adults join in play by directing it or telling a child, "That's not a sword, that's a magic wand," "Find all the blue blocks," or "We only write nonfiction in this class."

Social Risk

It's not *safe* to ask someone on a date. We might be rejected. We might feel terribly embarrassed. We might stumble and say the wrong thing. We might find out the other person has a low opinion of us. Kids worry about taking social risks for the same reasons. For an outgoing, gregarious child, approaching other kids to play comes naturally. For others, it's a tremendously big risk.

Support the risks your child makes socially. Simply acknowledging it's a risk can be a big help. "I know it can be hard." You can outline the risk involved: "She might say yes; she might say no." The most important part of taking social risks is giving your child the freedom to do it. If your child has a few special friends, let her invite those friends to her birthday party. Don't feel compelled to invite the whole class so no one feels left out. Allow kids to face occasional rejection from playmates. The better kids get at practicing risk, the better they will be at trying new relationships and gaining resiliency for temporary setbacks.

For some kids, social risk is saying hello, talking to adults, or asking a question. Kids aren't ready to do all these things at the same time. Offer opportunities, but don't force. Acknowledge the social risks kids take.

Emotional Risk

Emotional risk is simply running the risk of feeling bad. It may not seem like much of a risk, but often it's the one that scares us most. We react by shielding our children from bad feelings. When we protect them from emotional risk—the possibility of feeling sad, scared, embarrassed, angry, or any other negative emotion—then we deprive them of the chance to practice dealing with these difficult emotions and recover from them (see Rule 14: Don't Remove Ogres from Books).

Assessing Risk

When we holler to a child, "Stop running! You'll break your neck!" we're removing the chance for her to assess her own risk. Kids need the opportunity to try and judge their own risks without adults leaping to the conclusion that it's "too dangerous." As kids get more practice balancing on wobbly boards or stepping along slick logs, they become better judges about just what their bodies can do, how physics works, and what their personal limits are.

My husband and I both wondered if our oldest child would ever be able to safely cross a street on his own. Myles was perpetually daydreaming, and never seemed to notice the hazards of traffic. So I observed him on his own. Without me holding his hand or being a few steps away, Myles transformed into a different boy. He carefully checked for traffic, looked left and right multiple times, and waited at the curb, gauging distances of oncoming traffic much more cautiously then I ever would. Then he safely sprinted to the opposite sidewalk.

Without us constantly beside them, children assume risks they are comfortable with and take safety in their own hands.

Risk Makes Children More Careful

When you give a child a sharp knife, he understands its potential to hurt him. No child likes to be hurt. The result: He's extra careful.

With so many safety messages, kids can get the idea that they *can't* get hurt. Adults will always protect them. Rules will always protect them. Engineered surfaces, helmets, and playgrounds will always protect them. There's no need for caution. A child who feels no fear of his environment has no need to be careful. It's assumed everything's under control.

When you put risk back in children's hands, they tend to handle it carefully, taking the steps they feel comfortable with. Allowing children to take risks actually has the effect of reducing risky behavior.

Risk Helps Children Learn Who They Are

By taking risks that interest them, kids gradually piece together a sense of who they are. What sort of person am I? What am I good at and what are my limits? These are essential questions. As Gever Tulley reminds us, figuring out who they are is something that needs space and exploration through play and risk.

Think about a family, perhaps your own: Siblings' personalities vary; children and parents do not always share interests and values. A child developing within a home receives a heavy dose of who her parents are, but needs to venture out—take risks—to find out who she is. We are not all alike, and we need to keep in mind that the children we raise may not be like us. Children need ample room to explore so they can discover themselves and live the life they were born to live.

Try This—Add to Your Toolbox

Work on reducing real risks. Let kids explore age-appropriate risks that lead to growth, mastery, and independence.

Learn to Let Go

I still remember the five minutes I left my ten-week-old with a stranger. Sure, she was a licensed nursery professional, and I was only dashing out to get my jacket from the car, but those five minutes were a test of my ability to accept risk and independence in my child's life. For parents, letting go can be incredibly hard.

Allowing your child to take risks means you have to step back and let go. Move away to a different space. Stop words from coming out of your mouth. If you do your job well, your child will embrace independence and *need* you less. But needing is not the same as loving. Offering your child freedom and risk is one of the best paths to maintaining a lifelong, loving relationship.

Appropriate Risk

What's OK and what's too risky? Risk assessment is individual. Young kids should be supervised, but that doesn't mean they can't be out of sight and alone sometimes. Even if adults are watching, kids' play can proceed without intervention as long as it follows the Renegade Golden Rule: It's OK if it's not hurting people or property.

Ask yourself: What's the risk here? If the risk is mess, tears, bumps, or conflict, it's appropriate risk. If the risk is likely and involves serious harm, it's inappropriate risk. When assessing the likelihood, always modify for age. A toddler is likely to get hurt on a busy street, but most second-graders should be able to cross safely.

Take a Small Risk (for You)

Jessica Lahey, who writes about the importance of physical and emotional risk in her book, *The Gift of Failure*, says that U.S. parents are quick to chime in on conversations about kids' limited freedom with "Yes, we need more risk," but still shrink back when it comes to allowing those risks into their own family's life.

It's tough. Forgive yourself if the idea of risk ties you up in knots. Taking a risk means combating years of messages about danger and safety first. We can't defy that all-encompassing culture all at once. If this is tough for you, acknowledge it and recognize the emotions that are accompanying it.

Then choose a small risk to take. Maybe it's leaving your child with a sitter for the first time. Maybe it's a chance to play out in the yard alone.

SMALL RISKS TO START YOUR CHILD

Carry a message to a neighbor
Balance on a log or wall
Ride her bike "too fast"
Play outside by herself
Play in the house by himself
Use a public restroom solo

Cut a banana or an apple

Leave him with a sitter

Cross the street by herself

Ask a librarian, store clerk, or other person a question

Savor these small steps. When you're ready, take another one. You'll find that when you loosen up, your child may bloom with newfound feelings of power and responsibility. Be prepared to experience pride and growth, too. It's liberating to live with more joy and less fear. The biggest change might be in you.

Enlist Support

Especially with a firstborn or only child, parents can lose sight of which risks and freedoms are appropriate. It's OK if it's hard. Find someone who can boost your confidence.

Enlist a trusted adult to help. If you are too emotional to let your child play by himself in the front yard, have him do it on your friend's watch. Explain you want to get over this hurdle. If it's too traumatic, you can even ask for outside support. Lenore Skenazy, author of *Free-Range Kids*, makes house calls to help nervous parents let go. With her help and encouragement, parents let their kids play outside in the front yard, cross a street, or use a hammer. As Skenazy says, "I have learned that change can come fast. . . . All it takes is the ability to recognize just how safe and smart your kids already are."

Interview Grandparents

Ask grandparents and neighbors about their childhoods. Find out what others were allowed to do as children. Maybe you still feel that "things are different" today, but these stories give perspective by reminding us what children are capable of doing. Oh, your cousin cooked eggs when he was six? Your sister built a birdhouse with real nails at age five? When we live inside a shroud of safety messages, we forget. Soak up stories of what kids can do, and then try something with your own family

The point is not to reenact the past exactly. Although many five-year-olds used to fetch milk from the store, you don't have to send your five-year-old to the store alone. The point is to realize your children are capable. Kids, even at young ages, can do much more than you think, and do it well.

Find Appropriate Physical Risks

1. Kitchen Knives
   If you haven't given your toddler (or older child) a knife yet, start with a banana and a butter knife. Move on to hand-friendly choppers or yes, sharp knives. Sharp knives come in blunt-nosed styles to protect fingers. Toddlers can help chop fruits and vegetables of all sorts with training and proper tools.

2. Hammers and Saws
   If you have the space, set up a work area for kids ages four and older to practice sawing and hammering. Wood secured in a vise frees up both hands for directing the blade.

3. Going Fast
   When kids charge off too fast on their bikes or their legs, let them go. Most of the time they'll be fine. Sometimes they'll crash and learn their limits. Kids have a need to go fast and "too fast."

4. Climbing
   Kids feel power and learn about their limits when they practice climbing into high spots. Let them climb and balance with trees, ladders, walls, and other non-playground

heights. When you give kids an outlet for reasonable climbing, they are more ready to stay away from dangerous climbing.

5. Rough Play

If your child loves wrestling, rough tag and chase games, and even punching games, let it flourish. Rough-and-tumble play does a world of good for both the brain and body. Set limits on location, but if both kids are having fun with rough physical play, let the minor knocks come.

6. Crossing Streets

Remember, you've been teaching this one from babyhood on. Chances are your child knows more than you think she knows. Teach and train, then let her try it on her own. Practice different types of street crossings, and talk out loud as you cross together ("That car is coming fast, let's wait") so your child picks up ideas for judging speed and distance.

7. Nature Play

When you're practicing risk, it can help to seek the woods. Logs to balance on are generally lower than city walls, and there's no concrete to fall on. Streams and rocks invite games of leaping. Plus, an added bonus, there are fewer judging eyes to watch and say, "Be careful."

8. Access

Offer a measuring cup with a spout and let young children pour their own drinks. Look for other simple ways to promote independence. Are the broom and dustpan stored too high up? Are the glasses out of reach? Put common tools where young kids can reach them. This gives them a chance to develop skills and claim independence.

Find Individual Risks

Deciding what risks to take is extremely personal. It also differs by child, and by stage in that child's life. Children will be ready for some risks and overwhelmed by others. I was terrified of speaking on the phone as a child, a social risk. For eight-year-old Tasha, it was staying alone for half an hour; she burst into tears and ran to the neighbor's. Experiment. Not all risks are right for each child right now, but all children need some risk.

Words to Say

TO OTHER ADULTS

It's OK with me if kids go up the slide.
They look as if they're doing fine.
Are you worried about this game?
Let's talk to the kids and sort it out.

TO KIDS

Looks like you want to go up and she wants to come down.
What could you do?
The red slide is too high. If you want to climb, use the
   blue one.
Do you feel safe? Hmm. That looks high to me.
When I don't feel safe, I climb down.
I'll watch you, but I won't do it for you.
You might make a mistake.
I think you're ready to cross the street. We've practiced.
   Are you ready to try it?
I see you're going fast.
Your stick is too close to my body.

Move away from other people if you want to do that.
What's the worst that will happen?

Words to Avoid

You'll get hurt.
Get down from there. You'll break your neck.
Stop running!
Be careful.
Don't let me ever see you do that again.
You'll put somebody's eye out.
We'll just invite everyone in the class.
Everyone has to play together.
It's not safe to play by yourself.

Your Take

Feel good that you're open to increasing healthy risk in childhood. Maybe you're not the most free-rangey parent you know, but if you continually take steps forward you'll be taking the right steps for you. The key is to gradually give your child a range of healthy experiences. Deciding what age is right for your child to take certain risks is purely personal. Some kids might be ready to cross the neighborhood street at age five. Others not until eight, or even later depending on where you live. Risk gives us confidence and growth. Risk gives us science and poetry. Instead of limiting healthy risk of all types, we need to limit structured time and grant kids more independence. Train your children. Set smart limits. Let them practice. Then let them go.

RULE
2

It's OK Not to Kiss Grandma

Gabe, age six, ran from the room after his grandmother enfolded him in her arms. "Oh, juicy kisses! I don't like juicy kisses!" he cried, and rubbed his face in a pillow.

Renegade Reason

Manners are about respecting people. Respect a child's wish not to be touched, even by a loving grandmother. It's an excellent safety lesson, too.

We expect children to greet people politely. "At least say hi," we coax. When Grandma's involved, we expect kids to submit to hugs and kisses, wanted ones or not.

Greetings are tough. We want to look like "good" parents, and show we're doing a decent job raising a polite child. We want our family to be charmed by our child, or at least feel our child meets expectations. Social pressure can be intense because our competence is on public display.

Manners are essential for social harmony, but teaching them

needs to be done with respect. After all, respect for others is what good manners are about. That means respecting our children during the learning process. When it comes to greetings and good-byes, respect children's rights to learn at their own pace and to say no to unwanted touch, even if it comes from Grandma.

Renegade Blessings

When we model respect, kids pick it up. It's important for a child to understand she has rights even within the family.

> I know what people do to greet each other. When I'm
>   ready, I can do it myself.
> Sometimes I feel scared. Grown-ups understand.
> I do better when I'm comfortable, not pressured.
> Even if it's someone I love, I can set limits. I can tell people
>   what I like and don't like.
> My body belongs to me. I can decide whether to share it.
> Just because they're family doesn't mean they can touch me.

Why It Works

Kids have legitimate developmental reasons why they hide their heads, refuse to say hello, or respond in otherwise odd ways. "The social graces around greeting people often elude young children," say Laura Davis and Janis Keyser, authors of *Becoming the Parent You Want to Be*. Social greetings are best learned through modeling. Don't insist on set words and actions; there are alternatives, and the child has a right to remain silent.

Young children often fear strangers and difference. They may have strong, irrational fears about people wearing funny hats, glasses, beards, or other novelties. Ignoring visitors is often due to developmental factors, say Davis and Keyser. A child who doesn't seem to hear a polite "How are you, Kayla?" may not be rude at all, but simply deeply absorbed. A preschooler who refuses to say hello may be at a developmental stage of wanting to assert independence. You can still set expectations and encourage and model social graces, but at a young age, your child needs wiggle room. She may not be able to do what you're asking.

"Oh, don't mind her," we say, embarrassed. "She's just shy." Labeling a child as shy or rude undermines her learning. Labels stick, and children tend to internalize the labels we assign them, says pediatrician and parenting consultant William Sears. Kids may think: "I guess I'm a rude kid. I'm bad," or "I'm shy. I can't change. I'll always be like that." We often label to cover our own embarrassment. Labeling a child "shy," "uncooperative," or "rude" may backfire and doesn't help her learn social conventions.

Children are so much smaller than adults that they are easily overpowered. "Kids don't have much chance against grandparents coming at them with full force," says Deb Baillieul, a longtime teacher at the School for Young Children in Columbus, Ohio. As for Grandma's kiss, it may not seem like a big deal, but imposing unwanted touch of any kind sets a bad precedent. It can be a gateway for more. A child needs to know she has a right to set limits.

Hugging and kissing friends and family mixes two topics: bodies and manners. Sometimes in our effort to promote politeness, we forget that both are important. Kids need to learn what's appropriate for both. Be your child's ally. The idea is to teach manners, safety, and boundaries without scaring kids or confusing them. As child safety advocates caution, children need to be taught early on that they are the "boss of their body."

When can you expect children to say hello graciously? Around mid–elementary school. By this age, many developmental reasons for avoiding social situations are fading, such as separation anxiety or fear of new people. Mid-elementary children may not value greetings and other manners as much as you do, but they should be able to rise to the occasion. Set expectations ahead of time, practice at home, and let your child know how good it feels to be greeted nicely. For example, this may mean explaining to your child that as a visitor he needs to say hello to everyone he sees in the house when he arrives for a playdate.

Social abilities vary greatly, however. Josh, age ten, couldn't bear being an usher at church and saying hello to strangers, while his six-year-old brother greeted people easily. Keep in mind greetings may be incredibly hard for some children. Continue modeling the behavior you want to see and give children time.

Take Off Your Adult Lenses

When we meet and greet others, it can feel as if our parenting ability is on show. Is my child polite enough? Am I meeting my own mother's or father's expectations? Am I doing a good job raising considerate, well-mannered children? It's not about you. Your child has legitimate reasons for not speaking or hugging. Manners are all about respect, so respect your child and give room for his feelings. Besides, there are safety issues at play here. Children need to know you'll be an ally when they don't feel right about someone touching them. The goal is for them to say hi or hello and acknowledge each person they meet respectfully. Remember it's a goal and it may take some time to get there.

Fears of Older Bodies

"Why do your hands have worms on them?"

"Grandpa smells bad."

"What's that tube thing up her nose?"

Lumpy veins, neck wattles, liver spots, wrinkly skin, raspy voices, and distinctive smells—these may not be the first thing on your mind when you see a beloved older family member, but for young kids, such differences can be off-putting or downright scary. Will I "catch" old age? Are those really worms on Grandma's hands? What's that machine she walks with? Why is there a tube up her nose that goes *puff*? Why can't Granddad hear me the way other people can?

My grandfather had a scratchy chin, a smoky smell, and a voice that rumbled and coughed. When I spoke to him, he couldn't hear me. Another elderly relative had a touchy hearing aid that would emit high-pitched screeches whenever I got too close. All this was a bit scary when I was five.

Older bodies are different, and young kids are often scared of people who look different. This includes people with beards, hats, wrinkly skin, walkers, wheelchairs, and oxygen tanks. Give your child a chance to talk and ask questions about older bodies.

Family as Strangers

"Aliya, come and give me a hug!" Aliya, age two and a half, stared at the unfamiliar woman in the doorway. Her grandmother lived in New York and Aliya and her family lived in Ohio and only saw her once a year. Aliya took one look at the strange woman reaching out for her and hid behind the car.

When it's time to visit Grandma's house, young children are often expected to fly into her arms, or at least greet her politely with a smile. The trouble is, Grandma, Uncle Rodney, or cousin Sara may be a stranger to your child. As parents, we often warn our children to be careful of strangers, yet sometimes we forget our relatives seem like strangers.

There are all sorts of strangers we expect kids to cuddle up to. Gretchen took her three-year-old and baby to visit Santa at the mall. She placed them both on Santa's lap, hoping to get an adorable picture to send to family. The photos showed something else. "It was not joy on my kids' faces, but worry. They didn't feel safe sitting on a stranger's lap."

How long has it been since the last visit? If it's been more than a month, chances are the child needs some orientation. "Aunt Jenny is coming for a visit. She hasn't seen you in a long time." If you think your child might hide behind your legs or be nervous about the new person, go ahead and set expectations on both sides: "Aunt Jenny likes to hug people. I'm going to hug her. You can hug her if you want." And to the visiting relative: "I know you haven't seen Jack since spring and can't wait to see him, but Jack doesn't remember you well. He might take a little while to warm up." Or: "Jack doesn't like kisses right now. He's good at shaking hands."

Take time to acknowledge fears and establish (or reestablish) trust.

Phone Calls and Video Visits

Cayden didn't want to come to the phone. His uncle Phil was calling to wish him happy birthday, but Cayden shook his head. His uncle was offended and his aunt and grandmother both weighed in: *A boy who's six should talk. He needs to learn what's polite.* "Cayden is only willing to speak to relatives on the phone when he's seen them recently," said his mom. "Otherwise he refuses."

Kids live in the moment. On any given day, they may talk, or they may not. Don't push it. It's not that they're shy. It's not that they don't like you. It's not about manners. Virtual visits can be hard on kids.

When I go out of town, sometimes one child is in the mood to talk when I call, and other times he's not. Face it, we often ask ridiculous questions when we talk to kids on the phone. Example: "What are you doing right now?" Answer: "Talking to you on the phone." You are more likely to have a good conversation if it's a willing one. Over time, children will get used to the phone or video call and it will be hard to get them off.

Being the Boss of Your Body

Samantha's mom loved to greet people with kisses. One day, Samantha ducked and didn't want to kiss her mom when it was pickup time at school. "You don't have to kiss me, but I'm going to kiss you!" her mother said and forced a kiss on her.

In some ways, Samantha's mom was being flexible: It's OK if you don't feel like kissing me. But she's sending a bad message: *I'm going to kiss you whether you like it or not. Your body is not your own.*

With hugs, kisses, tickling, and other such touching, a child has a right to say no to unwanted touches. Yes, sometimes kids need a bath or a doctor's visit. Sometimes they need to be physically restrained from hurting someone, but when it comes to greetings, good-byes, and general affection, children have the right to be the boss of their own bodies.

This message needs to be simple and consistent. Your body belongs to you. You can share it if you want. You can say no to touches. A child's right to her own body is about respect, privacy, and safety.

When you teach your child about body safety, it's common to talk about good touches and bad touches. At its simplest level, a bad touch is any touch that doesn't feel good. If it feels icky, it *is* icky. Kids need to understand they have a fundamental right to body privacy.

This lesson can take a while to sink in. My six-year-old was kissed by another child at school. He didn't like it and repeated what the teacher said: "There's no kissing at school." Later we talked about it.

"You have a right not to be kissed if you don't like it," I said.

"No kissing at school," Zach repeated.

"You don't have to be kissed anywhere," I reminded him. "Not at school, not in the grocery store, not on the bus, not at home, not anywhere."

"Oh," said Zach, looking relieved.

But isn't it different with family? Isn't Grandma's kiss or Uncle Harry's hug and tickling fest in a different category? No. Perhaps it's even more important with family. Despite common worries about stranger danger, more kids are hurt or sexually abused by people they know (see Rule 4: It's OK to Talk to Strangers). "Family" status doesn't matter.

Kids have a right to set limits on their bodies.

Power of Modeling

It's not necessary to make your child perform: "Say hello to Ms. Jackson" or "Give Grandpa a kiss." Children pick up social greeting conventions by modeling.

A hello or good-bye may seem easy, but there's a lot going on. Kids are encountering a new space, new people, and new experiences. Arriving somewhere can seem overwhelming. So can new people arriving at a child's house. Before kids can focus on social niceties, they need to feel safe first. "I see you want to be next to my leg right now."

You can supplement modeling by giving children information and training at other times. Debra taught her kids how to give firm handshakes. They were eager to pull out their new skill when meeting their dad's colleagues. If you know visitors are coming, practice with a puppet show or give information. "When someone comes to our house it's nice to come to the door and say hello. That helps people feel welcome."

Kids like knowing what to do. It helps them feel competent. But remember, even children who know what to do may not be able to do it all the time. Sometimes fears and feelings swamp them.

Respect for others is what
good manners are all about.

Try This—Add to Your Toolbox

Ask the Child

Find out what your child doesn't like about Grandpa's hugs or Granny's kisses. Whiskers? Big bosom? Funny smell? Perspiration? Perfume? Juicy kisses? Tight squeezes? Kids could be scared of liver spots (*Is it a disease? Am I going to die if I touch her?*) or scratchy voices or deafness (*He can't hear what I say. I don't feel safe.*).

Once you've identified the main concern, talk it out. Sometimes there's nothing to change. "Yes, Grandpa's whiskers scratch and tickle a bit, don't they?" Sometimes you can set a limit. "Ada doesn't like big kisses, only little ones right now."

Keep People Familiar

Penny posted photos of extended family at child height on the fridge. Their faces became familiar, and the children often heard stories about Uncle Eric or Aunt Melissa. When someone was about to visit, Penny took the photo down and let her children touch it and get a good look. "Aunt Melissa made chocolate chip pancakes with you, remember? I wonder what she'll do this time." Find a way to keep long-distance folks familiar.

Break the Ice

Young kids are good at action. If she doesn't want to hug, maybe she can take the visitor's coat. Prep the situation ahead of time: "When my friend Greta comes, we can offer her a drink." Then invite the child to participate: "Could you get a cup out for Greta?"

If Grandma wants to snuggle, suggest reading a book together. Your child may start out at the far side of the room, but soon he'll be drawn into the story and cuddled up against Grandma. Children can be quick to love and accept new people, but it rarely happens at initial greeting.

Model Behavior

Model behavior. Go ahead and hug Aunt Brenda yourself. Your actions show your child this person is safe. Your words and actions also demonstrate that hugging and kissing are ways we greet our extended family, just as shaking hands and saying, "Nice to meet you," are all appropriate ways of saying hello in our culture. Whatever your culture is, children will pick it up from modeling.

Guide, Don't Force

Don't force a performance. We've all heard it, and we've all at one time or another said it ourselves. "Say hello to Mr. Morgan." "Go give Grandpa a big hug." If you want your child to do these actions, talk about it ahead of time. Let them know what's normal or expected. Reminding a child is OK ("Do you want to give Grandpa a hug?"), but forcing doesn't respect feelings.

Give Alternatives

Give your child an alternative. "You could wave. You could smile. You could say hi," or "You don't need to talk. Just come to the door with me." Or "You don't have to talk for a long time on the phone, just try saying, 'Hello Grandpa!'"

Give Information

Most children learn by modeling, but if your child doesn't easily pick up social conventions, give information to guide him. Five-year-old Hank didn't acknowledge other people when they said hello to him. His mother told him, "When someone says hello, they're waiting for a hello back. It's friendly to say hello when someone says hello to you." Hank didn't pick this up by modeling, but he started saying hello once the concept was explained to him. If you have a child like Hank, point things out in direct language. "When someone says hi, you could say hi or wave."

Another type of information is basic knowledge about bodies and body safety. There are many good books for children about "good" and "bad" touches, but sometimes affection from relatives can be a tricky line to walk. Children's books such as *Miles Is the Boss of His Body* address how to set personal boundaries with well-meaning relatives.

Help your child set limits, if necessary. "Nana wants to give you a hug. Do you want a hug right now? No? That's OK. You can tell her. She'll understand."

Give relatives information, too. This helps prevent misunderstandings and can enlist visitors to your side. As the Family Help Center in Buffalo, New York, suggests: "Tell relatives that you are teaching your children to be bosses of their bodies as part of teaching them safety about touching, so they are not offended by your children's behavior."

Adult Bodies Have Rights, Too

Grandma also has a right to set a limit on her body. Greetings and playtime can get too exuberant, and not every visitor is comfortable with young kids' physical affection. If this is an issue, let visitors know they have a right to set limits and say what they don't like, too.

Good-byes Can Hurt

Every time it came time to say good-bye to Grandpa and Granny, my son Myles would vanish. He wouldn't say good-bye; he'd quietly disappear inside the house. He couldn't bear the sorrow.

Saying good-bye can be a true ordeal for many children. If a beloved friend or relative is about to leave, a child may react by being silent, running away, or hiding. "Oh, come on and say good-bye to Uncle Rodney," we may chide. Separation hurts. It can hurt so badly—even if the visit was short—that kids can't cope with the enormity of their grieving emotions. If your child has a hard time with good-byes, work on hellos first, and wait until he's older before you tackle partings.

Give Children Time

Mohammed, age seven, rushed to fetch a visiting mother a drink and take her coat. When she entered the room, he always stood up.

Sam's mom didn't insist on big greetings, but wanted a quick hello. "Say hello, and then you can go play with your cousins. It's important to Aunt Louise that we greet her. Like washing hands in the bathroom, this is simply what we do."

Ideas about proper greetings are rooted in family culture. Acknowledge they are different. Strive toward the standards you set, but don't expect your child to be able to cope at every age, all the time. If you continually model and show what behavior you'd like to see, children will eventually be able to meet your family standard. Experiment with the level that feels right to you, while respecting your child, yourself, and people around you. Then give your child time.

Words to Say

GREETINGS

We can say hi together.

That's OK. Adults like to say hi. Sometimes kids need a
   little extra time.

It's important to Aunt Jenny to go over and say hello.

This is hard for her right now.

That's OK. He greeted me in his own way.
I know he heard me say hello.
That's fine. I saw her and she saw me.

SETTING LIMITS ON FRIENDLY TOUCH
(EVEN FROM GRANDMA)

You can hug Grandma if you want.
Looks like you don't want to hug.
It's been a long time since she's seen you.
Let's tell him hello together.
No kisses for me.
I don't want a hug right now.
Maybe later.
I heard Ada say, "no kisses."
Kyle doesn't want hugs.
No means no.
Touching has to feel OK.
You are the boss of your body.
Sometimes kids don't want to be hugged. That's OK.
Do you want help getting her to stop?
Is there something you're worried about?

Words to Avoid

She's just shy.
Don't be shy; say hello to Mrs. Vogelberg.
Oh, I'm sorry, she doesn't usually hide like this.
Stop being rude.
Say hello to Mr. Jackson.
Go give Grandpa a kiss.
Give Nancy a good night hug.

Your Take

Feelings about greetings and good-byes run high among adults. At times you'll find your family rules clash with others' expectations.

If other parents insist that a child greet you politely with "Hello, Ms./Mr. Thomas" and are embarrassed because the child won't do it, let everyone know it's OK. "That's OK. I see she greeted me in her own way."

If you're about to visit Great-Aunt Cynthia, who has high standards, talk about it ahead of time. Role-play and practice at home. "Aunt Cynthia likes to shake hands. Let's try it. A firm grip . . . not limp, not too hard . . . yes, like that."

What happens if we override a child's feelings and let Grandma kiss him? Be easy on yourself. Try to respect boundaries about bodies, but if it doesn't always happen, your child will be fine.

RULE
3
Model Mistakes

Five-year-old Colin hated to make mistakes. When he tripped and stubbed his toe, he would blame his sister. When he sneaked jelly beans from a bag of birthday treats he would say: "She made me do it." Colin's habit of blaming others whenever he did something wrong drove his mother crazy.

Tristan, age three, walked off the playground by himself. His teacher found him, explained the mistake, and told him he needed to stay on the playground. His reaction was to freeze. For the rest of the day, he hardly moved and became absolutely silent.

Renegade Reason

Model making mistakes in front of children. Seeing you goof up helps kids accept themselves, keep trying, and take responsibility.

Big Bird has been helping kids like Colin and Tristan for years. He sings a *Sesame Street* song encouraging kids to accept mistakes as part of living. You can still listen online to Jeff Moss's classic song

"Everyone Makes Mistakes": *Big people, small people, matter of fact, all people. Everyone makes mistakes, so why can't you?*

Many kids have a hard time accepting mistakes. Some deny them: "Not me!" Some blame others. Some freeze up and stop taking chances for fear they'll commit another dreaded mistake. When it comes to mistakes, kids often get blinders. They see their own mistakes vividly, but don't notice other people's. Simply pointing out mistakes when you see them can be a huge help.

Renegade Blessings

Saving face is sometimes the number one priority for young kids. When you teach them about mistake making, the lessons can last a lifetime.

> I might make a mistake sometimes. That's OK.
> It's not just kids who make mistakes. Everyone does, even
>   my mom and dad.
> When I do make a mistake, I might feel terrible, but I
>   know how to cope.
> I can accept responsibility for my mistakes and try to fix
>   them.
> I won't stop trying just because I might not be perfect.

Why It Works

It's no wonder kids often react strongly to mistakes. They are constantly trying new things and living with adults who seem to do the same tasks so seamlessly. Pour milk? No problem. Stack a tower? Easy. Put on a shirt with buttons? Five seconds. Mistakes happen every day for a child—whether he crosses a behavior boundary (hits his sister) or spills his milk.

"Children need models more than they need critics," said Joseph Joubert, French philosopher from the 1700s. It's long been known that children learn through imitation: watching someone else and repeating the behavior. Modeling is a great way to teach kids to accept mistakes in a healthy way, say parenting authors Laura Davis and Janis Keyser. Children watch us intently. When we are vocal about our own mistakes, kids learn how to cope with being "wrong" and making amends. How we deal with a mistake is more important than the mistake itself.

Some children feel shame when they make mistakes, either from the mistake itself or from the way we react. Shame is an inner feeling of "I'm a bad person." It attacks self-worth. Kids may react by lashing out, avoiding, hiding, or denying the mistake to protect themselves. A healthier feeling for kids to develop is guilt, which includes regret and remorse, and the desire to fix a mistake rather than avoid it. Psychologists such as June Price Tangney say parents can help kids avoid shame and develop a healthy attitude toward mistakes.

Take Off Your Adult Lenses

Our first instinct is often to moralize when children blame others. We tell them not to lie. We might give them a lecture about responsibility. That's not what kids need. It's common for kids to be mistake averse. Concentrate on their feelings first. Help children realize they are not alone—everyone makes mistakes, even you. Model your missteps and help kids take action to make amends when they goof up.

Shame and Making Mistakes

A mistake carries with it a mix of feelings, and some kids feel these powerfully. They may feel shame, anger at themselves, frustration, sadness, guilt, or hopelessness.

When your child spills her milk or rips her brother's picture, help her learn to acknowledge, accept, and make amends for mistakes. This is no easy lesson. How many of us as adults can admit our mistakes immediately and openly, and then make up for them? This is another life skill that serves our families and communities well, yet takes years of practice. The easiest way to accept mistakes and keep your cool as an adult is to learn it from an early age.

> **How we deal with mistakes is more important than the mistake itself.**

Fear of mistake making hits some kids harder than others. Mistakes are often hardest for boys, only children, and firstborns. As psychologist William Pollack, author of *Real Boys*, writes, boys are "shame-phobic." Many boys will do just about anything to avoid losing face. They are also typically interested in all things powerful, which makes them averse to shame. Firstborns and only children often feel more pressure to do things right. When kids live in an all-adult household, they may see themselves constantly failing as they compare themselves to the grown-ups around them.

Model Making Mistakes

As a child, my brother, Scott, hated to make mistakes. My mother noticed what really bugged him was being observed. He hated the shame of it. If he was going to make a mistake, he wanted to do it privately. One day at preschool, Scott fell backward into a pan of water. He howled. It wasn't just being wet and dirty. He hated the shame of making a mistake, and this embarrassment was mixed in with fear: Would Mom get angry?

For children who are mistake averse, modeling can be an enormous help. Teachers at the School for Young Children advised my mother to teach Scott it was OK to make mistakes by opening up about hers.

"Oh no, I made a mistake and all the markers fell," she would announce loudly. "I just have to pick them up."

Other days she would stamp her foot for emphasis. "Oh! I made a mistake!" she would holler. "It's OK to make mistakes. Everybody makes mistakes: kids and teachers, moms and dads."

As my mother stopped hiding all the little mistakes she made every day, Scott eased up on himself. Finally, he was able to admit a mistake, too.

> ## Model making mistakes in front of children.

Kids are always within earshot, listening, watching. Once you start announcing your mistakes, it's amazing how many pile up in a day: spilling coffee, forgetting the car keys, running late, misplacing your cell phone. Fortunately, most of them are little, and easy to announce and resolve. Give your child a vocabulary to express disappointment and move on: Oh no! Darn! Rats! Oops! Uh-oh! I made a mistake! Silly me. Oh, well. I guess now I'll have to . . .

> ## Admitting a mistake takes courage. Help your kids get into the habit.

My son, Myles, tried to write long before his fingers could manage a pen. Often he fell short and raged at himself. Striving for perfection is something he may well struggle with his whole life. I knew I had to model mistake making around Myles as much as possible. Starting when he was two, I made sure to vocalize my daily mistakes. Soon he was hearing a litany of oopses from me.

Getting kids to recognize that making a mistake is not a calamity is a huge first step. Knowing how to fix the mistake may take adult help. Does fixing the mistake involve a sponge? An apology? A new attempt at a drawing? But the day will come when your child not only admits a mistake, but calmly comes up with a solution. My reward came when I heard Myles's voice from his bedroom:

"Oh, no! I made a mistake!" Pause. "Silly Myles. Now I need tape."

Try This—Add to Your Toolbox

Don't create a perfect facade. Let your child see how often you mess up and what you do about it. Model mistake making when your child is within earshot. Modeling might help you accept your own imperfections, too.

1. Announce your mistakes
   "Oh, no! I made a mistake!"

2. State what went wrong
   "I spilled coffee on the table."

3. Accept your mistakes
   "Oh, well. That happens sometimes. Everybody makes mistakes, even dads."

4. Explain how you can fix it
   "Now I have to get the sponge and clean it up."

Despite all the spills and mess, let your child try things on her own as much as possible. Rushing to the rescue with an "I'll do it for you" can send the message that only perfection will do.

As kids grow, mistakes may get more complex, often involving social missteps. Instead of spilling paint, it may be a mistake involving gossip and hurt feelings. As adults, despite our best intentions, we do this, too. When I made a social gaffe recently, I knew my kids were watching me. I was angry at myself and was in no mood to model, but I summoned up my most gracious self. What's most important is demonstrating how to admit a mistake and make amends.

Words to Say

MODELING MISTAKES

Uh-oh! I made a mistake.
Rats! Darn! Oops! Uh-oh!
I spilled coffee on my grocery list.
Sorry, you're right. I was wrong.
I shouldn't have said that. This would be kinder.
That didn't work the way I wanted.
Silly me.
Sometimes that happens.
Oh, well.
Hmm. What could I do? How could we fix this?
I guess now I'll have to get a new piece of paper.

EMPATHY AND INFORMATION

Even mamas make mistakes sometimes.
Let me tell a story about a mistake I made when
    I was four.
It's not easy to pour milk.
I still love you even though you made a mistake.
It was an accident. Sometimes we do things and we
    wish we hadn't.

Everyone makes mistakes. Moms and dads, kids and
   teachers and grandmas.
When we make a mistake we can set it right.

Words to Avoid

There's nothing to be upset about.
What did I tell you? Look at the mess you made.
Colin! Don't be so clumsy. That's the third time you've
   spilled milk today.
Why are you lying to me? I know you did it.
You can't do anything right.
Here, I'll do it for you.

Your Take

Mistake making is one more area where you can help your child
cope with negative emotions and develop resilience for life. Of
course, if you're visiting Aunt Hattie, whose house is impeccably
clean, it's not the best time for your child to practice pouring milk.
Allow plenty of time for that at home (put liquids in a small plastic
measuring cup with spout) and say, "I know you usually pour your
milk, but at this house I'm going to do it." Also, many people don't
like their mistakes pointed out. Highlight your own, but don't am-
plify others'.

RULE

4

It's OK to Talk to Strangers

Ten-year-old Logan turned his face to the wall in the women's bathroom, as his mother told him. Already a fourth-grader, Logan blushed deeply at being sent to stand in the corner as women flushed in the stalls behind him. His mother didn't trust he would be safe standing by himself outside a public restroom.

Gabby, age eight, stood stock-still as a neighbor walked by and said hello. "I'm not supposed to talk to strangers," she said. Samantha, three, refused to talk to people. When her parents warned her about strangers, she became afraid of everyone she saw.

"Stranger danger" advice doesn't work. First, it doesn't protect kids. Second, it creates unwarranted fear and confusion. Children need different messages and tools to stay safe.

Renegade Reason

Stranger danger confuses kids and doesn't protect them. Give your child tools, not fear.

At the crowded fairgrounds, a mother scolded her five-year-old for wandering away. Like all parents, she was scared. "Stay right by me," she said. Then she invoked the fear of kidnapping. "If someone comes and steals you, then you'll be in *big* trouble."

Kidnapping continues to be U.S. parents' number one fear. A study by the Mayo Clinic found that almost *three quarters* of parents are afraid their children will be abducted. Chances are, you worry about this, too. Yet it is more likely that furniture will fall on your head. Every half hour in the U.S., a child is rushed to the emergency room because a giant flat-screen TV tipped over, seriously injuring and sometimes killing them, according to the Consumer Product Safety Commission.

"Worry is an aspect of parenthood, but it shouldn't define it," says Kim John Payne, author of *Simplicity Parenting*. It's hard to live in fear all the time. When fear consumes us, we don't parent our best. We live in worry. As we learn more about the relative risk of strangers and how we can take powerful steps to protect our children, then we can define a new life. Instead of being defined by fear, we need to define safety.

Kids need room to practice the skills that will keep them safe. It may seem counterintuitive, but that *includes* talking to strangers.

Renegade Blessings

Children need our help to navigate the world safely. Part of this is supervision. Part of it is giving children tools and independence. A child who interacts with a wide variety of people gains insight into trust and risk.

Most people are nice.
Lots of people can help me.
I can talk to strangers, but I know better than to go
    with them.

If I don't like something, I know to speak up.

No one has the right to touch me in a way I don't like.

If it feels icky, it is icky.

I know what to do if there's trouble: yell and get away.

I can take care of myself in small ways.

I can do so much! My parents believe in me.

Take Off Your Adult Lenses

Most of us with young children repeat what we heard in our childhoods, which included "Don't talk to strangers." We know more now. We know strangers are an exceedingly rare threat to our children, and most abduction and abuse happens to children from people they already know, our family and friends. It's still hard to shake the mantra: "Don't talk to strangers." The reality is, strangers are most likely to be our kids' helpers. Our fear needs to focus on the real threats, primarily car accidents. We cannot rule out every bad event in the world, but we need to approach childhood safety with measures that can truly protect them: standing up for their rights, learning to set limits, gaining street-smart independence, and yes, even defying adults when things seem wrong.

Today's Fears

"Ben doesn't walk to school," said Sheri, mother of a seven-year-old only child. Ben's school was just a few blocks away and he lived in a small town. "You can't *these days*, what with the world the way it is."

We toss around the term "these days," but the truth is the world is far safer today than it has been for years. According to the U.S. Department of Justice, violent crime rates are at their *lowest level* in forty years.

I was stunned when I realized that. Really? Wow. We're scared, but the news about low crime is not getting out.

The more I looked into it, the more I realized a secret fact: We live in a very safe era—much safer than when I was a kid. All the bad stuff—rape, murder, crimes against children—is down, and not only down, but down significantly. In fact, violent crimes in 2014 were close to *half* the level they were in 1994, according to the FBI. This dramatic decline is also occurring in other Western countries.

This is nothing short of amazing.

What is climbing is our mutual fear. Perhaps it's fueled by media or social media, but whatever the reason, our belief that the world is dangerous for our children is out of step with reality.

Currently there are seventy-five million children in the U.S. The chance of a child being kidnapped by a stranger is .00000153 percent.

Life has never been safer for children. We're past the era of open fireplaces in children's bedrooms. We've instituted child labor laws to keep kids out of dangerous farm work and factories. We've produced modern medicine to protect them from childhood disease. The real-life risks are vanishing. Now we need to help each other adjust our mind-set.

Why It Works

Figuring out who's a stranger and who isn't is often confusing for children. Most adults are strangers in a child's life, even Aunt Gloria who comes to visit once every two years. David Warren, a British psychologist, says, "Research suggests that children don't really know what a stranger is. They feel that once someone tells his name, he ceases to be a stranger." Children often think a stranger is somebody big or mean, or maybe somebody who wears funny clothes. Talking to strangers is not the problem; it can even be a solution. Strangers are often the ones who help a lost child reconnect with her family.

The "Don't talk to strangers" rule is increasingly irrelevant. Besides crime rates plummeting, kidnapping remains extremely rare, and almost 80 percent of abducted children are taken by their own family members, often in custody disputes. Ninety percent of sexually abused children know the offender. As Gavin de Becker, author of *Protecting the Gift*, says: "The Rule actually reduces safety in several ways. One is that within the message Never Talk to Strangers (because they may harm you) is the implication that people you know will not harm you."

"Don't talk to strangers" doesn't protect kids because family, friends, and acquaintances are typically the ones who hurt them. Since children are usually hurt by people they already know, it's vital that kids understand they have rights and can set limits on others, including defying adults. This includes saying "No!" when a person touches them in a way they don't like. It also includes adults accepting kids' fears and feelings. De Becker calls healthy survival instincts "the gift of fear." Kids need to experience "uh-oh" feelings to understand and trust this instinct. They need to begin by learning to trust when they feel safe and don't feel safe (see Rule 2: It's OK Not to Kiss Grandma).

A family's job is to socialize kids, but we can't socialize them within the confines of the car and our home. As sociologist Frank Furedi says, children are socialized through interacting in their community, and denying them exposure to their neighborhood hurts this vital social learning. Kids need experience learning how to meet a variety of people and gauging whether to trust them, whether it's a new sitter, the dentist, or a store clerk. Taking small social risks and assessing trustworthiness is necessary work for our kids. Talking to strangers is part of that.

Developing street smarts is a good step. Kids with street smarts tend to be safer than kids who are sheltered. These kids know how to read people they meet and can navigate new places, ask for help, trust their gut, and know what to do in tough situations.

"You can't protect people from very rare events," says Lenore

Skenazy, author of *Free-Range Kids*. Stranger-related crimes are rare and unpredictable. That's partly why they attract so much media attention, but the sensationalism boosts our idea of probability all out of proportion. Security expert Bruce Schneier, author of *Liars and Outliers: Enabling the Trust That Society Needs to Thrive*, says: "I tell people if it's in the news, don't worry about it. By definition, news is something that almost never happens."

Kids need to feel safe so they can explore, grow, and live. They have their own fears (in the Mayo Clinic survey the top fear for elementary school boys: being forced to eat food they don't like) and don't need the extra burden of ours. Kids who are shielded too much are less competent in real-world situations. Psychologists find that kids who don't build up this competence are indecisive and anxious, and fear growing up. Maybe this is the real fear parents should focus on: avoiding raising a thirty-five-year-old kid who lives in your basement.

Recognizing "Uh-oh"

Last summer I encouraged my nine-year-old to ride the city bus solo. We tried the route together first and then he was on his own. "Alone?" friends asked. "Are you sure he'll be OK?" No, I wasn't absolutely sure. Even though we live in a small city, the bus station is adjacent to an addiction treatment and mental health services building. The ride involved crossing town and successfully navigating one busy street without a crosswalk. I wasn't sure, but I was willing to take the risk. He bounded off the bus each day radiant with pride in his independence.

One reason I was willing to let my son try the bus alone was that I'd watched him react in "uh-oh" situations. One day at the library Myles came up to me with a troubled expression and said: "Some guy keeps following me. It makes my stomach feel weird." We were in the children's section. He pointed out the stalker, a teen who seemed to have issues judging personal space. "You did just the right thing," I told him. "Your instincts told you something wasn't right. Always pay attention to that uh-oh feeling."

This ability to trust your instinct is what Gavin de Becker insists is most helpful for protecting ourselves and our children. De Becker, who is a leading expert in judging threats, and regularly advises the President, U.S. Supreme Court, and CIA on high-profile security, advises families to talk to strangers, but be wary of strangeness. If something doesn't seem right, it isn't right. Our survival radar tells us something is amiss, and we heed it by moving to find safety—trusted adults and public, well-lit areas.

Stranger Confusion

The concept of a stranger is difficult for a child to grasp. Most people, including other children, are strangers to young kids. Your son may not recognize your old friend because it's been four months since you last saw each other. A new sitter is certainly a stranger, yet parents go out and leave the child alone with this person.

"Parents use the word *stranger* too early," says Jan Waters, from the School for Young Children. "Preschoolers don't even know what a stranger means. The word becomes loaded and confusing."

Outgoing kids naturally talk to the grocery store cashier. Quiet kids hide from everyone outside the family. These kids both need practice talking to people they don't yet know well. Interactions with people of all types help kids develop the skill of judging when things are OK and when they're not.

Risks We Accept

I asked my doctor once, "Is it safe?"

"Safer than driving to the grocery store," he answered.

Driving a child to the grocery store, school, or Grandma's house certainly doesn't seem like a dangerous activity, but chances are it's the worst risk you expose your child to every day. Car crashes are the leading cause of death and serious injury for children.

This is the irony. To protect kids from bad strangers, we actually endanger them more. We drive our children walkable distances to keep them "safer." We keep them away from the outside world, removing the chance for them to build street-smart social skills. We teach them our fears. Kids who are afraid can't try new things, take healthy risks, and learn to use good judgment—the very skills kids need to grow, succeed, and stay safe.

Driving carries risk. It's a risk we're willing to accept. We minimize the risk by buckling up and by staying off the roads on icy days, but we don't unnecessarily frighten our children and we don't get rid of our car.

Discarding Extra Fear

We live in a world of five-point-buckle car seats, helmets, safety warnings, Internet scares, and alarmist messages. For a while my daycare provider forwarded all the safety recall messages she received. As e-mail alert after e-mail alert flew in, my tension shot up. Suddenly the world seemed mighty dangerous. Cribs causing death. Toys causing poisoning and strangulation. The constant barrage of messages assaulted me with fear, even though we didn't have any of these items in our house.

Watch what makes you tense and worried. Is it legitimate, or is it extra fear? If we worried about everything, we couldn't function. I remember a childhood friend who stuck raw spaghetti in her ear and punctured her eardrum. It probably never occurred to her mother to say: "Don't stick raw spaghetti in your ear." There are simply too many rare events that may happen. It's possible to reduce commonsense dangers (hide the bleach, use car seats, teach your kids to swim), but we cannot remove every conceivable danger. We must learn to live with some risk.

Our job is to sift through the world's messages and focus on what's statistically likely and preventable. Too much fear distracts us.

Legitimate Fears

As adults, we should carry a degree of worry and concern for our children. My top concern is car crashes, partly because of the number of erratic drivers. Besides drunk, drugged, and texting drivers, I know there are legions of cell-phone-talking and sleep-deprived parents driving out there. Still, we must coexist with cars. When my kids are old enough, it's my job to teach them defensive-driving techniques. For now, they need to learn defensive skills as pedestrians.

As a society, we ought to be worried about many unsafe trends affecting our children. These include depression and anxiety, which lead to a host of social ills, including suicide. The American Academy of Pediatrics reminds us that loss of free-play time causes depression and anxiety in children (as do loss of recess and too much homework; see Rule 7: Recess Is a Right and Rule 8: Ban Elementary Homework). The nonprofit Alliance for Childhood finds kids aged ten and up spend more than ten hours a day relatively motionless and less than fifteen minutes physically active. These are legitimate concerns, but they are also concerns we can do something about.

Try This—Add to Your Toolbox

Preschoolers don't need to be wary of strangers. At that age, it's your job to keep them safe. By the time kids trek off to elementary school, they need to know basic personal safety, since kids this age interact with a wider world.

Stranger Sense

The mantra "Don't talk to strangers" should change to "Don't go with a stranger." This basic stranger safety lesson remains the same. There's no need to shock a child with imagined horrors; just give him basic knowledge, the same way you would with what-to-do-in-case-you're-in-a-burning-house. If there's a house fire, go outside immediately. Don't stop, even for your toys. If a stranger asks you to get in his car, don't go with him. Even if he gives you candy.

Find Helping Strangers

If a child's in trouble, she needs to be able to identify the helpers. These are strangers.

In many communities, helpful strangers include police officers, firefighters, medics, and other officials, along with store clerks. More often it's another parent, a friendly face in the crowd who understands kids.

You can teach this as "Find a mom or dad," or "Find someone with kids." Make sure you discuss how to tell if people are parents: They have their kids with them. Tell kids: "Find a parent. Parents are used to helping kids."

Some parents, particularly mothers, are only comfortable using a "Find a mom" rule, saying that women are safer. It seems better to include dads. There are so many caring fathers out with kids, on the playground and at kids' events. Even though you may not explicitly say, "Find a mom because I don't trust dads and you shouldn't either," kids pick up on this unspoken fear. Greg, a stay-at-home father of a preschooler, says, "I don't want my child to fear men."

Teaching your child to find a parent can begin early. That simple message is not fear inducing. It's clear. Kids know what moms and dads are. This safety tip makes sense to them, and no kid likes being lost. Gavin, age three, heard the message and decided to try it out next time he was at the mall play space. A few minutes after they'd arrived, Gavin came up to his mother with another mother in tow. "I was practicing finding another mom," he said proudly.

Kids like to know what to do when they're lost. Basic knowledge of what to do gives kids power and reassurance. It helps them feel safe.

Don't Be Nice

"Be good." "Did you play nicely?" Phrases like these are confusing to kids and can lead to trouble. Too often adults toss around *good* to mean: Do what grown-ups tell you. *Good* means obedience and compliance. Being good and playing nicely could mean doing what a pedophile wants. We tend to teach obedience, but staying safe means teaching a child that she can also defy adults.

Instead of using vague "Be a good boy" or "Be a good girl" statements, reinforce a child's right to speak up and set limits in everyday life and play. "Did you like it when Kyle pushed you and took your truck? No? Then tell him." Kids need to know that they can set limits and say no to people of all ages, whether friends or strangers. These "I don't like it" limits apply whether it's to a child who grabs a toy, an overzealous grandma slathering them in kisses, or a friend's older sibling who crosses the line of safety.

"That's how you start," says Gudrun Herzog, a teacher at the School for Young Children. "It's really important for kids to know they have rights."

Learn Street Smarts

Offer plenty of opportunities for kids of all ages to build up common sense and courage. For a young child, this could be something as simple as asking the librarian for a book she wants. It could be ordering her own ice cream or making a phone call to set up an appointment. Many small steps of public courage help kids understand how the world works and gradually gain street smarts.

When out and about, encourage kids to be observant. A college self-defense course taught me cool karate moves, but also basic ways of interacting in public to avoid stranger disaster: Look at people, smile, and say hello. Simply being aware and engaged in your surroundings gives the signal that you're alert and not a victim. Many groups give tips on how to present non–stranger-based safety lessons to kids.

Foster Independence

Many of us adopt a habit of worry. My parents may have worried from time to time when I was school aged, but mostly they assumed all would be well. After all, I had a quarter in my pocket for a phone call in case of emergency.

Kids have a need to explore independently, even if it's just around the block on their bike or in a hidden corner of the backyard. This gives them creative freedom and confidence. Most important, it gives them a chance to rely on themselves. Children can't build these skills if they are always being watched.

Parents used to give kids challenges at young ages to test out their growing competence in the world. Jamaica Kincaid describes this ritual beautifully in her coming-of-age novel, *Annie John*. In the story, the mother sends her five-year-old out on an errand after training her carefully. The child has been to the store before and knows the shopkeeper. She returns triumphantly with three small packages and her mother bursts into tears. It's a tale of competence and independence.

An elementary school in California's Silicon Valley recently stepped up to a similar challenge. Oak Knoll School asked kids to try an independent act, such as riding the bus or playing at the park alone. According to Lenore Skenazy, who helped coordinate the school's project, the kids felt powerful, but the parents were transformed. They suddenly realized how responsible their children could be, and this newfound competence and responsibility extended into family life.

Give your child space that's free from constant watching. It could be a room you're not in. It could be biking around the block. For an older child, it could be going to the store and buying milk. No need to check in and worry. Agree to the plan, and make sure your child knows to contact you if the plan greatly changes. Then practice this yourself: Assume all is well.

Shield Kids from Fear, Not the World

Acknowledge your fears. My husband, for example, has a deep-rooted fear of snakes, passed on by his dad. He knows logically that the little garter snake we find in the backyard can't hurt him, and he doesn't want to convey this fear to our children. When we find a snake, he does his best not to yell, and then calmly says, "Look, guys, a garter snake." You cannot always shake your deep-rooted fears, even if all the logic and statistics stand against it. If you secretly worry about kidnapping or other rare occurrences, let it stay a private worry.

Today most parents are worried about sex offenders. The registry system makes it easy to know who lives nearby. I typed my address into the Michigan sex offender registry list and found eleven offenders within two miles of my house. I admit, seeing their faces staring back rather unnerved me.

Sometimes knowledge creates fear, but sometimes it reduces fear. These people have always lived among us. Knowing where they live should help us be safer and less fearful. Looking a little more deeply, I learned only one offender was considered dangerous. If you are going to check your neighborhood for offender addresses, take the time to check the tier system, which is designed to let the general public know which offenders are low risk (charged with possessing pornography, for example) and which people are serious, repeat offenders. Many people required by law to register are not threats. Knowledge should make us safer.

What do we do with the knowledge that there's one known dangerous person in the area? It's best to give basic safety information, but don't overreact. Think of the danger as you would a house fire: It could happen, but it probably won't. Here's what to do, just in case. When you talk to children, use a calm voice to talk about scary subjects. Be matter-of-fact when presenting safety information. This helps kids focus on your words and message, not your fear. If fear is overpowering you, your child will only pick up that you are scared.

Share adult fears with other adults. Project to your child this message: The world is mostly a good place.

Words to Say

Stay where I can see you.

Stay with me.

Stay where the adults are. The adults are taking care of you.

Find a mom or dad with kids.

You came here with me. You leave here with me.

Go together. Come home together.

Who's a safe adult at the gym?

That's Mrs. Greene. She lives in the brown house.

You can ask the clerk yourself.

Did you like that? Say no! Say stop.

Words to Avoid

Don't talk to strangers.

What if somebody steals you?

Somebody might come and kidnap you.

You'll be in big trouble.

Be good.

Play nicely.

Do what Mr. Johnson tells you.

Your Take

Statistics may not sway you. You may hear the logic that strangers rarely hurt children, but you can't get past the what-if thought that strangles your heart. If you can't shake the fear, try to keep it in perspective and among adults. Give your child the freedom to practice stranger interactions and gain the social skills she needs, especially the uh-oh reaction. This is for her safety.

Depending on your family background and personal life experience, you may feel particularly vigilant about one kind of danger, whether it's sexual abuse or drugs. What matters most to your family is up to you. Whatever the individual cases, children learn most about staying safe by consistently having you reinforce their rights: the right to stand up for themselves, to speak up when something's wrong, and to defy adults when necessary.

Section II

NAVIGATING TECHNOLOGY

*Enjoy present pleasures in such a way
as not to injure future ones.*

—SENECA

RULE

5

Embrace Amish iPads

The Amish are known for a horse-and-buggy lifestyle that bans cars. But not even the Amish are Luddites. They are technology selective. Many use cell phones. Some kids text. Some Amish communities reject bicycles but allow in-line skates. Why? A bicycle can take people too far away from the community.

Renegade Reason

Set tech limits to protect family and community. You are teaching lifelong habits.

Despite having a horse in the stable, many Amish use telephones, voice mail, copy machines, refrigerators, LED lights, and even word processors. When something new appears, they look at it, often restricting how and where this tool is used. Perhaps the Amish should be best known for their example of evaluating technology.

Here's the essence of their approach:

- Reject what impairs deepest values and community.
- Accept helpful tools.
- Adapt certain tools to avoid harm.

Adapting the Amish approach to modern, non-Amish life, the idea might be summed up as: "Go slowly. Be careful. Set limits to protect what you cherish."

Amish communities vary in their acceptance of technology according to their viewpoint and values. This is rather like families. As Donald Kraybill and his coauthors in the PBS series–based book *The Amish* say, the Amish blend of progress and tradition is a "continuous and complicated struggle." Sound familiar?

If you are one to rush to get the newest device, this chapter may not be for you. If you sometimes feel overwhelmed by technology and struggle to achieve the right balance for your family, then you may find useful ideas to adopt from seeing how others set limits.

Renegade Blessings

Children may complain that your house is the last to get a certain modern gadget, but that is not what will hurt them. Kids are hurt when they don't have meaningful family connections and don't have help establishing lifelong healthy habits.

I know how to talk to people.
My real life is important and wonderful.
Computers are just one part of life.
My family cares about me.
Just like junk food, too much screen time isn't good
    for you.
Nighttime is for sleeping.
There are manners for computers, too.
I'm in control of my mind. I have the strength to stop
    playing on computers.

Just because everyone's doing it doesn't mean it's good.

Things are always changing. I can cope with change.

Take Off Your Adult Lenses

We want our kids to "get ahead" and have all the advantages we can provide, but that doesn't mean handing them a smartphone or other digital device without guidance. Before the advent of junk food, parents didn't have to worry much about what children ate; food was relatively nutritious. Now with huge aisles devoted to chips, soda, and various corn syrup concoctions, we understand that one of our duties as parents is to teach good eating habits. Moderation, balance, healthy habits—this is the same with technology. Like teaching kids how to make food choices and achieve a balanced diet, we must take on the new role of teaching them how to make technology choices and achieve a balanced life. It starts with being aware and deliberate. It involves setting limits.

The Amish iPad

The car is banned in Amish life because it brings too much mobility. Mobility can bring a disintegration of community. Likewise, a dishwasher is banned because it takes away from the deeply held value of collective work and family cohesion that comes with washing dishes together. However, for non–Old Order Amish, a refrigerator is OK because it serves roughly the same role as an icebox. It stores food. The Amish modify their fridges to run on propane, however, since they do not connect to the electrical grid. Being tied into the grid goes against their principle of keeping separate from the world. Many modern conveniences, including lawn mowers and clothes dryers, are adapted to run on propane, compressed air, or batteries.

The telephone is probably the most relevant example for non-Amish families. A phone's insistent (and sometimes incessant) ring was viewed as disruptive to family life and face-to-face communication. The telephone could not be in the home, but many Amish agreed to the idea of public phones, or phones in a workshop, barn, or basement, with time constraints. The answering machine became a welcome tool for Amish furniture makers and others to receive messages from clients. Part of this meant designating a window of time: "Please leave a message. I will answer the phone between seven and seven fifteen p.m."

ESSENCE OF THE AMISH iPAD

Go slowly and be careful.
Wait.
Watch and see how it impacts people around you.
Ask people about the good points as well as the bad.
Decide what you deeply value in life.
> As commonly used, does this technology
>   improve life?
> Can you adapt this technology's use to match
>   your values?
Draw up a bucket list of your highest life priorities.
Run a pilot project.
Note the results, including mood, family cohesion, and
    time devoted to your life's highest priorities.
Modify again if you need to.
Set time or space constraints.
Possibly reject. Possibly adapt.

Look at your family values, and see what you cherish. If you don't relish following an Amish example, try following Steve Jobs's.

Smart Parents Set Tech Limits

Steve Jobs, the founder of Apple, set strict screen limits as a parent. "We limit how much technology our kids use at home," he told *New*

York Times reporter Nick Bilton, sharing that his kids hadn't yet used an iPad. Instead the Jobs family discussed books and history around the dinner table. He wasn't the only one. Many computer programmers and tech executives who develop the digital world create low-tech home environments for their kids. Interviews with Jobs and others show that techie parents ban screens from the bedroom, set strict time limits, and fill their kids' lives with old-fashioned books, board games, and nature.

Parenting in a Digital World

Five-year-old Isabelle is jumping up and down. "Kill him! Kill him!" she shouts gleefully. She's not playing a video game, but she's watching. On the screen is a shoot-'em-up game being played by two boys, ages seven and twelve, the kind of game with bodies littering the ground and copious amounts of digital blood. Isabelle loses interest after a while and reads a story with her mother while the boys keep playing.

Technology creates challenges, not least of which is we don't know what we're doing. It's new territory. But each generation has had new parenting challenges to face. When the car was invented, it changed family and social life. We came up with rules: Don't play in the street. We invented playgrounds. We made rules to set the age of sixteen for kids to drive and created driver's ed. Parents established family rules for governing when a child was responsible enough to get a license. We changed it from a problem to a rite of passage.

We need to do the same thing now with screens, games, and ever-changing digital technology. We are the ones to evaluate and invent these rules. Just as "Mud is not bad, but I don't want it in the living room," video games are certainly not bad, but some games and some use of them are unhealthy.

There's really nothing different here. It's all about setting limits, modeling healthy behavior, and being "good" ourselves (not swearing at home, not overusing smartphones). This chapter has some guidance and rules to help you do that. But first, before we can decide on sensible rules, we need some information.

Why It Works

When I give talks about renegade sharing and the idea that children have a right to take a long turn (as long as they like, until they are "all done"), someone in the audience invariably asks an excellent question: What about screens? Should children have as long a turn as they want with screens, too?

The answer is no. Screens are different.

Screens uniquely stimulate, and they overstimulate children's brains. Kids can't let it go. Maybe you've tried this with your child. Most kids will binge on screens, despite headaches and sleep loss. As adults, we find shutting down the computer or turning off our phone hard enough. Young children haven't yet fully developed the section of the brain that governs impulse control. Since they can't stop, we need to parent it.

Dealing with technology is basically the same as dealing with an angry toddler. You set limits. You offer tools and coping skills. You decide what's important. You stick to it. Tablets, smartphones, and the next best thing will come and go. Our kids need to prep for a lifetime of rapid change. They can meet this challenge best by developing creative thinking, being part of a strong family, and learning healthy habits.

> **Young children can't handle unlimited time with screens. They don't know when to stop.**

You've heard it before: Babies and toddlers should not be exposed to screens. For years, the American Academy of Pediatrics recommended *zero* screen time for children age two and under. No TV, no tablets, no handheld screens, no "educational" games. Kids this age need face-to-face, real-world experiences to develop socially, mentally, and physically. Despite this, we know most toddlers play with screens, averaging more than two hours a day, according to research by Common Sense Media, and almost a quarter of U.S. infants have a TV in their bedroom. By the time kids are in elementary school, screen time dominates their waking hours. For kids age eight and older, it's often seven-plus hours a day.

People talk about "screen time" because time indeed is the biggest issue. How do kids spend their limited time in childhood? It's a simple matter of opportunity cost. What is the child doing? What is the child *not* doing because of screens? Vital human skills—empathy, anger control, impulse control, conflict management, social abilities, flexibility, and focused thinking—take time to develop. Children need real-world experience, interaction, and practice to master these challenging parts of being human. When too much time is used up in virtual ways, kids miss the chance to develop in certain other ways. "Our brains are constantly being shaped by actions we engage in," says Richard Davidson, a neuroscientist at the University of Wisconsin–Madison. Screen time strengthens certain parts and neglects others. You can think of it as a corollary to the old adage "You are what you eat." When it comes to screens and brain wiring: "You are what you do."

Children have the right to interact and move through the real world for the majority of their day. It's how they learn the complex task of being human. As Nicholas Carr, author of *The Shallows: What the Internet Is Doing to Our Brains*, says, Internet use reinforces distractedness. Being distracted, Carr says, means we're more likely to follow the crowd, skip original thought, and have a harder time feeling empathy and compassion.

Younger kids need at least 80 to 100 percent of their waking hours off screens. For zero- to four-year-olds, this amount probably approaches 100 percent. Some early-childhood educators, such as

Ann Pelo, strongly advise no screens for children younger than seven. No matter what percentage or age cutoff you use, younger kids need real-life experiences even more than older children. Some video games, for example, let kids don virtual dress-up clothes and play in virtual sandboxes. Real sand and buckets and real dress-up clothes are far more useful to a four-year-old's developing mind.

When we provide vegetables for supper, kids are more likely to develop healthy eating habits. Research is showing that the more time kids spend with screens, the more they will watch as they grow older and the harder it will be for them to turn them off. Screen watching is habit forming, and adults tend to repeat the actions of their childhood.

On the social and emotional side, screens bring a mixed bag. On the plus side, children laugh and form friendships over video games or other screen play. However, older children often try social media before they've mastered the nuances of in-person friendships. This can lead to loss of real-life social skills, bad cyber manners, and friendships without depth. Children need adult guidance to learn both real-world and online etiquette.

> Parent technology the way you
> would parent nutrition.
> Model and moderate.

Some advocates for play, such as psychologist Peter Gray, disagree with screen limits and say children who have the chance to play outside with other kids and the chance to play with computers will choose a pretty decent balance. "The problem is not the computer," he says. "It's the lack of really fun alternatives—especially lack of opportunities to have adventures with other kids outside without continuous adult interference." If you can provide this sort of child-rich environment you may not need to rely on screen limits, but many families find that child-friendly play opens up when we set screen guidelines.

Screen limits are most important for younger children ages two to nine. Young children have the greatest need to interact with real-world objects, people, and environments. As children reach upper elementary school their relationship with screens will grow and change.

Boys' Brains and Video Games

Video games are "addictively" appealing, especially for boys. There is something about how boys' brains are wired that makes them susceptible to the high action and constant reward system (going up a level, gaining points) of common video games. In boys' brains, more than girls', the reward centers of the brain get triggered when they play video games. This makes games more attractive to boys in general, and for some boys, irresistible. Researchers from the Stanford School of Medicine studied brain images and saw much more activity in the area that deals with reward and addiction for males when both sexes played video games.

"Boys are particularly vulnerable to getting 'hooked' on first-person shooter games," says neuropsychologist Jane Healy, author of *Your Child's Growing Mind*. Boys are more likely than girls to display compulsive behavior toward gaming, develop unhealthy social relationships, and be unable to stop. Leonard Sax, a psychologist who studies gender, uses Friedrich Nietzsche's phrase "will to power" to explain why some boys are so attracted to these games. Boys' keen interest in power isn't bad, but it can be met in other ways, including real-life adventures, competition, and sports.

Go Slowly and Watch

"Don't vilify all video gaming and apps," my friend told me. "There's a lot of good out there."

Agreed. There's wonderful fun and learning with screens. I love the information the Internet's opened up, including cool world maps and interactive constellation apps. You may love blogs, long-distance games with friends, or YouTube videos, and your children may love video games or coding. Deciding what's useful, what's harmful, and what's time wasting takes consideration. I prefer to be the last one on the block. That gives me ample time to assess new screen use and check out the common benefits and pitfalls.

We laugh now at generations of past parents who worried about the unhealthy introduction of pool halls, comic books, and even chess. Characters from the period drama *Downton Abbey* are terrified of the toaster and of electricity leaking out of wall sockets. Perhaps someday we'll laugh at our reactions to technology today. New inventions take getting used to. It's not all good; it's not all bad. It comes down to how we use it as a tool to support the best in human life.

Develop Impulse Power

As an eight-year-old, my son, Myles, was eager to play video games. The other kids at school talked about it. His cousins played. He seemed old enough to try.

What I first noticed was that my stable, easygoing child snarled and snapped at me when game time was supposed to be over. He'd been happy before he started, and happy during the game, but ending it produced rage. This happened every week. It was transformative rage—the kind that made sweet Bilbo Baggins transform into a hideous evil guy in *The Lord of the Rings*.

I had two goals here. One was to allow my child to participate in the modern world he was growing up in. The other was to teach him life habits of impulse control for technology.

Knowing boys are particularly vulnerable to the allure of video game play, I told my son that video games weren't bad, but they could overpower his brain. To play video games in a healthy way, he had to prove he could be stronger than the video game. He nodded, seeming to take this logic in. I could see his mind was itching to start Minecraft.

I knew I had to step out of the role of Video Game Stopper. Just as parents should avoid becoming the Homework Cop, an important part of setting screen limits is stopping anger from being directed at the parent and increasing friction between parent and child.

We shifted responsibility to Myles. To prove he was mature enough to play video games, he had to set his own timer for the game and—this was the hard part—turn the game off immediately when the timer rang. "It's going to be hard," I told him. "But every time you do it, you'll be building up your brain and getting stronger. If you're not strong enough to turn it off, you're not strong enough to play video games right now."

He knew the stakes were high. He decided to set the timer to give himself a five-minute warning so that stopping in the middle of a game would be easier. The difference was dramatic. No more screen-time clock watching for me. No more raging eyes and parent-child conflict. Instead, when the timer went off, Myles hit the Off button. When he stood up, he was smiling and told me about his game.

The conflict had shifted to its appropriate opponents: my child's impulse strength and the computer itself. Part of his smile came from his new sense of power. Computers are powerful, yes, but he was powerful over a computer's draw.

This technique combines willpower (development of impulse control) with family rules. Myles had to stop. He knew if he didn't, his screen time would be eliminated next time.

Technology use must be parented. Set limits.

Distraction and Temptation

In the children's book *Frog and Toad Together*, Toad bakes cookies and the two friends try to rustle up enough willpower to stop eating them. Despite putting the cookies in a box, tying up the box with string, and setting it on a high shelf, the chocolate chip cookie temptation is too much for them. They finally settle on feeding the cookies to the birds.

Freshly baked chocolate chip cookies are like digital messages. They seem to exact a magnetic pull. When I realized a little yellow icon on my screen meant I had new e-mail, my concentration dropped. Instead of checking e-mail only two or three times a day, I found my eyes constantly seeking the icon; it was difficult to resist checking messages.

You know the powerful pull of a smartphone's ping or another device's call to action. We can't berate ourselves. It's the way we're made. Sometimes willpower isn't enough. We can always strengthen our willpower, but we also need stronger options. These come from setting technology habits through family rules. As Kraybill quotes an Amish elder saying, "Individuals are not wise enough to make private choices about technology." In some ways, Amish families have it easier. Their church tells them what constraints they must live with. As parents we must take on this role for our children. But we must also do something harder: We must set these rules for ourselves (see Rule 6: Discipline Your Phone).

Video Games and Addiction

"Mom, I'm closing my eyes and Minecraft is playing in my mind," said eleven-year-old Anna. She held out her iPad Mini to her mother. "Please hide this," she said. The pull of the video game felt so all-consuming to Anna that it scared her.

I remember when *Pong* came out in my childhood. This early video game wasn't much, just a little white square going back and forth trying to look like a Ping-Pong ball, but I remember struggling to break away. How much more entrancing and sophisticated games are now.

Video gaming is habit forming and kids say they can't pull away from it. Whether it can be termed clinically addictive or not, it has many of the same pulls as addiction. Fast-moving video games cause dopamine to be released in a way that's similar to the effect of taking addictive drugs. Besides the fast action and fun figures bouncing on the screen, kids get grabbed by video games because of the built-in reward system of gaining points and advancing levels. When you take the screens away, kids can get grouchy and agitated.

The answer for an addict is to never touch the addictive substance again. That doesn't work with technology. Kids can't get away from screens. They're everywhere. We need to coach kids to watch for danger signs, monitor mood signals ourselves, and help kids set healthy habits for developing moderation and impulse control. Sometimes that means taking a break.

Push Pause

My son Zach had a terrible time stopping story time. If we stopped reading in the middle of a long book, he grew frantic. To him, the whole story had collapsed. Bookmarks saved us. The simple act of inserting a bookmark helped Zach realize the story wasn't over; it was just on pause.

Games are never over. You can always do more, score higher, advance to the next level. To cope with the never-ending nature of screens and video games, it can help to introduce words such as *pause*. Even young children know what the Pause button does. It stops a show and lets you resume later. Some parents call this "saving the game." Let kids know it's never going to be "all done," but it's time to stop.

Keep Games Fun and Social

Video games are fun. That's why kids and adults play them. Fun should be part of every child's day, whether it comes in the form of video games or not.

If you like gaming, it's easy to see the good. If you're worried about violent games and gaming's incredible magnetic power, it's hard to see anything but bad. For example, one charge is that video games are mostly sedentary. That's really not the main concern: Book reading is also sedentary.

As a child, I played *Dungeons and Dragons*. My mother looked at it and decided the game was fine, even though other mothers were worried. She saw it was creative and social. When we played, my brother and I cooperated and laughed a lot. It even taught me about mapping, mythology, and how to spell *miscellaneous*. Without calling it that, my mother used the Amish iPad approach. We can all do that when evaluating new digital inventions. Is it creative? Is it cooperative? Does it foster social relationships or hurt them?

James, age nine, lived in a low-tech household but longed to play video games. When kids at school talked about them, he claimed he played them, too. His schoolmates could tell James didn't know what he was talking about and shunned him. My son Myles plays minimal computer games. In fact, with thirty minutes on Wednesdays and one hour on Sundays, I've learned through a classroom poll that the only kid who plays fewer video games per week is the librarian's child. The amount of time Myles plays is small, but the social benefit seems big. He can talk and laugh with other kids his age about Creepers and redstone and be part of his generation. The social benefit seems good.

Video games offer the allure of a fictional world, a virtual reality not grounded in this one. It's fun to pretend temporarily to be someone else and have adventures. People who live inside imaginary characters' heads and create entire fictional worlds are not just video gamers, they're also authors. It's OK to love an imaginary world. The danger is when the virtual world supplants a child's real-world life. Does he have real friends? Does he care about other activities? Does he express passion for the world he actually lives in? It's fun to indulge in fantasy games, but connection to real life needs to stay primary.

Most video games are plain old fun. How much fun from screens do we want to include at the expense of other life? Video games, good and bad, take children's time. Studies have shown this screen time is not displacing reading—most boys stop reading for pleasure by age eight, soon after they learn to read—it replaces outdoor playtime.

Indoor Time

Technology keeps kids inside. Video games and other screens are displacing outdoor playtime. A National Wildlife Federation program estimates U.S. children now spend significantly less than ten minutes a day in outside play.

Outdoor play improves both bodies and minds. Kids who play outdoors not only gain better coordination, but they improve their ability to concentrate. This is especially true of children with signs of ADHD (attention deficit/hyperactivity disorder). Kids need outdoor time for running and physical fitness, but also for mental sharpness and mental health. Kids who play outside also have better anger management and disease resistance. Simply being outside among trees significantly reduces stress in people of all ages.

If we care about our kids, we need to get them outside. Without enough outside time and real-life connection, kids begin to feel empty, bored, and turned off. Leonard Sax describes kids' need for real-life experiences in his book *Boys Adrift*. Nothing gets them excited. They lack passion and fall into apathy and depression.

If we care about our planet, we need to get kids outside. It's people who have fond childhood memories of nature who donate time and money to protect the planet. Nancy Wells, of Cornell University, found that the best way to stimulate kids to care about the environment was for them to play in the woods or do things such as camping, hiking, and fishing before age eleven.

The Beauty of Wandering Minds

One of the most common questions for authors is: "Where do your ideas come from?" Mine come from walks. I come up with book titles on long car rides and entire fiction plots on cross-country skis. You know this phenomenon: "It came to me in the shower!" or "I just thought of this while walking the dog."

This is the gift of the wandering mind, the part of our brains that functions differently, often more creatively, when we are not actively focused on a task. Larry Rosen, a research psychologist and the author of *Rewired*, says our brains go into a stage of daydreaming as a default mode when we're not fully focused. The wandering mind gives us our aha moments. Kids who are constantly plugged in don't get this downtime for brain calm and creativity.

Educational Benefits

Some "educational" computer games are best ignored. Young children can learn colors by interacting with the world. They don't need an app to teach the sound a cow makes. Many games claim to teach math and reading skills but may not offer much.

When it's time to teach specific skills, however, some families find conveying basic concepts through a computer can have an advantage over human instruction. "Cayden memorized his times tables in a way that was so fun and painless," said his mother. "In contrast, my dad drilled me. It was very stressful and unpleasant . . . [he used to] wake me with 'What's seven times seven?'" Her son also learned cursive writing and telling time from an app, and her five-year-old daughter uses an app to learn Hebrew letters.

Some school programs distribute laptops to every student, often in middle school, but sometimes younger. A Duke University study by Helen Ladd and Jacob Vigdor tracked thousands of these students. They discovered that reading and math skills *declined* when laptops were introduced. The weaker the student to begin with, the more severely her scores declined.

The true value of computers as teaching tools is likely to burgeon in the coming years as we learn how to refine their benefits. For example, girls can significantly improve spatial rotation skills—the ability to envision an object rotating in three dimensions. Research by Jing Feng and other psychologists at the University of Toronto suggested that playing an action video game improved girls' spatial abilities, and the effects lingered even five months later. The trick is to "extract the critical training components from first-person shooter games," said Feng. Researchers hope using video games in this way could help smooth out gender differences in fields such as engineering.

It's easy to be wowed by what computer learning offers. But we must stay amazed at the richness the real world offers. We tend to overvalue quantifiable, academic learning and undervalue the less linear type of learning and exploration of ideas children do on their own. Both have their place. Our job is to make sure one type of learning doesn't shoulder out the other.

Video Games and Violence

My first book contains a chapter called "Bombs, Guns and Bad Guys Allowed." I'm not against violent fantasy play. Backyard sword fights, toy gun play, and "you're dead" games are all healthy aspects of child development.

Prepackaged violence changes the equation, especially visual images of violence. Any prepackaged play (ready-formed idea handed to a child) is less valuable to a child's mind. Children are extremely sensitive to visual imagery, and seeing repeated images desensitizes our brains to violence. It's one thing for a child to imagine a battle between good guys and bad guys, and another thing for a child to see lifelike images of gore and destruction. Video games present two types of visual violence: 1) traditional shoot-'em-up games against an enemy (soldiers, zombies), and 2) violent games against societal norms, such as killing babies on bicycles and raping women. Shooting zombies may be fine. Researchers say killing babies—even digital ones—is likely not. Douglas Gentile, from Iowa State University, says content matters. He found that video games impact children's empathy. Kids who played pro-social games showed more caring behavior. "With violent games we see the exact opposite," he says. Leonard Sax says research results on this are as clear as the established hazards of secondhand smoke.

Tech Check

Time to set new, clear limits if your child . . .

- Snaps and gets angry after playing on screens
- Can't turn screens off
- Spends little time outside
- Seems stressed and tired
- Spends more time with screens than in person with friends
- Isolates himself from family life

Practice

"Dude, why don't you just text? It's easier." My nine-year-old was calling a school friend to set up a time to play together.

He's completely right. Texting is easier. That's precisely why my child is calling. He needs practice. It's my job to give my son abundant opportunities to make personal phone calls and be at ease with people face-to-face. I'm not worried that my child won't be able to learn to text. Face-to-face and one-on-one social interaction are hard, however. Kids need practice.

What about social media? Kids need practice with real-world friendship skills and impulse control first. Can your child control her anger? Does she frequently blame people, and have a hard time owning up to mistakes? Does she show good judgment about when to share secrets and when to be silent? These friendship and emotional skills come with maturity. If your child hasn't developed them yet, then she's not ready for social media.

Cell Phones

First it was teens, then tweens, now younger and younger children are being granted their own cell phone. These phones are typically smartphones, which come with great interactivity and temptations built in.

The same rule applies to cell phone use as other technology: Be intentional.

When Holly gave her fifth-grade daughter her first smartphone, she used the idea of a phone contract, borrowed from another parent. Among the list of agreements: Turn your phone off in restaurants, don't text anything you wouldn't say out loud, and don't send pictures of your private parts. She was shocked by how much her daughter didn't know. "We assume our kids know things we consider common sense. In reality, they don't. They don't have our life experience."

Low-tech Kids Need Tech Teaching, Too

"We don't even have a TV," says Nadia, mother of a three-year-old. "I try not to expose her to all that." Even kids from non-tech houses find tech everywhere. Babysitters bring phones and show videos. Kids on the school bus play handheld devices. Mobile technology is simply part of our children's world. Every child needs to be taught about technology, no matter what kind of home you provide.

Be aware that forbidden fruit can be the most tempting. Your child needs guidance coping with the temptations of technology. It's not enough to give a child a low-tech childhood; we must give her the skills, knowledge, and habits to live with technology. When this child turns eighteen she needs to cope on her own with a digital world. It's up to us, because nobody else will.

Children's Rights in a Screen-Filled World

A right to engage in the world in which she's growing up

A right to interact with the real, non-screen world for the majority of his day

A right to learn and practice face-to-face social skills

A right to times of quiet

A right to learn healthy boundaries for technology

A right to adequate sleep

A right to receive regular, full attention from people around her

Try This—Add to Your Toolbox

When things seem amiss, it can be tempting to dismiss all technology and completely unplug. Unplugging can certainly help re-center families, especially if screens have gone too far. However, online life is part of daily life—it's how we pay bills, get announcements, keep up with friends, plan trips, gather information, and more—so eventually we need to set a balance.

When it comes to setting good limits, concentrate on time, space, and developmental maturity. Align screen tools to your values.

Find the Right Screen:Life Ratio

Researcher Larry Rosen is a self-declared technology advocate. He's been studying the psychology of technology for more than thirty years and loves most of it. But in the past few years, he has become worried by a lack of limits on technology. He suggests a ratio of 1:5, in minutes, for children under twelve. That means half an hour of tablet play is balanced with two and a half hours of outdoor play or other non-screen time. The ratio can adjust as kids grow older.

Ratios like this can work well when applied to kids' free time. That means non-school, non-sleep, non-scheduled time. For example, a four-year-old who naps, goes to preschool, and has a gym time has about four hours of unstructured free-play time. Screens should be no more than twenty-five minutes of that. Another good guideline is 80 percent or more of an older child's waking time should be off screen, and nearly 100 percent for a child aged zero to four.

Screen time opens worlds, while also closing worlds by taking away time for other things. If you value free play and outdoor play, make sure your kids get a healthy dose of both every day.

Does It Promote Community?

Two-year-old Eli giggled as he waved at his grandma. Grandma lived a continent away, but with a video call they could connect and remember each other.

All screen use is not the same. If video calls help keep your family close, then freely incorporate them into your life. There's no substitute for being there, but video calls allow even young children to interact and enjoy distant relatives.

Create Sacred Spaces

Back in the 1970s, my parents set a rule to promote family connection: no reading at the table. We made an exception for breakfast, since everyone was too groggy anyway and my parents wanted to read the paper. They also made another rule: no phone calls answered during dinner. For a half hour, we would be together as a family.

Today it's not books and newspapers that encroach on family time; it's tech gadgets. Decide what parts of the day will be sacred spaces to build family connection. Meals are typical times. What works for you depends on your family. Maybe it's the car. When everyone's stuck together for the ride without a gadget, great laughs and conversations can take place. Find your spaces and stick to them. The message your kids get is simple and strong: We are important as a family. There's a time to be interrupted and a time to be fully present.

Set Time and Space Boundaries

Six-year-old Jacob and Dylan were wrestling during library story time. Wrestling itself isn't the problem, since these games are good for kids. It's the wrong time and space. The same limits apply to technology. Advances have made computers mobile, but that doesn't mean we can't limit their mobility. Set limits on tech times and space.

This might mean no screen use on school days, because there's already little time in the day for family, outdoor time, and unstructured free play. It could mean half an hour a day. The American Academy of Pediatrics originally recommended no more than one to two hours of entertainment screen time a day for children, even on weekends.

"All technology stays on the main floor in our house," says Melissa, a mother of two. "That goes for adults, too. It's always out in the open." Her family finds togetherness time with technology. Being in one space means more sharing, and helps the adults keep an eye on how screens are changing the kids' moods.

Other families balance days on and off, including tech-free weekends, or the 5:2 screen diet. Marta's family tried this—five days online and two days off-line each week—and liked it. Her kids were reluctant at first, but soon enjoyed the off-line days, which had less yelling and more family time. Cheryl tried screen-free Sundays, and found it made a difference especially with Milo, her son with autism. "What a nice couple of days! Milo was especially more interactive than he normally is—getting out puzzles, blocks, and books. There was remarkably little pushback."

Set Limits on Tech Time and Space

SAMPLE BOUNDARIES
Thirty minutes a day, or
No screens on weeknights
One to two hours per day on weekends
No screens in bedrooms (parents included)
No screens at the table
No screens after supper
No screens one hour before bedtime

Education Versus Entertainment

Some families distinguish between screen time for entertainment and screen time for education. In a young child's world (age four and younger), screen time is screen time. Whether it's educational or entertainment, it takes young kids out of the real-world experiences in which they develop best.

In our family, screen time is simply what kids choose to do on computers. What parents choose to share in addition to that is what we term educational, whether it's a movie, online video, or other information.

Many screen guides suggest so many minutes on computers a day "except for schoolwork." Since there is no documented value in home-work for elementary-aged children, screens should not be needed for school-related work (see Rule 8: Ban Elementary Homework).

For older children, about age ten and up, the real question is about creativity. Creative screen time may be creating computer code or creating videos. Entertainment versus education is not necessarily the question. Just as with all children's play, what's most interesting is usually a combination of fun and learning.

Change the Parent-Child-Computer Dynamic

No parent likes to play timekeeper. If your child lashes out at you for enforcing screen time limits, it's time to step out of that role. Change the parent-child anger dynamic by transferring responsibility for tracking time to the child. Some parents use a built-in timer that automatically shuts down the game, but try a timer that forces the child to exercise impulse control. This helps kids strengthen their own self-control—a useful skill for so much—rather than follow the automatic shutdown.

Screens as Rewards and Punishment

If kids break a specific tech rule (for example, beg for more time or disregard the timer), a screen consequence might be appropriate. Be clear about tech rules. However, most misbehavior is about unrecognized feelings, so focus on feelings and problem solving rather than meting out screen punishment.

Once you've set your family screen time, try not to use extra screen time as a reward for good behavior. Want to reward your child? Try giving her alone time with you.

Guide to Setting Tech Boundaries

1. Find a good screen:life ratio. Of your child's waking hours, what will it be?

The American Academy of Pediatrics' original guidelines said no more than one to two hours of screen play a day, a ratio of about

1:7. Some researchers say a 1:5 ratio is good for children under twelve. That means half an hour of tablet play is balanced with two and a half hours of outdoor or non-screen play.

2. Put all phones and screens away at least one hour before bed.

3. Remove screens from all bedrooms. (Kids check messages during the night.)

4. Shift conflict, anger, and control away from an adult-child dynamic. Put the child in charge of controlling her impulses and monitoring her screen time.

5. Set clear expectations, including no grumbles, negotiations, or begging for more time. These behaviors signal kids need a break.

6. Make plentiful time for real life. Does screen time squeeze out other interests, including free play and outdoor physical play, in your child's day?

7. Create "sacred spaces." These are screen-free areas. This might include the family dinner table.

8. Teach technology manners. This includes valuing the person you're with over the person on the screen.

9. Talk about the feeling of being "grabbed." Help your child pay attention to times she can't stop thinking about a video game or can't stop playing. That's a signal it's too much.

10. Set time windows for when tech is allowed. For example, it could be between four and six p.m.

11. Set times when screens are limited or not allowed: zero to thirty minutes on weekdays and perhaps one to two hours per day on weekends.

12. Alternately, declare a weekly Internet Sabbath, or perhaps a monthly week or weekend free.

13. Create a welcoming space that's public. Allow children to use screens only in the living room, for example.

14. Follow the rules yourself.

If something is bothering you, it's time to make a change.

Observe the Sabbath

Whether it's Fridays, Sundays, or another day in the week, decide on a day for an Internet Sabbath. This is a weekly time when phones are off and computers are shut down. Let close family and others know you won't respond on the Tech Off Day. Or maybe you'll choose a TV Off Day. If you can't get away for a complete day, set aside a weekend afternoon, or only allow tech for half an hour first thing in the morning. We like to feel in contact, but the truth is, most of it can wait. Make sure one or two people know an emergency method to reach you. Beware: The effectiveness of the Sabbath depends on *you*. Kids can do it. You have to, too.

During your off-screen time, notice what you do instead. Are you outside more? Talking and laughing more? Taking walks? Whatever it is, this activity is typically being replaced by screen time.

Make Bedtime for Sleeping

My son's math class was learning about graphing, so they did a quick class survey: When's your bedtime? "I go to bed at nine p.m.," many kids said, "but then I get to stay up playing video games." One eleven-year-old regularly stayed up until midnight with games in hand.

Playing video games in bed is about the exact opposite of counting sheep. Looking at screens before going to sleep causes sleep problems. It stimulates the brain to be awake and suppresses melatonin, the hormone needed to help our bodies fall asleep. One of our fundamental jobs as parents is to teach and model good sleep habits. For elementary school–aged kids, that means nine to eleven hours a night, early bedtimes, and rituals to help them wind down and become drowsy. Kindergarteners need even more hours of sleep.

Be a Technology Renegade

It can seem cruel to set limits in your house when other families are letting their kids run free with tech choices. Don't worry about hurting your children. They're not missing vital computer skills. As Google executive Alan Eagle told the *New York Times*, "At Google and all these places, we make technology as brain-dead easy to use as possible. There's no reason why kids can't figure it out when they get older." Eagle's own kids go to a Waldorf school, which is full of hands-on learning and nature.

Research reported in the journal *Pediatrics* found that using a computer once a week was better for kids than using it every day. Technology research professor Sherry Turkle, of MIT, interviewed thousands of young people and found kids long for family, full attention, and a meaningful life. Give them that. Fit in some tech. They can do the rest. Just like a family that sets chores, bedtimes, and family responsibilities versus one that doesn't, you are doing your kids a favor by giving guidance with technology's pull.

Words to Say

> You set the timer.
> It's up to you to prove you have control.
> Screens are good, but only sometimes.
> It's hard to stop. How will you do it?
> Looks like you've been grabbed by the computer.
> That's a signal to say: Whoa. Slow down.
> I know it's hard to stop.
> Games are made to go on forever.
> You're not finished, but it's time to stop.
> Save the game. Put it on "pause." Don't worry, it
>   saves everything until you play again.
> You need to show me you are stronger than the computer.
> Apologies are best in person.
> Would you say that in person? (regarding social media)
> When it changes your mood, it's good to take a break.
> We all need an Internet break.

Let's try it.

Sure, you can play it, but not right now.

No phones at the table.

You know the rule: No screens in the bedrooms.

Outside time now.

Words to Avoid

Sure, that's fine. It's educational.

OK, one more minute.

If you don't hurry up, you'll lose your screen time.

I guess it's OK. Kids are always on screens.

Your Take

Especially when it comes to technology, there is no one-size-fits-all approach. Some households are techy; they may include parents who are computer programmers, and find joy playing interactive video games as a family. Other households are non-tech or extremely low-tech. Most fall somewhere in the middle, letting the tide carry them along. Whatever comfort level you have, think about it, set some limits, and find technology parenting tips that work for you. Be intentional. Screens are part of our world, but the youngest children thrive primarily off-screen.

RULE
6 Discipline Your Phone

S onia, age two, was playing with her mother. When her mother picked up her cell phone, Sonia burst into tears. Jamie, another two-year-old, took more drastic measures. She put her mother's smartphone in the trash.

"I felt horrible," said Sonia's mother. "To her the phone meant I was going to a place where she couldn't join me—an adult cyber world—and she felt left out."

Renegade Reason

Kids learn manners and life habits from watching adults. Modeling healthy tech behavior starts with you.

When it comes to screen time, most parents think of children zoning out on screens. But adult tech use may be more out of control. Not only are kids jealous of adult devices, but they are watching you.

Where is your phone during school pickup time? Dinnertime? Bedtime story time? When was the last time you felt caught up, relaxed, and on top of life? "Today children contend with parents who are physically close, tantalizingly so, but mentally elsewhere," says MIT professor Sherry Turkle.

Being a model can be draining. Some days it's the hardest part of parenting. We have to be constantly on show, displaying our best, most kindly spoken, disciplined selves. Just like modeling a healthy lifestyle, we must model good screen use. Part of parenting today is acting as a living model when it comes to healthy use of technology.

Kids do most of their growing and learning from the real world. They need caregivers who are present, not disconnected and distracted. If we want a child who's not consumed by video games, one who's responsive to family members and finds joy in life, then we must look at ourselves first.

Renegade Blessings

Just like with modeling manners and good sleep habits, modeling technology manners and good screen habits is the best way for kids to learn to manage daily life. Demonstrate restraint and balance. Children will learn:

I'm important and valued.

It's polite to give your attention to the people you're with.

My parents greet me in person when they see me. I don't have to compete with the phone.

Sometimes really important things come up. I can wait. I know it's an exception.

I know when my mom has to work.

Working hard is good, but not all the time.

Inventions keep changing, but some of the best stuff in life doesn't change.

My family matters.

Being together feels good.

Why It Works

It's easy to focus on what's "wrong" with the kids when faced with parenting challenges. It's harder when the focus is on us.

Turkle, a clinical psychologist from MIT, has studied technology use for decades. She was surprised to find that it was the kids who were devastated and frustrated by the parents' tech use. "My dad's always on his phone," kids say, or "My mom says 'just a minute,' but then she keeps playing on her phone and she's gone." Kids of all ages—from tots to teenagers—are longing for the elusive respect of full attention.

Multitasking is part of parenting. We can't take a shower or prep supper without multitasking with a child in the house. We wash dishes while tracking a toddler in our peripheral vision and listening for the baby to wake. Screen multitasking, however, diverts our attention away from our surroundings—and our kids. "There's a very big difference between your mother doing the dishes and not giving you her full attention, which is what most people grew up with, and your mother being immersed in e-mail or texting," says Turkle. The pace and intensity has shifted. Kids notice it. They feel it. They view the screen as competition.

It hurts parents, too. More than a third of U.S. adults check work messages routinely during dinner. Half check work e-mails or texts in bed in the middle of the night or before getting up in the morning. This constant on-call pressure to respond instantly is stressful— so stressful that other countries are instituting bans on the practice. It's currently illegal to contact workers on holidays in Germany, and that may extend to evenings also. "There is an undeniable relationship between constant availability and the increase of mental illness," says Andrea Nahles, Germany's labor minister, in a 2014 article by *The Christian Science Monitor.*

Larry Rosen, who's studied the psychology of technology for more than thirty years, says adult smartphone use is rightly called an obsession. We check, we scan, we update, we check again and drop everything else when a new message appears. All this attachment to technology doesn't give us much pleasure. Instead it gives us worry, a constant feeling of being behind, out of date, out of touch. As Rosen explains, obsession differs from addiction. Addiction compels people to seek pleasurable experiences. Obsession compels people to repeat a behavior to reduce stress and anxiety.

Rosen says people immediately think of technology fasts or digital detox to solve their problems, but setting limits and boundaries works better. By retraining our brains not to follow the constant urge to check in, we don't feel the impulse so strongly. When we check in, we are trying to calm our anxiety. Messages come at unpredictable intervals, which makes checking in even more habit forming. Each time we check in, our brains release neurotransmitters and the cycle is reinforced. Taking breaks, limiting check-in times to certain periods of the day, and balancing our screen-to-life ratio can reset our adult brains and model good habits for kids.

The more we learn about children's brain development, the more we learn kids need us. Catherine Steiner-Adair, a psychologist and the author of *The Big Disconnect: Protecting Child and Family Relationships in the Digital Age*, says neuroscience in this tech era is reinforc-

Take Off Your Adult Lenses

My phone is my world, we say. Or: I have to be available—what if someone needs me? Our children need us to be fully available in the present. What we are more likely missing when we don't set limits on technology is time to live the life we value. We check our phones partly because our brain chemistry compels us to check. We can retrain this urge. We check our phones partly because we're afraid of missing out. If we put the phone down, we may miss out on a friend's social media update and photo of a sunset. If we don't put our phone down, we may miss out on our social relationship with our child and the real sunset outside.

ing two age-old truths about children's learning: 1) human-to-human interaction builds the brain uniquely, and 2) the role of parents is critical. We need to be there for them.

Limits Are Possible

A friend who used to text three thousand times a month stopped by. Last time I'd seen her, our conversation had been distracted. Every few seconds her eyes and attention would dart away, drawn as if by the pull of an invisible string down to her handheld device. Now she seemed much more present. What was the big change?

"I dropped my phone on a concrete floor," she said. While the phone was broken, she found she wasn't in a hurry to get it fixed. "It was nice not to be bothered."

This forced break prompted Elena to change her ways. She called friends to talk and only texted for quick logistics. She began to turn off her computer when she was done. At night she turned off her now-fixed phone, instead of keeping it on as an alarm clock.

Now for the first time in years Elena uses a regular alarm clock again and sleeps through the night. "I'm finding my limits," she said. "I love the freedom and space."

Most parents haven't found that balance. Here's what kids see: adults setting no limits for themselves for time on phones and other devices. Adults interrupting meals and story time for a "quick text." Adults using home time for work, checking business e-mail at all hours and saying, "This will just take a minute"—then disappearing for much longer. Kids see no boundaries. Adult attention appears to be a fleeting thing. What children are learning by example is: 1) it's OK to interrupt someone constantly, and 2) the online world is better and more important than this one.

It's OK to Be Inaccessible

The only thing I want to do 24-7 is breathe.

You can be inaccessible. Yes, even to your kids at times. Chances are, if they are really in trouble, they can find another adult with a cell phone.

I received an e-mail the other day that included this note in the signature line:

"I reply to e-mails from 12 p.m. to 2 p.m. and after 8 p.m. on weekdays." That made sense. The sender was a mother with young kids. Twelve to two p.m. was nap time. After eight, the kids were in bed. Weekends were for family. She set clear limits and notified people.

When I worked for nonprofits, I often spent long field days in the woods, visiting sites for my job. As cell phones grew common, I took one with me, but only turned it on at lunch or during other natural breaks in the day to respond to messages. "How am I supposed to reach you?" a coworker asked. "You should have it on all the time." The new technology had changed expectations. I discovered being constantly accessible hurt my ability to do my job. I couldn't answer office questions and be present in the woods. I needed to concentrate on the people I was meeting and the area I was visiting. After a while, I took to turning it off again and checking for messages a few times a day. There's a time to be available and a time to be off-limits. If I'm available to everybody, then I can't help anybody.

Be accessible to the present moment, not the phone.

Setting Work-Life Boundaries

You may think your boss won't take kindly to being unable to reach you outside work hours, but she might be relieved. It could be she's overworked and overconnected, too.

Consider what has created an overly porous work-life boundary in your life. Doctors and plumbers need to be on call at times. Most of the rest of us do not. It's true you may not have complete control, but work at setting stronger work-life boundaries.

We bemoan the lack of privacy in our personal lives. It may annoy us to answer a work message on the weekend, but it still boosts our sense of being needed, of being valued. "Oh! A message for *me*." Somebody wants us. We're important.

The other common work-life trap is using technology to work from home. As a freelancer myself, I know this one. There's the allure of being able to be with your kids and your job. What ends up happening to many parents is constant stress and not handling either job well. If you work from home, work in blocks and hire a sitter. You'll find your work time (even two hours) is much more productive, and you can be fully present in both times. We say we're "doing it for the kids," but kids don't need you there constantly. They do need your clear absence or presence. Make it clear to yourself, too.

> Make it clear. Are you absent or present?

Importance of Announcements

When you see people with heads down, eyes scanning, shoulders hunched over a screen, they all look the same. They could be reading the newspaper, scrolling through Facebook, or concentrating hard on work. It's hard to tell what they're up to.

Our kids don't know either. "I thought you guys were playing video games all day," one eight-year-old told his parents. That's what he liked to do, so it made sense to him that his parents were playing video games when he saw them glued to their computer screens.

A computer or digital device is a portal to everywhere. We don't know what's going on. We don't know if the person is bored or ab-sorbed. Our children don't know how involved or excluded to be. Announce it for them. Rachel, Sonia's mom, now does this when she makes a phone call: "See, I'm calling Daddy." Kids need information so they understand how interruptible you are (your child may think: *Oh, he's just looking at maps; I can talk to him*) and whether it involves or impacts them (*Oh, cool, she's on the computer looking up my soccer camp. She's busy at the moment, but I know I'm important*).

The more I parent, the more I find young kids and parents-on-computers don't mix. Still, there are times I'm home with my kids and I have to get stuff done. Even simple errands—renewing the library books, buying tickets, paying bills—involve online time. With the kids absorbed in free play, it can be the perfect chance for me to tick some of these chores off my list.

The trouble is, the kids can't tell what I'm up to when I face the screen. They just see me staring at it. It's a different relationship than if I'm around the house busy with my hands. I may be distracted, but they can see what I'm doing, and chances are I can still talk.

So before I head to the screen, I announce it. "I'm making plans for our vacation." Or "I'm checking to see if your book has come in." Or "I'm doing some research on new tires." These are all tasks that require little thought, and I can be interrupted. Sometimes I say: "I'm working now. I need quiet."

Explaining to the people around you what you're doing is polite no matter what their age. The other day I saw a non-tech woman in her seventies take offense when the man she was talking to started tapping away on a device in the middle of a conversation. "Are you listening or messing around with your phone?" she asked, annoyed. "Oh, I'm listening. I'm actually taking notes here on what you just said," the man answered. "This is my notepad." Explain what you're doing or nobody will know.

Care of Deep Relationships

Before social media, we lavished time and attention only on our closest friends and family. Acquaintances were people we ran into from time to time but didn't devote much time to.

Now the situation has flipped. Kathryn, for example, a mother of two, has five hundred friends on social media. Several times a day she comments on people's profiles, many of whom are nice folks but not deep friends. Being on social media helps her feel in touch and caught up, especially since she's home with young kids, but she realizes she doesn't spend in-depth time with close friends anymore.

As Georgia O'Keeffe said: "Nobody sees a flower really; it is so small. We haven't time, and to see takes time—like to have a friend takes time."

Deep relationships take time. These are the people we live with and the ones closest to our hearts. Look where your time is spent. Is it allocated to your loved ones or your acquaintances? Are you nurturing your deepest relationships, or spreading yourself too thin?

If we hope our children will find deep relationships of their own—friends and someday a spouse—then we have to demonstrate deep care and the time-consuming nature and wonder of important relationships. We must model how to treat the folks who matter most in life.

Untether the Kids

"But what if she really needs to get in touch with me?" Our sense of always needing to have the phone on so kids can get in touch is linked to our cultural sense of crisis. We live on constant alert. When kids don't text right back, we shoot up to high alert. Part of this is due to our perception of risk in daily life (see Rule 1: Safety Second).

Let kids truly be untethered sometimes. Let them go without a phone in their pocket. There are plenty of people with phones who can help if they truly need to make a call. Let kids go with the understanding that they need to report back to you if their original plans change greatly. Letting them go means being prepared for them to get into a fix . . . and get themselves out of it.

I try to be near a phone during school hours in case the office calls saying, "He's sick." But there are times I'm not available and my husband isn't either. If we can't be reached and it's truly bad, that's what the emergency contacts on all those forms are for.

Our kids' job is to explore and establish independence. They don't need to check in every half hour. You'll both worry less if you set reasonable boundaries and don't stay by the phone.

Renegade Tech Guide

Be in one place at one time.
Put your phone in a basket or other designated area.
Set calling hours.
Practice saying, "I'm not available."
Realize you have a right to not be reached.
Value the ones who are present.
Balance tech with calm.
Shut things off at night.
Shut things off at sacred times.
Value single-use items (use an alarm clock).

Try This—Add to Your Toolbox

Each family must find a "right" tech balance. What's most important is that you set some guidelines, both to model moderate behavior to your children and to follow your own life values.

Value Who's Present

My first high school job was at a bookstore. At sixteen, I didn't know what to do when the shop phone rang and I was serving a customer. The store rule was: "The person in front of you deserves your attention." This is still true. The people in front of us are our families, children, neighbors, and community. They must see us as people, not as bodies with phones.

Screen worlds make people in the same room absent from each other. We don't know if a person is with us or not. Maybe you think you're with your kids all day, but your glazed eyes and "What?" tell a different story. Be truly absent or truly present.

Model Tech Etiquette

When we leave the table in the middle of a meal, we say, "Excuse me," to the people around us. When we know we're going to be late for a get-together, we speak up.

When we're in the same physical space as our kids but our attention needs to be elsewhere for a while, it's polite to announce it. For example, when I'm going to be on the phone for an extended time I let the kids know: "I'm going to be on the phone talking to the doctor. I need to listen carefully to what she says. Can you help by doing noisy things in your room? I'll let you know when I'm done." This gives me quiet call time, and it helps kids know that they can still be noisy, but have to shift the location.

The same goes for the Internet. "I'm going to be [writing a letter, researching health insurance, whatever]. I need to concentrate. You can still talk to me if you have a question. I'll let you know when I'm done. Then we can go to the park."

Sportscast Your Screen

Announce what task you're doing, so kids know why your face is glued to the screen. "I'm calling Daddy" or "I'm checking the weather." If you don't feel comfortable announcing your actions, that could be a sign that the task is better saved for a time when you're not with your children.

Set Windows of Time

Advances have made computers mobile, but that doesn't mean we can't limit them in time and space. Practice saying, "I'm not available." Practice saying no and setting limits to reclaim your time. Too many tiny texts, calls, and posts also fragment our brains, leaving us feeling overwhelmed and spent.

I remember when answering machines first became commonly accepted. "What's wrong with your phone?" a friend asked. "All it did was ring and ring." The phone was working fine. It was our answering machine that had broken, but his comment showed me how this form of communication had become culturally expected. Now, years later, we expect instant replies and online connection from those around us.

You will be going against current cultural expectations if you carve out your own space. You don't have to conform, but it's polite to notify. You might try options like these:

"I reply to e-mails once a day."

"Thanks! I'll respond when I can. I'm engaged with young children and don't use the computer every day."

> If I am available to everyone,
> then I cannot help anybody.

Set Sacred Spaces and Deliberate Habits

Where is your phone at school pickup time?

Turn off tech to delineate the day. We do best with rhythm, including daily rhythms for sleep, action, relaxing, and togetherness.

Our phones and computers can connect us to everything night and day, but just because they can, it doesn't mean it's best to use them that way.

Decide what times of the day are best for you to be tech-free. Try to start with the times when your family needs space to be together, not the times when you feel you won't be missed. I turn everything off before the kids come home from school. Then I can welcome them with full attention. Remember, children need to see *you*—not you on your phone. It's a time of family reunion.

Each tech item is a gateway to so much. The phone is for photos, games, work e-mails, alarms, fitness checks, a reference guide, and so much more. This very limitlessness calls for limits. The multiuse nature of tech forces us to continually make choices.

Set habits to help you. We can't resist constant temptation, so remove it. Put the phone in another room, or set a family practice of putting phones in a basket, a cookie tin, or an empty fishbowl. Make a ritual of turning things off. When I'm not using my computer, I drape the screen with a cloth. It's off, totally and symbolically.

Examples of Sacred Spaces

Dinner table
Bedrooms
School pickup time and homecoming
The park
Being together in the car
Walks
The kitchen
Restaurants
When guests are over
On playdates
Other social times
Unwinding, relaxing times
Vacations

Understand What Calms You

Shoot baskets. Walk the dog. Have a cup of tea. Go outside. We all should know activities that are proven to calm the human brain (exercise, downtime, meditation, time with nature) and what refreshes us individually (knitting, tai chi, wrestling with the dog). Teach your child to include calming activities each day, and help him recognize what refreshes him. Model calming times and include your child in these activities. Lifetime tools like these balance the overstimulation of screens.

Take Mental Photos

Be aware how often you put a camera in your child's face. We love our kids, and some photo memorializing is OK. But constant photo shooting takes us away from the moment.

At the park, I watched a preschool teacher snapping photos of the kids' antics with his phone. It was a lovely day, and the kids were digging in the sand and giggling when they found ants. Nick was zipping off pictures of the children to their parents so parents at work could share the scene.

Before he got a smartphone, this same teacher would have been engaged with the kids instead of with the distant parents. "Oh, look at what you found! That's a big hole. Look at that ant moving fast." There was still some friendly banter, but the process of snapping multiple photos and sending them off takes some time. His face and attention were disengaged. Even "instant" tasks take longer than we think.

Don't Occupy Your Life

The definition of *occupy* is to take up space or time. If you reach for your phone to stave off boredom or because there might be a message, then you're beginning to use the distraction of computers to occupy time and take up dead space.

Online devices are alluring, but they're attention stealers. Will we say on our deathbed: "I wish I'd spent more time browsing social media"?

Write a bucket list and update it regularly. What are you making time for? What do you really want to do with your one precious life? Memorial services, cemeteries, and cancer screenings are healthy reminders of mortality and help get our priorities straight. If you don't know your priorities, try putting your phone down and let your mind go. There's a proverb that says, "If you want to know where your heart is, look to where your mind goes when it wanders."

Or, as Steve Jobs said, "Your time is limited, so don't waste it living someone else's life."

Hold fast to what you consider good. These are your life priorities. Here are some universal rules that can help you determine if your tech use supports or detracts from these goals.

ASK YOURSELF:

Does it draw your family closer?
Does it allow deeper friendship?
Are there more smiles?
Does it preserve your sacred spaces?
Does it allow you to follow your passion?
Is it the right timing?
Is it the right location?
Is it the right duration?

As Turkle reminds us: "We don't need to reject or disparage technology. We need to put it in its place."

Words to Say

I'm calling Nana.

I'm checking the weather to see if it will rain when we go
to the park.

I'm going to be working now. Noisy games in the
basement.

I'll let you know when I'm done.

Hello! It's good to see you. How was your day?

You're right. No phones at the table.

Sorry I had to be on the phone. Thanks for waiting quietly.
It's good you know what to do when I have an
emergency call.

I'm not available then. I have my phone off in the morning.

Words to Avoid

This will just take a minute.

Mmm-hmm. I heard you.

Shhh.

Be quiet.

Uh, what?

Your Take

As you discipline your screen use, you are also influencing your
grandchildren. If your children feel you're being fair, they will likely
repeat strategies you use effectively with their own children. Setting
limits and modeling healthy behavior can be effective through the
generations.

Screen life will keep changing. We can't predict what will come, only that change will come. Whatever new gadgets and developments appear, your child can be ready if she knows how healthy people set limits and care for each other. She will need to navigate a time in history of constant technological change. That's why she needs your guidance now. Kids need us to establish rhythms and boundaries in family life, healthy habits that can set the pattern for the future.

CHILDREN'S RIGHTS at SCHOOL

The mind can only absorb what the butt can endure.

—PROVERB

RULE
7
Recess Is a Right

My son Myles wandered out of the school building during his first week of school. He was restless and ready for a change, so he headed to the playground. The teachers brought him back to class, explaining about recess time.

Kids know they need a break from class. Recess helps children's brains learn more, not less. Regular recess is a child's right.

Renegade Reason ||||||||||||||||||||||||||||||||||||||||||||||||||||||||||||||||||||||||||||

Recess boosts memory, learning, and focus, as well as happiness and interest in school. Recess is as essential as lunch to the school day.

||||||||||||||||||||||||||||||||||||||||||||||||||||||||||||||||||||||||||||||||||||||||||||||||||||||

Ten-year-old Robin, an active runabout, despaired when he entered fifth grade. Although fifth grade is still an elementary grade in most communities, Robin's school considered him a middle schooler, and middle schoolers got no recess.

Robin's not alone. Across the nation, 30 percent of schools offer little or no recess time for elementary-aged kids. It starts with children as young as five.

What Recess Is

Recess. It brings an instant image of kids bursting out of the school doors, running and chasing each other with exuberant screams. In our minds, recess is action.

Though most kids enjoy an action-packed recess, it's vital to understand that the point of recess is not necessarily movement. It's a break. Some kids use the break to run, climb, swing, and shout. Others use the time more quietly.

Gavin played soccer. Harper built tiny houses with twigs. Emily played the modern version of dodgeball, gaga, with seven friends gathered in an octagonal pit.

"I wrote a poem at recess today," my son Myles told me once. Some days he played lively games; other days he talked with friends or invented an ant language. This is all recess. As a third-grader, I played nonstop jump rope or chase games, but in fifth grade I often used recess time to sit on a bent root that served as my bird's nest, side by side with my friend Dana. We took a break from the noisy crush of classmates to commune and think our own thoughts. This, too, is recess.

Recess is not primarily about exercise. That's easy to miss, especially with valid concerns about the obesity epidemic. Recess is a break from being told what to do. It's a break from structure, from adult control and dictated choices. Recess is a psychological, emotional, cognitive, social, and physical break that often involves vigorous movement.

The Centers for Disease Control and Prevention defines recess as "regularly scheduled periods within the elementary school day for unstructured physical activity and play." The Robert Wood Johnson

Foundation calls it "physical and social activities of [children's] choice."

No matter what they do, kids come back refreshed. It's a liberating time of free choice. A time to be with playmates of their own choosing, a time to think their own thoughts, a time to move their bodies as boisterously or gently as they like.

Kids have a right to recess. It's as essential as lunch for healthy learning. Schools with only ten to twenty minutes of recess a day are hurting children. Simply looking at educational outcomes and brain power, kids need more recess, longer recess, and—no matter how badly they are "acting up"—never to have recess time taken away.

Renegade Blessings

When kids get adequate recess time, here's how they
  benefit:
I love going outside.
It feels great to move my body.
I feel ready to concentrate again when I come back in
  from recess.
Class time is time to pay attention. Recess is my time.
It's not easy to agree on rules for games, but we can sort
  it out.
My friendships are strong. They help me when times at
  home or school get tough.
Making my own choices at recess makes me feel respected.
School is a place where I can be myself.
School is a good place to be.

Why It Works

Recess is an ally in the school day. Recess amazingly boosts academic learning *and* classroom behavior. Regular recess helps kids absorb new material, improve accuracy, and recall facts. With recess, test scores go up. Kids goof off less, fidget less, poke their neighbor less, and generally pay better attention to the teacher when they get a good dose of recess.

The American Academy of Pediatrics (AAP) considers recess a necessary break from academics that offers vital cognitive, social, emotional, and physical benefits. Recess is so important to children's health and growth that the AAP issued a policy statement in 2013 stating: "Recess is a crucial and necessary component of a child's development and . . . should not be withheld for punitive or academic reasons." No taking recess away. Not for behavior. Not for any reason.

Olga Jarrett is a prime researcher of recess. Jarrett, a professor at Georgia State University, found that fourth-graders were more attentive and less fidgety after they returned to class from recess. Anthony Pellegrini, a psychologist from the University of Minnesota, researched third-graders and found that kids grew increasingly inattentive the longer class time extended before recess came. This reality is supported by the nation's principals. In a 2009 survey of two thousand elementary school principals conducted by the Robert Wood Johnson Foundation, almost all agreed that recess helped kids approach classwork with renewed focus and better behavior.

As many parents and teachers recognize, kids need recess to get their ya-yas out. Sometimes we think of this as just physical energy, but kids explode into high action partly as an emotional release, too. Children feel a variety of emotions in a school day, ranging from frustration about classwork and tasks such as holding a pencil right to anger at a perceived injustice or school rule to the emotional intensity of being among other classmates. Kids feel emotions intensely and express them with their bodies, says early childhood author Dorothy Briggs. Recess gives kids a chance to yell out frustration and run out momentary outraged feelings.

Daytime recess is as important as sleep at night. It replenishes and refreshes young minds. It restores balance and dignity. It's a time of free choice in an otherwise structured day.

More Recess Is Better

A 2009 study in the journal *Pediatrics* showed that third-graders' test scores went up with additional recess. From the time of the ancient Greeks, people have noticed a link between mental and physical abilities. Now modern brain research is shining a light on the idea that yes, physical activity is linked to the intellectual, because it strengthens executive function, the mix of cognitive skills that include concentration, learning, goal setting, impulse control, memory, and accuracy. With physical action, the brain enlarges the hippocampus and improves areas such as memory and spatial navigation.

Study after study shows that classroom behavior improves if children have recess. Not only that, but the more recess, the better. This is particularly true for kids who have a hard time sitting still and paying attention. Olga Jarrett says kids with ADHD were more likely to have their behavior improve with additional recess time. Neuroscientist Jaak Panksepp, at Washington State University, agrees. He's extensively studied ADHD and its link to play. He says children and other social mammals must have their need for play met before they're ready to advance to more mature developmental stages. When kids are restless, that shows there's an unmet need for play. If motion is the problem, recess is the answer.

Kids who poke their neighbors and can't sit still, however, are often punished by being made to stay in for recess. That means kids who need recess the most are frequently deprived of it. This counter-productive discipline habit reinforces the "troublemaker" label and denies children the chance to learn to their optimal ability.

Take Off Your Adult Lenses

All that noise and running around can seem aimless. *What a waste of time*, we may think. *School is for education and these days there's so much to cover in the curriculum already. Besides, they run around in gym class.* Recess is not a luxury from a bygone era; rather, the breaks help kids' brains process what they've learned and get ready for the next lesson. Academically, recess is essential to the school day. It's usually filled with physical action, but it's a mental and emotional release as much as a physical one. Recess is a break from being told what to do. It's the one time in the school day children are allowed to fully be themselves—a liberating and refreshing thing that imbues them with renewed energy and focus to concentrate on classroom learning.

Why Recess Needs Rescuing

By 2005, 40 percent of U.S. school districts had reduced recess time or eliminated it altogether, according to a study in the journal *Childhood Education*. Investigative research by public radio station KUOW, in Seattle, showed that the number of schools offering little or no recess doubled every two years in Seattle-area public elementary schools. In 2010, one school fell in that category. Two years later six schools did. By 2014, eleven schools had no recess or negligible recess (twenty minutes or less).

My elementary school had three recesses a day: a twenty-minute morning recess, an afternoon fifteen-minute recess, *plus* almost an hour in the middle for a lunch-and-recess combo (of course, all sensible children dashed through lunch so they could head out to the playground). It's easy to dismiss tales of the Good Old Days as starry-eyed, irrelevant, or even misremembered. Turns out my memory isn't faulty. According to education researchers, such as Rhonda Clements, a professor at Manhattanville College, three recesses a day was standard for elementary schools across the United States until about 1990.

School without recess, or with too little recess, leads to discontent. "I hate school," six-year-old Amir told his mother. Last year, he'd loved it, and the difference was recess. If his first-grade class got outside at all, it was only a few minutes before the final bell.

Benefits of Breaks

The human mind needs breaks. We can't sustain attention for long periods, not without a change of some sort, whether it's a new location or other novelty. Eric Jensen, author of *Teaching with the Brain in Mind*, explains how attention goes in cycles. We concentrate in rhythmic cycles typically lasting 90 to 110 minutes. As I write this chapter, I just stood up to take a break. We all need mental breaks from extended concentration. That's how the human mind works.

Acknowledging this, some countries incorporate multiple short breaks into the school day. Elementary children in Finland get a mandatory outdoor recess lasting 15 minutes after every 45-minute lesson. The same age group in Japan gets a 10- to 15-minute break every hour, since attention begins to wander after about 40 to 50 minutes of instruction. Breaks are also important for establishing information in memory. Breaks give kids "processing time," time for brain chemicals to move information into long-term memory.

One way kids process new information is by playing it. This is true of many kinesthetic learners. As soon as I finish reading a story, my six-year-old leaps up to act it out. Once he plays it—whether it's facts about a tornado or history about Paul Revere's ride—he makes it his own and remembers it. Having free time to incorporate new ideas into their play helps some children embed class learning into memory.

Don't Use Recess as Punishment

"Your assignment is late. You can't eat lunch today."

We would be appalled if a teacher said that. A midday meal boosts energy and helps kids concentrate on afternoon schoolwork. Recess falls in the same category. It's sacred. A child has a right to recess during the school day. Still, even when schools schedule recess into the day, kids aren't guaranteed to get it.

Lucy was in kindergarten. An active, social child, she thrived with lots of time to bounce around. When she talked too much to her partner or came late to circle time, the five-year-old had to stay in for recess. Ryan, age six, was getting restless and didn't finish his math assignment on time. His teacher had him finish it during recess.

All children deserve recess, no matter what their behavior or classwork status. It's simply how kids thrive and learn.

The American Academy of Pediatrics recommends *never* taking away recess as a punishment. Still, teachers persist in disciplining children by depriving them of recess, or enforcing class rules with the threat of taking recess. It's an easy method; they know children want recess desperately.

Recess is taken away for multiple reasons. Behavior is number one, but that's followed closely by not finishing homework or classwork, or even additional instruction in the guise of special services.

Jack was slow to say hello and smile at people, so he was offered special services from the school counselor. They met and played games to improve social skills. But Jack's social services time was scheduled during the most social time of the day: recess. Likewise, Claire, a Native American, was given additional ethnic learning resources. Her family was thrilled she'd learn more about her heritage, but not during playtime.

As for schoolwork, "no recess" punishments impact a growing number of children who are burdened with excessive homework (see Rule 8: Ban Elementary Homework). In one classroom, kids had to miss recess if parents didn't sign their spelling lists. In another, unfinished math problems meant kids had to stay in. Children need reasonable expectations and need to face consequences when they don't meet those expectations, but the punishment must fit the crime. Recess is unrelated to spelling, math, and late homework, except for this: Kids need recess to concentrate on these very assignments.

A 2013 study from the Robert Wood Johnson Foundation found that most school districts, 63 percent, had no policy about withholding recess. Creating a protective policy at the school district level makes a big difference in kids' access to recess, especially if it's two-pronged: 1) Recess cannot be withheld for poor behavior, and 2) recess cannot be withheld for non-completion of schoolwork.

I respect teachers. I respect educators enough to believe they can find alternative ways to discipline their classes without depriving kids of recess.

Gym Class Is Not Recess

In 2011, half the kindergarten parents signed a petition asking for more recess at P.S. 101 in Queens, New York. Kindergarteners were only getting one short recess a day. The principal gave them an extra gym period instead.

Gym, or physical education, is a class. It's formal instruction time that is teacher led. Kids certainly move around in gym class, but as Olga Jarrett has found, there's often less movement in gym class than at recess. Kids sit or stand while they wait their turn or teachers explain rules. Gym class is valuable on its own terms, but it can't give a child the creative, emotional, and social benefits of free recess play. As one child said: "In gym they tell you what to do and your friends aren't on your team."

Classroom stretching and movement is also not a real break. "Our students are always moving," teachers frequently say. "They don't sit at desks all day. They're very active learners."

Motion itself is not the point. Adults often confuse the notion of motion and structured activity with recess. Ask any kid and she'll quickly correct you: "Recess is when I play with my friends." "At recess I can do what I like." "Recess is fun!"

With kids indoors so much and news about the obesity epidemic, it's easy to assume recess's main benefit is exercise. That could be why many adults shrug off reduced recess. There's an assumption that kids get physical needs met in other ways: Children move about the classroom, the teacher does stretching time, or they get gym twice a week. Some schools only schedule recess two or three times a week, on non-gym days.

Recess is not gym time. It's not stretching time. There should be no substitution.

How Much Recess?

Designing the elementary school day for optimal learning requires six recess components:

- Daily recess
- Balanced recess
- More recess
- Longer recess
- Recess protection (no "off" days, gym substitution, or withholding)
- Age protection (recess for all grades at the school)

1. Daily Recess
   Recess needs to be daily. Kids' attention, thinking skills, memory, and attitude toward school depend on it.

2. Balanced Recess
   Frequent breaks help students' brains learn best. Recess needs to be scattered throughout the day, so balanced recess means at least morning and afternoon. A recess/lunch combination alone doesn't offer enough breaks for healthy learning. Neither does the practice of holding "recess" during the last few minutes of the school day.

3. Number of Daily Recesses
   Children of elementary age need two or three recess periods a day. Research on fourth-graders led Olga Jarrett to recommend a minimum of two recesses a day. Younger children benefit from even more recess time for their best learning and growth. Kids third grade and younger should have three or more recess times.

   - Pre-K–3rd grade   3 times a day
   - 4th–5th/6th grade   2–3 times a day
   - 6th–8th grade   1+ time a day

4. Duration of Recess
   Each recess period should be twenty to thirty minutes long, or longer. Shorter breaks allow kids to run, but they miss out on social and cognitive benefits. When kids have only a few minutes they can't develop meaningful play.

   Watch encroachments on recess time. Recess should not include lineup time or put-on-your-coat time. In some schools, excessive lining up eats up five to ten minutes of scarce free time. If the recess period is thirty minutes, that should mean thirty minutes of play.

5. Protected Recess
   Recess is recess (no gym class substitutions). Recess is also free, unstructured play, a time of freedom to choose playmates and play ideas. Recess is considered a child's right, and is not withheld for behavior or academic reasons.

6. Ages for Recess
   Children up to age eleven or twelve need daily recess. This covers 100 percent of elementary school as well as the younger grades of middle school if fifth- and sixth-grade students are classified as middle school students. Some schools offer recess only to younger children and remove it as early as third grade. Recess for all students pre-K to eighth grade is an excellent goal.

Schools often reward kids with stars for certain behaviors, including sitting still and listening. Here's a "star chart" for elementary schools to see how they measure up. Is your school a star?

RECESS STAR CHART
How does your school rank?

No daily recess	Unacceptable
20 min. or less	★ Losing learning potential
30 min.+	★★ On the right track
50 min.+	★★★ Star material

Recess for Preschool and Pre-K

The term *recess* should apply to only elementary-aged children. Preschool kids need more than recess. For young kids, unstructured free play, both indoor and out, should be the majority of the day. Designating a twenty- to forty-minute "recess time" is not enough for this age group.

When preschoolers are housed in an elementary school building, they often follow a schedule appropriate for only older students. The idea of "recess" does not apply well to kids age five and under. Children this age need free play in blocks of one to two hours or more for meaningful learning to occur. Research shows kids play at a superficial level when limited to short play periods. They curtail sophisticated play because they know they will soon be interrupted.

Recess Rules and Conflicts

Even when kids are out at recess, there's no guarantee they get to play.

Jayden, a first-grader, saw orange and red maple leaves on the school playground. He picked them up to make a leaf bouquet for his mother. A recess aide made him stand against the fence and miss the rest of recess for violating the school rule of "not picking things up from the ground." Myles, age five, was in trouble for scuffing paths through the wood chips on the playground. He had to miss recess and sit against a wall.

Recess rules can be bizarre. At my son's school, kids were not allowed to pick up snow. This was a problem, since snow covered the playground two thirds of the school year.

School staffs set these rules to avoid conflicts during the semi-chaos of recess. But one of recess's prime values is for kids to gain practice dealing with peer conflicts. It would be better to set a rule such as "no hurting people" and train the school community in conflict resolution. Kids need practice when a conflict opportunity comes up. The educational value is immense.

Benefits of Recess Time

BREAK AND RELEASE

The mind can concentrate for a time, but then it needs a break. Recess breaks help kids return to class with renewed focus. It also gives them time to unleash pent-up emotional and physical energy.

BETTER BEHAVIOR

Misbehavior is often a result of kids growing bored, wanting to talk with friends, and being at the limits of trying to control their bodies. Disruptive class behaviors decrease when kids get enough recess.

PHYSICAL ACTIVITY

Exercise, action, and motion help keep children's bodies healthy, combat obesity, and stimulate blood flow to improve mental energy.

ENHANCED ACADEMIC LEARNING

Regular recess breaks help sharpen memory, learning, and focus, all vital executive functions needed for cognitive thinking in the school day.

FRIENDSHIP

Recess gives kids social time to form bonds with other children. Besides developing friendships, kids gain social skills by interacting with other classmates on the playground.

CONFLICT MEDIATION PRACTICE

This is an oft-overlooked benefit. Recess is full of sorting out rules and differences. Conflict mediation is complex social work—and some of the most important work humans can do to prevent wars, bullying, and violence. Although recess conflicts can vex playground supervisors, the greatest benefit comes when kids work these differences out themselves. Some simple peacekeeping training can guide them.

FREE CHOICE AND EXPLORATION

Recess gives children a chance to follow their own ideas and interests, essential for people of every age.

HAPPINESS

What's most children's favorite subject? Recess! The happiness recess brings enhances children's emotional health and positive attitude toward school.

Structured Recess

Imagine not knowing what to do at recess. That's been the case with a generation of children who have never experienced recess and don't know what to do with free playtime. Schools in Chicago and Boston recently reinstated recess, and there's momentum to bring it back around the country, especially in urban school districts.

As recess is reinstated, it often comes with new structure. Structured recess means trained adults are on hand as "recess coaches" from companies such as Playworks and Peaceful Playgrounds to lead group games and help kids resolve disputes. In schools in Bellevue, Washington, for instance, positive behavior intervention specialists organize kids into group games of soccer and freeze tag.

Some school cultures may need this additional help as they transition. Structured recess, however, should not be the end goal. The very structure—adult-led games and organized activities instead of child-led ones—negates the essence of recess. Peaceful Playgrounds, for example, emphasizes movement and fitness and suggests adding enhancements such as number grids and the alphabet to playgrounds. Recess is more than that. It's about a child's freedom and choice.

Playworks and other groups say that behavior issues decrease and student physical activity increases when they get involved, but studies by Martha Bleeker and colleagues, reviewed by the U.S. Department of Education, show there is no real difference. Teachers report that kids are moving more, but data from accelerometers showed no impact. Student behavior *does* improve with access to more recess, but it tends to improve anyway, not because of Playworks.

When two boys lingered apart from the structured group games, a recess coach approached them, as reported by KUOW public radio. "Make a decision!" she said. "Recess goes fast." One of the boys smiled. "We're just looking at the clouds," he said.

Children don't want to be herded all the time. If professional structure helps reinstate recess where recess is lacking, it's a good first step, but children have a right to real recess.

Try This—Add to Your Toolbox

Reclaiming recess is a joint process between families and educators. Some steps are relatively easy, while others take a broader effort. Recess is worth it.

Protect Recess Rights

Depriving a child of recess has health and learning concerns. Try writing a note to the teacher as a preventive measure that explains your view that recess should not be used as a discipline tool (see sample letter, Appendix p. 341). You might write a similar letter to the principal or school board (see sample letter, Appendix p. 342). Most schools do their best to listen. At the very least, you'll be opening up a dialogue.

Easy Steps

Long-term change takes time. Some of these simpler steps may help fill the gap until then.

1. Early Recess
   Our local school squeezes in a third recess by opening up the playground twenty minutes before school starts. The principal encourages kids to play vigorously before the bell rings. Active play like this is particularly important because most kids arrive by bus (sitting) or car (sitting). Early recess is a fairly simple way to sneak in an extra recess with little cost to the school.

2. Volunteer Recess Supervisors
   Sometimes school staff is spread too thin. Volunteer to round up fellow parents who can supervise an extra recess. This parent team could even take conflict mediation training. With approved volunteers watching the crowd, teachers are freed up to prep their next lesson.

3. Movement Within Class
   Movement programs, such as Brain Gym or Instant Recess, should never be mistaken for true recess. They are structured, teacher-led exercises performed in the classroom. However, it may be the best your school can do for now. Short stretching breaks do add movement and blood flow to a crowded day.

4. Free Play
   If school schedules can't immediately accommodate new recess time, individual teachers may be able to open time for additional play or free choice time in their classrooms. This serves as a social, emotional, and cognitive break.

Be a Recess Hero

Caring adults across the country are rallying to the recess cause. You can be one of them. Just google "parents want more recess" and see what you get. Story after story chronicles communities' quest to reinstate recess time. Here you'll discover ideas and allies.

You may not get all that you ask for. Parents in Lee County, Florida, rallied to restore recess after the district eliminated it. They asked for a minimum of twenty minutes a day and got fifteen; they asked for daily recess for K through 8 and got K through 5. Ideally, all kids before high school should get recess, but you may have to pitch your battle strategically.

By helping your child, you are helping all children. The first step is to be aware, since many adults don't realize recess is rare.

RESEARCH RECESS

1) Start with the kids
   Kids are quick to identify problems about fairness and recess. Ask what the recess reality is. Do kids ever have to miss recess? How long is recess? Listen without judgment. Some stories may be exaggerated, but the child perspective often uncovers issues you never thought about.

2) Learn the school's official recess policy
   Find out what the scheduled recess times are. How many recess periods a day? How many minutes? Is it daily, or

does the recess schedule vary? Do any ages or grades at the school receive more or less recess? Can recess be taken away for any reason?

3) Observe recess time
Ask if you can visit school during recess time. Watch what truly goes on. See how often kids are "benched" (forced to sit or stand against a fence) during recess and for how long. This could be a sign the school needs help gaining better conflict mediation or "peacekeeper" skills for recess supervisors. A recess spent sitting down away from play is no recess at all.

4) Ask what teachers need
What are teacher concerns? What support could help? Change comes through respectful partnerships.

FIND PARTNERS

1) Find allies
Ask around. Start the conversation. Find others who feel this way. Share stories about the benefit of recess with parents and educators and see if you can get a group of allies to support a recess discussion.

2) Find examples of schools with more recess
Maybe the school across town has two recesses and yours has one. Local is best, but if you can't find a model nearby, find one in the news and contact them. The key here is to make a personal connection between a principal who has more recess and your school. Change is often scary, but people are more willing to try something if it's already been done successfully.

3) Educate policy makers respectfully

People in education care about kids. Let your local principal know your views and plans to elevate the discussion of recess. Share research findings and the American Academy of Pediatrics policy report with policy makers.

4) Enlist outside experts

When you're ready, bring in outside experts to offer testimony at a public meeting or event. This adds legitimacy to your cause.

ADVOCATE

1) Gather signatures

Recess advocacy generally includes petitions and signature gathering. Many schools get hundreds fast.

2) Attend school board meetings

Get to know your school board. Show up and offer comments to support recess during the public comment section. As one mom who successfully got recess reinstated at her daughter's school said, "The squeaky wheel gets the grease."

3) Involve the kids

You can bet kids care about recess. Enlist their energy. Have them write letters, give speeches, draw posters, make videos, and do interviews with the press. This is guaranteed to be a lesson in democracy they won't forget.

Don't let fancy playground equipment and price tags stop you. My early recess days were spent on a square blacktop lot surrounded by a chain-link fence. Besides a few old tires and painted lines for hopscotch, there was no playground equipment. No climber, no swings, no slides. All children truly need is empty space and time.

Words to Say

> I'd like to learn more about recess at our school. Can we talk?
>
> Research is showing that test scores go up with more recess.
>
> Did you know recess improves classroom behavior and academics?
>
> Our school only has twenty minutes of recess. That's less than half what's recommended for optimal learning for elementary kids.
>
> There's been some interesting research about recess. Have you seen it?
>
> Here's an article in the *New York Times* about it.
>
> I'd like to share a story.

Your Take

You may not see yourself as an advocate, but part of parenting is speaking up when you know something's wrong for your child. Take a look at schools around you, too. Maybe your own child's school has recess, but do they all? Recess deprivation is hardest felt in low-income schools. The facts are appalling. A national study by Jodie Roth and other researchers at Teachers College, Columbia University, found that 44 percent of U.S. elementary children living in poverty have no recess. Be an advocate for children everywhere.

RULE
8

Ban Elementary Homework

"My son *likes* homework. He comes home and does it cheerfully every day," Rebecca told me. Her son was six, and just starting school. The next year we talked again.

"My thoughts are evolving on that," she said. By age seven, Liam had lots more homework. "Sometimes he really needs to relax and be with us. We only have two and a half hours together in the evening."

His mother could well be right. After a seven-hour school day, plus extended care after school and travel each way, Liam may need rest and the warmth of family most of all. It might be best for this seven-year-old to unwind and play to be refreshed and rejuvenated for the next school day, or for his parents to support his school learning in their own way. The question is: Who gets to decide?

Renegade Reason

Homework does not benefit elementary school–aged children.
When school is out, children need space and time for other things.

Darren, age six, skipped out of the school yard swinging his backpack. His mother greeted him. "Hi, how was school today?" "Great!" said Darren. He grinned and ran around a tree. The next minute he threw his backpack on the ground with force, remembering what was inside. "I've got homework!" he shouted in an anguished voice. "I hate school!"

I'm tired when I come home from work. Sometimes I have to bring work home, but my most productive hours are already spent. I'm ready to collapse, take care of family needs, and prepare for the next day so I'm at my best. Kids need this, too.

Homework is a hallmark of modern schooling. We want our children to be good students, and we assume homework helps them. Why else send homework home, even in kindergarten? Some parents like it, some teachers hate it, but when both sides of the homework debate argue, they largely use beliefs. Research results are surprising: Homework does not help elementary school–aged kids academically.

When you dig into the peer-reviewed homework research, it's astounding how strongly it backs up the case against homework in the younger years. In high school, homework makes sense; in middle school, some is OK; but in elementary school? Research says no. What's more, homework in elementary grades is shown to hurt kids' attitudes toward school and learning.

Homework Load

Homework generates passion among students, but it's not passion for learning. Kids wear shirts that read: "Homework-free zone," "Homework: Stop the madness!" and "Homework? The cloud ate it." And perhaps one of the most perceptive ones: "I think my mom is happier than I am when I don't have homework."

"I have tears in my eyes as I write this," said one grandmother.

"My nine-year-old grandson spent from three p.m. until eight thirty p.m. doing homework. How much do you think he likes school?"

Elementary school homework has ratcheted up steadily since 1980. A 2004 University of Michigan study of nearly three thousand children found that homework time had increased 51 percent since 1981, and a study from the University of Maryland found homework time over a similar period was up 145 percent. This time takes away from other activities and exacts an emotional toll.

Take Charlie's case. Charlie, a second-grader, had homework in four subjects: spelling, Spanish, math, and writing, plus twenty minutes of reading and a requirement to log in to an Internet homework site. "We logged on and my tired son could not figure out the math and started throwing a fit, crying and kicking," said his mother. "No child should have to be this tired . . . or have to do two hours of homework in second grade. My heart just broke."

Is it too much? It's hard to pin down how much homework kids have because homework load varies. It varies between individual teachers, schools, and communities, and each child takes different amounts of time to complete the same assignment. Averages are not important here. What's most important is how homework is influencing your child.

Nine-year-old Taylor's teacher assigned homework every day. "It was brutal," said his mother. "He had short-term daily homework and long-term projects." Taylor reacted by hiding homework assignments.

Many families in this country are fed up with homework. I know, because every day people stumble onto my blog post that explains why our family bans homework. Some of the search terms they google include:

Homework is killing my family
Why do kids have homework when they are already in
    school for 7 hours?
Third-grade homework is painful

Are there teachers who disagree with homework?
Write a letter to principal requesting less homework
I don't sleep enough because of homework

When I was in college, my classmate's mother came out with a book titled *The Second Shift*. This book, by UC Berkeley sociology professor Arlie Hochschild, focused on the double shift women faced doing housework and childcare after working a full-time job. Kids today—some as young as three and four—are facing a new second shift in the guise of their own good: homework.

Renegade Blessings

When we trust children's natural joy in learning and support academic learning in a variety of ways, kids gain so much. A focus on academic homework is more appropriate in the teen years. Give younger kids time to develop and mature in other ways—that's the best way to support academic learning.

I like school.
I have time to do what's important to me.
My own ideas are valuable.
I love reading books with my family every day.
It's fun to share with my parents what my class is doing.
My family cares about learning. So do I.
There's a time to work and a time to play.
After a long day, everyone needs a break.
My teacher's in charge at school. My parents are in charge
    at home.
Older kids get homework. There's a time to get serious.
    When I get older, I'll do that, too.

Take Off Your Adult Lenses

For many of us, homework is simply part of going to school. Kids may grumble about it, but we believe homework's good for them. The trouble is it's just a belief. Studies repeatedly show that homework at the elementary school level does not improve academic learning. Kids have already had a full school day with adults telling them what to do, and cognitive thinking is only one type of learning. Homework encroaches on time meant for other learning, including physical (outside play), social (family activities, dinner, and chores), and emotional (unwinding from the day). Homework is intended to reinforce school learning, but it can do just the opposite by making kids resent it and turn against school. If it's personal responsibility we're after, kids can learn that in other ways. A positive attitude and good sleep are more important.

Why It Works

"Oh, we use the ten-minute rule," my son's elementary principal told me. I looked at her blankly. She explained that ten minutes of homework per grade was recommended, so first-graders should have ten minutes a day, fifth-graders, fifty minutes a day, and so on. Harris Cooper's research is widely cited as the reason elementary schools, the National PTA, and others have adopted the ten-minute rule. Since studies can be found to bolster both sides of nearly any debate, Cooper, a psychologist and neuroscientist from Duke University, compiled research from roughly 120 studies on homework in 1989 and another 60 studies in 2006. The result? Time spent on homework had no correlation to elementary school students' academic achievement.

Most schools misuse the ten-minute rule. Cooper suggested it as a way to limit elementary school homework. This means it was designed to protect children from *too much* homework, rather than establish a minimum baseline amount of homework to require.

"The research is very clear," agrees Etta Kralovec, an education professor at the University of Arizona, in her book *The End of Homework*. "There's no benefit at the elementary school level."

"No research has ever found a benefit to assigning homework (of any kind in any amount) in elementary school," writes national education expert Alfie Kohn. "We think kids ought to do homework *despite* what the evidence says."

Cooper himself, although he believes in homework even for first-graders, agrees with Kralovec, Kohn, and others: His own report states, "There is no evidence that any amount of homework improves the academic performance of elementary students."

Homework's benefits are age dependent. For elementary school kids, studying in class had superior results, according to Cooper's report. In upper grades, the analysis showed minimal correlation ($r = .07$) between homework time and achievement for middle school and modest relationship in high school. Even in high school, more than two hours of homework per night did not help. "It's only good in moderation," Cooper explains.

Research Results

GRADES K–6
- Homework does not improve academics in elementary school.
- Homework hurts kids' love of elementary school.

LATER ON
- Homework marginally helps middle school students. The relationship between academic success and homework is minimal, if there is one.
- More than two hours of homework a night does not help high school students.

Although the research does not show an academic benefit, Cooper's extensive analysis does show that homework in elementary school hurts kids' attitudes toward school. That's dangerous. With up to thirteen years of school or more ahead of them, it's best if elementary kids like school. Homework also stirs up frequent family conflict. A survey of twenty-five thousand parents by the *Today Show* found that 76 percent of families wanted a no-homework policy at their schools. Why? Too many tears and evenings lost to homework conflict.

We owe it to families everywhere to learn more about homework before giving children years of unhelpful and unnecessary homework. Future research on homework needs to focus on the unique needs of elementary school students.

> Dump the ten-minute rule—there's
> no science there.
> Adopt the "no-minute rule."

Hours in a Day

If the day had plentiful hours, a small dose of homework might be reasonable. But the opportunity cost is too great. "Even elementary school kids are staying up late to finish assignments," say Sara Bennett and Nancy Kalish, authors of *The Case Against Homework*. "Lack of sleep can contribute to depression, higher stress levels, and even learning and attention disorders."

When thinking about the time a child may devote to homework, it's critical to look at the twenty-four-hour math.

Pediatricians recommend nine to eleven hours of sleep per night for elementary school–aged children, and much more for younger children. A five-year-old should still be sleeping ten to thirteen hours. Daily routines (getting dressed and ready, going to bed) take time, especially with tired young children. With ten hours of sleep plus an hour at each end for getting ready, that leaves twelve hours out of twenty-four.

School is typically seven hours, plus transportation to and fro, adding another one to two hours. The average school bus ride is thirty minutes, though many kids travel farther than that each way, especially in rural areas. At best, that leaves four hours "free."

It's often less.

Jimmy, age seven, goes to after-school care. His parents, who both work full time, pick him up at six p.m. That gives the family just two hours to say hello to each other, have dinner, relax, and get to bed. Long days in school and extended care leave kids exhausted. Jimmy's not alone. Nationwide 6.5 million kids, most of them elementary aged, go to after-school care programs, and many go to before-school care, too.

My first-grader, Zach, gets home at 4:45 p.m. after an hour-long bus ride. Bedtime is 7 p.m., so after coming home from school he gets a mere two hours and fifteen minutes. During that time he has to squeeze in saying hello, unpacking his backpack and catching up on the day, forty-five minutes of play, family dinner, bath, pajamas, and bedtime story. There's no time for anything else. On days when his older brother has a piano lesson, Zach has to tag along and gets home at five thirty p.m.

Homework has no place in a young child's life.

Children need time to play and process their day to be ready for the next one. How is kids' time taken up in the after-school hours? Proponents of homework often say, "They're just playing video games anyway." Some do. However, for many kids, downtime is scarce. What kids do:

- Go to after-school care or "extended day" programs
- Pursue interests in sports, music, dance, art, etc. through extracurricular activities
- Attend siblings' extracurricular events and classes
- Shuttle between households for custody arrangements
- Learn cultural heritage (e.g. Chinese school, Bible study)
- Go to the grocery store or on other errands with parents
- Practice musical instruments
- Do daily chores
- Relax and unwind through play, TV, or other fun

The day is full already. When we choose to send our children to school, we shouldn't have to choose to send them overtime.

What Kids Need Instead of Homework

Physical motion
Release from being told what to do
Play
Reading for pleasure (emphasis on pleasure and joy)
Free time to explore their own interests
Downtime
Family nurturing
Family responsibilities
Outside time, in nature if possible
Regular and long sleep

Better than Homework: Reading

Schools that ban homework make the news, such as P.S. 116 in New York City, a public elementary school that banned homework in 2015; and Collège Saint-Ambroise, in Quebec, which banned it in 2014. As principal Jane Hsu explained in her note to P.S. 116 parents,

"The negative effects of homework have been well established." The school's new policy encourages families to limit screen time and promote play and reading.

The follow-up story is what's most important. Does it work? Few schools have taken this courageous step, but Gaithersburg Elementary School, in Gaithersburg, Maryland, is one example.

Gaithersburg banned traditional homework in 2012. Instead, principal Stephanie Brant asked students and their families to read for thirty minutes a night. It was introduced as a one-year pilot project, since it was a culture shift. As of this writing, the policy is firmly in place. Test scores have largely stayed the same without traditional homework at Gaithersburg. Kids are engaged in learning, and the emotional toll from homework has vanished.

What's fascinating about the Gaithersburg example is it's a low-income community. A whopping 82 percent of the students live in poverty, including 70 percent of them in non–English speaking families. This is one of the common arguments people use when saying it doesn't work to ban homework. "That's fine for *you* to say," I hear parents and teachers reason. "What about students from low-income households?" The idea is that low-income kids aren't getting educational support from home, so they need extra practice from homework. Low-income or high-income, most families care about their children's education and can support a reading-as-homework culture. Traditional homework may be hardest for kids with a stressful home life, regardless of income situation. Parental involvement comes in many forms, and homework is not the only path to achieve it.

Although reading habits are vital for school success, homework often *gets in the way* of reading time. Kids stop reading for pleasure in huge numbers after age eight, according to a 2013 Scholastic study. Think about that: Age eight is soon after children learn to read. As LeVar Burton, host of *Reading Rainbow*, reminds us, ages seven to nine are the key ages for children to become lifetime readers. The Gaithersburg students read two books a week.

Home Life Versus Homework

"Your job is school," parents tell their kids. "I'll clean up supper. You concentrate on your homework." This type of message puts parents in the unwanted role of Chief Maid, catering to their children. It also raises an entitled generation, who easily come to believe that menial tasks are beneath them. Wherever they are, at home or at school, kids need to chip in and participate in caring for their surroundings.

Families need family time to teach kids to wash the dishes, chop carrots, scrub the tub, help their siblings, exercise outside, make music, art, or other creations, and cuddle up with a good book. These skills form the rhythm of daily life. School assignments shouldn't shoulder out other types of learning.

Who's in Charge?

Homework by definition takes place outside school, on home time.

Homework sets up a potential clash of authorities. Who's the boss? If a child's tired and needs to go to bed, should the parent override the teacher? If parents disagree with homework or the amount of homework, do they have any recourse? The subject of homework causes stress for both teachers and parents, and certainly for children. In a child's life, the two biggest authorities are his parents and his teachers. Yet their roles and relative power remain unclear.

As parents, we're used to being in charge of our families. We know when our kids need to go outside and run off steam. We know when they're exhausted. We decide when to sign up for soccer and we set schedules such as bedtime. When kids hit school age, family life seems no longer our own. Who gets to decide what a child should do with her home time?

In a homework culture, there's an underlying assumption that schools have the right to appropriate a child's day after school. Nothing else is as important. Not family priorities. Not sleep. Not play. Parents protest when homework erodes family time. Family time is simply the peace and privacy to decide what to do with personal life. It's the basic human right of being able to run private lives without outside interference. The State, in the form of the school, extends into nonschool hours. The teacher's authority to set homework assignments clashes with the parent's authority to set family life. "Who controls the child's time?" asks Kralovec. "Homework forces families to follow the State's educational agenda."

Most families wouldn't mind if homework didn't occupy much time. From among the more than one hundred thousand people who read my homework posts, the ones who were most supportive of homework had something in common: They described reasonable schedules. Often it was no more than ten to twenty minutes of homework a night for elementary kids. In their view, homework was moderate and the family still had plenty of time for baths, play, soccer, and other evening activities.

However, even small doses of homework can hurt. "Shayla has very short, manageable amounts, but she doesn't like it," her mother says. "Every day it turns her off from school. When she comes home she's *done*." Plus homework designed for ten to thirty minutes often stretches longer. "The 'ten-minute-per-grade-level' rule is a joke," says Heidi, mother of a second-grader. "Perhaps that's what the teachers thought they were assigning, but it *never, ever* took that little time."

Many families nod in agreement. As Jennifer Senior, the author of *All Joy and No Fun*, says, "Homework is the new dinner." Family dinner is togetherness time, but it should be private, not prescribed. No outside force tells you what to eat or what topics to cover in your dinner conversation. Homework around the kitchen table, on the other hand, is directed time. The school has decided the focus. If homework becomes the new family dinnertime, then true family time is lost.

> ## The child belongs to the family. A child is not school property.

Parents are the ultimate authority in a child's life. The State may take over only in cases of abuse and neglect. Teachers and schools must concede that parents have the right not to have unwanted homework imposed on their family. Teachers are charged with doing what's best for a child's academic learning. Parents are charged with doing what's best for the whole child, and when the two collide, parents have the ultimate authority.

As state law in Michigan says:

Revised School Code (excerpt) Act 451 of 1976 380.10

Rights of parents and legal guardians;
duties of public schools. Section 10

It is the natural, fundamental right of parents and legal guardians to determine and direct the care, teaching and education of their children. The public schools of this state serve the needs of the pupils by cooperating with the pupil's parents and legal guardians to develop the pupil's intellectual capabilities and vocational skills in a safe and positive environment.

When Is Elementary Homework OK?

- When it's joyous
- When it's reading for pleasure
- When it's occasional (one to three times a year; once a term)
- When it's optional

- When it's independent. Children can do the entire assignment on their own; adults are only involved because of a child's desire to share
- When it promotes greater love of school and learning, such as an assignment that makes children more excited about a topic than before (often project-based learning)

When Should Homework Begin?

Most scholars, parents, and teachers agree some homework is important in high school. Classes are shorter then, life gets more serious, and take-home work can be important for complex projects or deep thinking, whether it's chemistry or essay writing.

It's unfair to expect a student to go from zero homework in elementary school to serious homework in high school without a transition period. That's why there's middle school. As one student who attended a no-homework school said, the sharp adjustment to high school was hard. She envied the more disciplined study habits of her classmates.

I also went to a no-homework elementary school and a highly academic high school. Middle school offered plenty of time to transition. Kids can benefit from limited "practice" homework in middle school before diving into the rigors of high school or, later, college.

There's a danger of going overboard, however. Middle school is a tender, in-between time. Even high schoolers don't perform well with more than two hours of homework a night. It's healthy to add occasional home assignments in seventh and eighth grade so kids can get used to figuring out personal homework routines, remembering assignments, and working independently. If middle school homework is viewed mainly as a training ground for good study habits, then this can be accomplished with thirty to forty-five minutes a night *total*, and not every night.

BEST AGES FOR HOMEWORK

Preschool & kindergarten	None
Elementary school	None
Middle school	Practice homework in seventh and eighth grade
High school	Less than two hours a day total; not daily in all subjects

Homework Is Not for Parents

Another problem with assigning homework prematurely is that children often can't cope or complete the assignment on their own.

Ilse's son, a second-grader, broke down in tears when he was faced with two hours of homework in a total of six subjects. "I did his homework last night and I don't feel guilty," his mom told me. "I will continue to do his homework for him so long as I know that he knows how to do [the material]." Parents frequently admit to doing their kids' assignments to save them from getting in trouble with the teachers. But teachers don't like the deception.

Helping kids who are over their heads in elementary school means they get in the habit of relying on parents to 1) do their homework or actively help, and 2) nag or remind them to do their homework.

I remember at age fourteen, watching my friend's mom tell her when to do her homework. My friend grumbled and moaned, but it was clear both parties were used to these roles: the Nag and the Grumbler. I was amazed. My mother never told me when or how to do my homework. I never expected her to. Homework was mine, purely my responsibility. She would occasionally ask, "What's your evening like?" but that was all.

Homework should be 100 percent the child's responsibility. When homework comes at an appropriate age, kids can do that. Parents should not be homework enforcers (see Rule 10: Don't Sign Here).

Homework-Happy Kids

"What should I do if my child *wants* to do homework?" parents ask. If you're not a believer in homework but it's your daughter's idea of fun, by all means don't stop her. Many children like to play school, and for some kids doing homework is part of that. My son Zach likes to write teacherly statements on a whiteboard at home, and go around checking imaginary students' journals. Playing school helps young kids process life. The key is that it remains in the realm of play: an action the child chooses to do on her own initiative.

Do check in. Many kids "want" to complete homework because they're scared of being punished at school if they don't. Find out what the penalties are. Ask, "What does your teacher say about homework?" or "What happens if kids don't do their homework?" Make sure it's freely chosen, not done out of fear. Fear hurts learning.

Homework-Happy Parents

If you're a parent who likes homework, you're not alone. Many parents believe a little homework every year helps their children develop personal qualities of responsibility and hard work better than other uses of time. Although research shows no actual academic benefit in elementary school—and often negative emotional costs—many families don't mind moderate homework and believe it's character building.

There are many right ways to raise a child. No matter what your stance on homework, it should be the parents who decide whether to allow homework for elementary-aged kids, not the schools. In other words, homework can be optional, a parenting tool available to families.

Some teachers are already using this method. "My son's third-grade teacher sends home an optional homework packet every week," said Robin. "Ty never does it, but two of his friends' parents have their kids do it."

Understanding Why Homework Exists

Those who advocate for homework want children to succeed, and believe homework is the path for them to do it. Besides academic reasons, parents and teachers often cite responsibility and a link between home and school.

REASONS TEACHERS GIVE HOMEWORK

To create a home-to-school link and communicate with parents

To teach responsibility, discipline, and time-management skills

To act on the belief that homework boosts student academic achievement

To please parents and administrators

REASONS PARENTS WANT HOMEWORK

To instill good study habits

To keep an eye on schools and see what kids are being taught

To ensure teachers have high standards and are doing their jobs

To give their kids the very best, following the belief that homework is the path to success

Let's look into these reasons.

The Home-to-School Link

"Homework's not so much for the kids as it is for the parents," an elementary school teacher told me. "Many parents don't pay attention to what we're doing in class unless it comes home as homework. It creates that school–home link."

Children from a supportive home environment—one that takes care of kids' physical and emotional needs and promotes the value of education—generally thrive in school. These parents create a home-to-school link of their own. Trying to instill a supportive home environment where one is missing is well beyond the scope of homework.

Parents say homework gives them a chance to see what kids are up to in school. Simple sharing is enough. You can see what your children have been up to by what comes home in their backpacks—no homework required.

Good Habits of Responsibility and Time Management

Adults often say one of the main reasons homework is important is because it helps kids develop responsibility and time-management skills. We can teach kids responsibility in other ways. When you're six, it takes responsibility to bring two mittens back home every day, plus a lunch box and a hat. When you're eight, it takes responsibility to get up on time and make your own lunch for school. As one mom put it, "That's what pets and chores are for."

Families set responsibilities and time-management skills at home already: *Make your bed first, then you can play. I know you're missing your favorite show, but you know the rule: The dishwasher has to be emptied first.* These are daily lessons in responsibility and time management.

Questions of character are often what families are most concerned about. "Does homework correlate to soft skills like grit and determination?" asks a father of a preschooler. He wonders if studies of self-control such as the marshmallow test have important implications in favor of doing homework.

Walter Mischel famously studied children's self-control and ability to delay gratification using marshmallows, and published his work for a general audience in 2014 with his book *The Marshmallow Test.* I checked in with my friend Tanya Schlam, a Ph.D. researcher and mother of two, who worked with Mischel on a follow-up study that tracked these preschoolers thirty years later. "Developing self-control is incredibly important," says Schlam. "But you don't need homework to develop self-control." Actions of many sorts can enhance self-control, from martial arts to music lessons to modeling by parents. For example, our family practices self-control at the grocery store. We don't buy candy as we walk through the gauntlet of sweets at the checkout lane. "Why is it there?" asked Zach. "To help us resist temptation and develop self-control," I reply.

Extracurriculars

"Extracurriculars cannot get in the way of school assignments," teachers often say. Most educators I've met believe schoolwork comes first.

Our role as parents is to consider the whole child. An extracurricular activity is an outside pursuit a family believes is important. Sometimes it's Hebrew school or Chinese language lessons. Other times it's sports, theater, or community service. The only thing "extra" about extracurricular activities is that they're outside the school agenda.

Non-homework activities are known to sharpen kids' brains, including music and exercise. We need to question what's extra in a child's day.

Especially with school arts programs being cut, time for other interests is important. Some parents schedule too many activities for their kids. That's true. But some children may only tolerate school but come alive when pursuing other interests. Who's to say what's more important to a certain child?

> Extra schoolwork is what's extra—not always extracurriculars.

Sleep Wins

If we want students to perform better on tests, absorb more information, and become creative thinkers and motivated problem solvers, the answer is not more homework. The answer is more sleep.

According to the National Sleep Foundation, our children suffer sleep deprivation from busy schedules, electronics, and yes, homework. Approximately one third of children have lost sleep in the past week due to homework. Elementary-aged kids are not getting enough sleep as it is, with 30 percent regularly sleeping seven to eight hours or less, and most not reaching the recommended nine to eleven hours. A five-year-old kindergartener should be sleeping even more: ten to thirteen hours. Sleep is not glamorous, but its scientific merit is being better understood each year. With enough sleep, children improve in academics, attention, and behavior.

Try This—Add to Your Toolbox

The issue of inappropriate homework is a big one. If it's bothering you, start by simply noting what you observe.

For example, Kathy, a mother of seven, played the dutiful role of Homework Enforcer when her first child entered elementary school. "I would fight with him daily over homework, taking on the role of drill sergeant because that's what I thought I was supposed to do."

Two years ago, when her daughter entered first grade, Kathy watched her cry and dawdle over daily worksheet packets. "She started complaining of tummy aches and saying she didn't want to go to school," said Kathy. "That's when it hit me: This was all just too much for a six-year-old." Kathy started reading everything she could find about homework and realized there was no basic value to homework in elementary school. She talked to teachers, removed and reduced homework for her children, and eventually home-schooled one child.

Watch your family and note what you see. What does your child need after school? How much time does homework take? What's the emotional toll? Are you playing Homework Cop or finishing his work for him? Is homework supporting a positive attitude toward school?

When you're ready, move on to Rule 9: Opt Out of Harmful Homework. This guide offers ideas both parents and teachers can use to open the conversation and start making changes.

Words to Say

Wow, that's neat. You've been learning a lot.

Have you been outside this afternoon? It's a good time to run around.

You look tired. How was your day?

Looks like you could use a snuggle.

Let's read together on the sofa.

You can play until supper.

Everyone needs a break.

Sleep's good. It makes your brain strong.

All work and no play makes Jack a dull boy.

Words to Avoid

Sit down and do your homework.

I don't care, you still have to do it.

The most important thing is your homework.

If you don't do your homework, you won't get into a
   good college.

Here, let me do it.

You can skip it tonight.

Incomplete homework means you miss recess.

Homework comes first.

Your Take

Like any complex issue, it's OK for your thoughts to evolve on the subject of homework. Perhaps your child is young or you haven't experienced any burden directly. Maybe your child adapts to assigned work without complaint, or maybe you did homework as a kid and didn't mind. Many of us start as big believers in homework, and it takes time to adjust and consider other possibilities. We want to be good parents, and the culture is overwhelmingly in favor of homework. Teachers' views evolve, too. As Sara Bennett, coauthor of *The Case Against Homework,* noted, the teachers who give the most homework tend to be newer and less experienced. Decide on priorities for your family. As your child gets older and has more homework, take the steps you need to restore balance.

RULE
9

Opt Out of
Harmful Homework

My elementary school had no homework. It did have amazing teachers and project-based learning. As a nine-year-old, I remember feeling school was so exciting that I couldn't wait for Mondays to come.

We don't all live near a school that has teachers who feel confident enough not to hand out homework. As a parent, I grew apprehensive as my son Myles entered elementary school. I knew from other parents that the homework load increased year by year, and by fourth grade it was expected to be heavy. Each September, I shared my unorthodox homework views with his teachers: no homework for children in elementary school. Yes, it is possible to opt out and still maintain respectful partnerships with teachers.

Don't be afraid to speak up and be an advocate for your child. You may meet a kindred spirit. Teachers often dislike homework, too.

Renegade Reason

Parents and teachers can agree to ban homework. When something's not working, it's time to make a change.

There is a growing movement for reduced homework, called Healthy Homework. Some schools have begun to adopt parent-negotiated homework policies. Healthy Homework strives to place sane limits on homework and balance school and family life. Healthy homework focuses on *no* homework for elementary kids—except for pleasure reading and occasional student-chosen projects that don't require adult help.

Many educators value family time and promote a no-homework or low-homework school culture. As Paul, a former third-grade teacher, says, "It's your child, your family, and your time. Parents should have the right to decide what after-school activities their families prefer, including whether or not to participate in homework assignments."

If you're a teacher or a principal, it's OK to ban homework for your school. If you're a parent, it's OK to opt out and explain the reasons for your family ban. Together, we need to keep both home and school learning joyful.

Renegade Blessings

Children gain many blessings when we halt homework, including better attitudes toward school and learning. When we advocate for our children, they have a better chance of getting their needs met. Kids also gain advocacy skills. They watch and learn from our example—another reason to advocate respectfully.

When something feels wrong, it's best to speak up.
Sometimes grown-ups don't agree, even teachers and parents.
People can disagree respectfully.
I don't have to take sides. I like both my teacher and my
    parents.
If you have a problem with school, it's good to talk to the
    teacher.

My parents really care about me.

Someday I'll stick up for my child.

Why It Works

Being an advocate for your child and family is part of parenting. For most parents, the first advocacy begins as children enter school. Remember the renegade guideline: "If something is bothering you, it's time to make a change."

Children show us something is wrong through their behavior. If a child flops and fights homework, she is sending a message that homework is not meeting her most urgent needs. Research shows homework is a top stressor in children's lives. Psychologists such as Madeline Levine say that stress is showing up in younger and younger children, too, with stomachaches, headaches, and depression in elementary school–aged children.

For a more complete discussion of what the research says on the disputed value of homework, see Rule 8: Ban Elementary Homework.

Speaking Up

Parents and teachers are partners. Partners tell each other when something is wrong.

You can say: "This is what's going on at home: [tears, stomachaches, staying up past bedtime]. It's not working for our family." Only you know your home situation. Share your support of classroom learning and your desire for your child to maintain good sleep, time for play, pleasure reading, and a love of school. Teachers know a supportive home is the best recipe for student success. You might be surprised how much they want to support your goals.

At a recent school orientation night, the teacher explained the school day, then asked for questions. Every parent question centered on homework. "How much homework is reasonable to expect for a third-grader?" asked one dad. "Do you expect a child to finish her homework even if she's tired and crying and ready to go to bed?" asked another mother.

"If it's bedtime, then go to bed," responded the teacher. "Or go ahead and modify the lesson." The parents looked shocked. "Sure," continued the teacher. "Do every other one. Change it if there's a frustration level. We want to cultivate a positive attitude toward school. It's called common sense."

Common sense is typically what both sides are striving for. If it's not working, notify the teacher. Parents often assume they can't question the teacher's plan when it comes to academics, but homework assignments are not inviolable law. For example: "It takes Sarah an hour to do the spelling and she cries every day."

"Oh, I only intended that spelling to take ten minutes. Just have her practice for a few minutes and then stop."

Or: "Nathan really struggles with reading and at night he's too tired and gets so frustrated he hates it."

"Do you already read him a bedtime story? That's fine. Reading aloud counts."

Chances are, if it's not working in your household, it's not working in others'. If your child turns out to be the only one who is struggling, that's also important for the teacher to know. Every child deserves the chance to receive the best education for her. As one mother put it: "Hooray for teachers who are willing to listen with an open heart!"

> Parents and teachers are partners.
> Partners tell each other when
> something is wrong.

Opting Out

More and more families are opting out of standardized testing for elementary kids. You can also opt out of homework. The Healthy Homework movement, spearheaded by the film and working group *Race to Nowhere*, asks teachers to support parents who opt out of homework for their child.

Opting Out with Teacher Agreement

Negotiated agreements can work. They take courage and openness on both sides. It starts by being willing to ask and listen.

Devon, a kindergartener, was so stressed about homework that he had trouble eating dinner and couldn't sleep. The five-year-old brought home daily math worksheets, projects, and reading, and due to his mother's work schedule, they didn't get home until six thirty p.m. His mother set up a meeting with the teacher, arming herself with a copy of Alfie Kohn's article on no homework and one by Peter Gray on learning and play. She was nervous, but decided to ask his teacher to substitute nightly reading for homework.

"His teacher was very understanding, but not totally on board," she said afterward. Together they agreed on nightly reading, with a mix of reading aloud and reading on his own. Devon would be allowed to fill out his reading log in the morning at school, and daily math worksheets dropped down to one a week. "Not perfect, but better than before," Devon's mother said. They had figured out a level both sides could cope with.

Each September, I made a point to meet my son's teacher and let her know why our family banned homework in elementary school. He wouldn't be doing spelling at home, or log sheets, math, or computer assignments. We tried to limit screen time, promote outdoor play, and participate in family life, which included music and reading. In third grade, I didn't have a chance to meet his teacher early on, so I wrote a letter (see sample letter, Appendix p. 343). Our unusual stance each year was met with puzzled but friendly acceptance.

"The parent is supposed to be in control of the house, not the teacher, school, or government," says Jessica, a fourth-grade teacher. "If the parent doesn't want or believe in homework, then the family should feel safe in sharing that with the teacher."

Sometimes negotiated parent-teacher agreements work, and sometimes you encounter a teacher who believes strongly in homework and won't budge. That happened to Kathy, whose daughter Tasha suffered stomachaches from homework stress. "I tried to reason with my daughter's first-grade teacher, but I was met with 'my way or the highway,'" she said. "I just wasn't going to make my daughter do homework anymore and it didn't matter if her grades reflected it." Despite the disagreement, Tasha's family maintained their homework ban and Tasha moved up to second grade with no problem.

Negotiating an agreement with a teacher is a year-by-year solution that requires continued energy and courage. For families with more than one child, it can mean multiple conversations and differing results. It also tends to get harder as kids advance into upper elementary school, when more homework is expected.

Fully Opting Out—Is It Legal?

If you don't negotiate an individual agreement, is opting out altogether legal? There's a frustrating silence on this question. Parents don't know if schools can compel a family to participate in homework against their will. Laws on school attendance are clear: Under compulsory school attendance law, children have to go to school. Parents have the legal right to homeschool, but this may not be possible due to jobs. That leaves few options. If you choose to enroll your child in school, then he has to go, but does he have to complete all assignments? It is unclear how much authority a school or teacher has to give children low grades or hold them back on the basis of not participating in homework, especially in elementary school. In Canada, dual attorney parents Shelli and Tom Milley sued their Calgary school for the right not to have homework for their three children and won. In Australia, the New South Wales Department of Education and Communities made it clear that homework was not mandatory for families.

Most families in the U.S. have no idea what their rights are. What is clear is that young children feel intense pressure to turn in homework. Teachers send "incomplete homework sheets" for parents to sign. Kids are punished with bad grades, shaming, and loss of activities and privileges at school. The most common punishment, guaranteed to bring anguish to any elementary child, is this: "Students who don't turn in their homework will miss recess." (See Rule 7: Recess Is a Right.)

Respecting Authority

"How has this worked out for your family?" one mom asked. "I don't mean academically; I mean in terms of viewing people in authority."

This is a biggie for people. "Respect authority" is a cherished value. In terms of homework, adults tend to believe respecting authority means obeying the teacher and doing what's assigned.

Respect is fundamentally about treating people well. There is no magic in simply respecting the institution of homework. We should treat all people—grown people, young people, teacher people, and non-teacher people—with respect. This is part of social community and basic human dignity.

Respecting a child starts with understanding her needs. If her greatest need is sleep, then we need to make room for sleep. If his greatest need is physical release—banging sticks on trees, running in circles—then we need to grant that. Among these many needs, homework may not be a priority.

Remaining Open

Andrea, a reading teacher and former second-grade teacher, said, "I used to think worksheets would help children bridge the gap of what they didn't know, but I've totally changed my view now." As Kat, a teacher and mother, said, "I'm a former high school teacher, and I assigned plenty of homework. If I did it over again, I would assign much less after all the reading I've done on education."

The person you approach may not be ready to hear a no-homework message. Changing beliefs takes space and time.

Try This—Add to Your Toolbox

The message "It's OK to ban homework" applies to both teachers and families. Each has different ways to help the homework situation.

What Teachers Can Do

A true educator listens to new ideas and makes decisions based on good research.

1. Open the Conversation
   Tell families your goals for the kids and your philosophy about homework. Don't assume parents know. Most families are frantic about homework—either wanting it or despising it. Share your viewpoint and let them know where you're flexible. Tell families what you most value: It could be kids who love to read, eagerly share the school day with their parents, and are well rested and unstressed

when they come to school. Help families find the right balance.

2. Educate Parents

"As a teacher, parents used to ask me what they could do to reinforce their first-grader's learning at home," said Dana. "I'd say, 'Read to them. Read to them a lot.' Most parents would blink and stammer on with, 'Well, yeah, but what else?'" Chances are, parents are new at guiding school-aged children. They're anxious to know what's best for them. Share what you know about learning styles and the importance of reading as a family. Younger parents, especially, are used to a heavy homework culture from their own school days and may expect you to provide it.

3. Share Research

"I'm a teacher who believes in no homework, but I have to assign it to keep my job." Sound familiar? As a single teacher, you have limited power. Burnout is just around the corner if you are consistently forced to teach against your principles. The children need you. Share research with colleagues and administrators, find allies, and see if you can begin the important work of internal change.

4. Support Homework Alternatives

For reading-as-homework to succeed, educators need to understand the barriers families face. It's possible to get creative about providing books and gradually changing reading cultures. Stephanie Brant, for example, principal at Gaithersburg Elementary, brought a bookmobile to families, even during summer months. If you don't have energy or time to go to those lengths, that's OK. Do what you can to identify the underlying issues, find partners, and get engaging books in kids' hands.

5. Find New One-on-One Time

"I used to have an aide, but that got cut with budget cuts," said Marilyn, an elementary school teacher. "Kids need one-on-one time when they're learning to read; it makes such a difference." Some teachers believe in homework for precisely this reason. "Kids actually get more one-on-one attention and instruction when parents help them work through their homework," said Angela, another elementary teacher.

Recruit more one-on-one helpers. Ask for parent and community volunteers. Our local school is hopping with retired-teacher volunteers, who donate hundreds of hours to the children.

6. Acknowledge the Impasse

Some parents clamor for more homework to give their child the best advantage, and others oppose it for the same reason. Both believe they're doing what's best for the kids. What to do?

Here is a case in which you cannot please everybody. Perhaps we need to recognize the split and not expect to breach it right now. Unless the school takes a strong stance based on homework research, acknowledge the divide. Give your opinion. Ask families which approach they would like to see for their children. Call reading at home "homework" for the pro-homework families. Ask other families to read at home with their children. Offer reasonable home assignments from time to time to satisfy families that demand or crave it, and let parents in non-homework families know it's optional. As one fourth-grade teacher says: "My parents thank me constantly for giving them peaceful tear-free evenings. If they want more, I am able to suggest tons of free learning sites."

When you think about it, this is not a departure from

what schools already do in other areas. There's a requirement that parents vaccinate their children, but some parents opt out. There's a curriculum requirement for sex education, but some parents opt out. Homework is simply another area where private philosophies may differ.

7. Support Families
The best foundation a child can have is a strong, supportive family. "Teachers should support involved parents," says Daryl, an educator. If a family's views are radically different from yours, give space for their way to succeed. Say, "Let's try it." You can always adjust if the method needs to be tweaked. There are many right ways to raise and educate a child.

What Parents Can Do

Have confidence. It's always scary to buck convention, but you have more rights than you realize. Stay respectful and focused on the child.

1. Thank and Encourage Teachers
Even a teacher who doesn't assign homework needs encouragement. Teachers are often under tremendous pressure to send work home, and they frequently report being caught in the middle, with pressure from both parents and administrators. Don't speak up only when something's wrong. Be vocal in your support of no-homework or reading-only teachers. They need your voice.

2. Don't Suffer in Silence
If your gut tells you something is wrong, it probably is. Watch your child. Observe your own behavior. If your family is suffering, it's not healthy for anyone.

3. Open the Conversation

Some parents prefer to skip homework, rather than bring it up with the teacher. One mother routinely ripped half the worksheets out of her son's homework folder before he even saw them. Another simply skipped all the assigned work except reading. Teachers understandably grow frustrated when assigned work isn't turned in. It takes tremendous courage to speak up, but it's the respectful path. "I have more guts now with my second child," said one mother. You can do it. If you don't know how to begin, see the following sample script.

Sample Script

Ready to talk to your child's teacher? It can help to start with the math:

"We get home at five p.m. She goes to bed at eight p.m. She's only eight years old and she's exhausted.

"We really want to support her learning, so we talk over the day and read a bedtime story together every night. Of course, you know how important reading is for school success. Our main goal as a family is to make sure Kate gets the rest and playtime she needs so she's ready for the next school day and stays positive and engaged with learning.

"This is what we're seeing: [Describe family stress and conflict]. This is what we need to do as a family: [Describe how you spend your family time together]. I've been reading some recent research that shows there's no benefit to homework for kids in elementary school. I'd be happy to share it with you. Based on all this, we'd like to propose doing daily reading at home as a substitute for homework. We firmly believe that's what's best for our family. How does this sound to you? Will you support our educational goals?"

4. Request Reading-as-Homework

Reading aloud to children every night is fundamental to school success. Maybe you already do a bedtime story, but it's five minutes at best. Read aloud to your child every day, and up the time commitment (at least twenty minutes). When your child starts reading on her own, don't stop reading aloud; there's no upper age limit. Set aside additional time for her to read by herself for pleasure. Give teachers examples of schools that use daily reading as homework, and offer to put them in touch.

5. Support Teachers

Be a partner with your child's teacher even if you disagree about homework. Support for classroom learning does not have to involve homework. It could be talking about classroom topics at home, augmenting subjects with books or outings, and pointing out concepts in daily life. Supporting the teacher can mean reinforcing the curriculum in your own way and volunteering in the classroom. Show your kids you love learning in your own style.

6. Ask for a Homework Bill of Rights

Schools from Los Angeles to Vienna, Virginia, have recently adopted school- and district-wide policies to control homework, called a Homework Bill of Rights. Some ban homework on weekends and holidays. Others deal with homework amounts or grading practices. It all starts with a committee of interested parents and teachers to explore the issue and propose new practices.

7. Change Schools or Teachers

Sometimes parenting and teaching philosophies are at complete odds. Acknowledge it if that happens to you. It may make the most sense to switch classrooms or scout out a new school that matches your learning philosophy. When a teacher at Dale's school did not agree with the family's learning style, the principal agreed to switch the child into another class. Other families decide to change schools or homeschool for more flexibility.

8. Remember Your Power

   You are the parent of your child. You are charged with doing your best to raise and educate your child and to resist things that hurt him. This includes unreasonable homework.

   You can influence teachers and principals. These educators are your partners. Be respectful and act as partners to address the problem.

   You elect school board members. Bring the issue up, in partnership with other concerned teachers and parents. The school board is meant to serve families and children.

Words to Say

FOR PARENTS—WHEN SPEAKING WITH TEACHERS

Is there a good time to talk?
I'd like to talk to you about homework.
Here's what's going on at our house.
I see Jack crying, having meltdowns, and saying,
   "I hate school!"
It's just not working for my child.
It's not working for us at home.

My goal is to give Elena a supportive atmosphere for
　　learning at home.

We do this by having early bedtimes, plenty of outdoor
　　playtime, and reading together as a family.

I've been doing a lot of research about homework. They're
　　finding that homework doesn't benefit kids in elementary
　　school.

Here's an article about it.

Instead of traditional homework, we'd like to have
　　Elena read every night. This is working well in many
　　schools.

Would you take some time to consider this? Then we
　　could talk again.

Will you support our educational goals?

FOR TEACHERS—WHEN SPEAKING WITH PARENTS

At this age, play is your child's most important work.

Homework at this age is simply reading together
　　every night.

My goal is to keep kids positive and engaged
　　with school.

I expect you'll read together for ＿＿ minutes.

If something's not working for you, please let me know.

I understand family time is important.

Please stop if the assignment takes more than fifteen
　　minutes.

Here's some information about the importance of
　　reading and the research on homework.

Here's how we already support responsibility and time
　　management in the classroom.

That's up to you and your family.

That doesn't fit with my philosophy, but I'm willing
　　to try it for a while.

I accept that.

Let's see how it goes.

Words to Avoid

I'm sorry, we can't make exceptions.

Your daughter will have to miss recess, then.

My son has better things to do than this stupid worksheet.

You're looking at this wrong.

Your Take

Bucking the system takes resolve, but take heart—you are not alone. Excessive homework is emerging as a global issue.

In Germany, educators banned homework for kids in grades five through nine at Elsa-Brandström high school. President Hollande called for a ban on homework in France to address inequality concerns. Finland, often looked to as a model for education reform, requires little homework in all grades, plus shorter school days, and supports consistently high academics.

Australia's New South Wales Department of Education and Communities, which includes its biggest city, Sydney, recently issued a clear statement that homework is not compulsory. Its Parent Guide to homework goes on to say: "Let the school know if you don't agree with its homework policy and discuss alternative strategies." The guide states each school must have a homework policy, and schools are reminded to develop policies that take the latest research into consideration; for example, "For primary students, there is no evidence that homework lifts academic performance."

Each school and school district is a unique environment. Maybe the teacher is sympathetic, or perhaps the principal is the one open to new educational ideas. Maybe you'd be satisfied with homework cut in half. Without a homework policy in place, navigating homework at your child's school is a balance of social relationships and respectful education on both sides. Take cues from your child. Do what you need to do to make sure she believes books are a joy, and that she remains engaged and positive about learning.

RULE
10   Don't Sign Here

I first met a request for my daily signature when my son Myles hit school age.

"You have to sign my spelling list," he told me.

I stared.

"You have to sign my spelling list," he said again.

I peered at the spelling sheet and its prominent blank line. A parent signature? I balked. That tiny act collided with everything I believed in about supporting a child's learning. Not only did it send a continual message to my child that adults didn't trust him, but it jettisoned me into a role I knew I didn't want: Schoolwork Patrol Cop.

I gently told him I wouldn't be signing these school papers.

"But you have to!" he wailed. "If you don't sign, I'll miss recess!"

"Your job is to learn to spell," I told him. "If I don't want to sign, it's up to me to talk to your teacher."

Signatures for schoolwork tell kids: We don't trust you. We don't trust you really did it. We don't trust you care about your own learning.

Renegade Reason ||||||||||||||||||||||||||||||||||||||||||||||||||||||||||||||||||||||||||||||||||||||

Parent signatures for children's work diminish trust and responsibility.

||||||||||||||||||||||||||||||||||||||||||||||||||||||||||||||||||||||||||||||||||||||||||||||||||||||||||||||

Nora came to her mother with a practice sheet for her viola lessons. "She was very anxious about me signing it," her mother said. Nora was worried her teacher wouldn't believe she'd practiced and as a result she wouldn't get a prize from the music teacher's prize box.

When I was a kid, my parents signed report cards and field trip permission forms. That was it. Now there's a maze of signature lines bombarding families. Sign here. Initial here. If you don't sign daily your child will fail, miss recess, or lose classroom rewards. For a family with multiple children and signature requirements, the daily ritual of homecoming and sharing the day becomes a series of check marks, initializations, and Quick-where-do-I-sign-so-that's-off-the-list?

Here's a sampling of items parents are asked to sign:

Reading logs
Reading contracts
Spelling lists
Daily planner or parent communicator folder
Math homework
Online Spanish labs
Online school portals
Music practice logbooks
Behavior contracts and school policies

It's enough to make a parent feel like a jailer. Tick off the time your daughter read a book, figured math problems, and practiced piano. How many minutes? Where do I sign? Sign, initial, check. Day after day.

Parent check marks take personal responsibility away from kids. They quietly undermine family relationships and build a culture of distrust between parents and children and children and teachers. We can do better by creating partnerships of trust.

Renegade Blessings

Children gain so much from relying on themselves, taking ownership of their own learning, and feeling the rewards of family interactions without dictated management tools.

> Learning is really up to me.
> It's fun to share with my family what I've learned at school.
> It's not my parents' job to make sure I've fulfilled my responsibilities.
> Grown-ups in my life trust me.
> Sometimes I make mistakes, but mostly I'm trustworthy.
> I can learn without worrying about being punished.
> Even when they disagree, my parents and teachers respect each other.
> When I disagree with someone, I'll try to do the same.

It can be easy to shrug off the small inconvenience of a parent signature in the midst of busy parenting. You may simply roll your eyes and say: "It's not a big deal. I'm not going to fight this battle." Still, a small thing like a signature matters.

Why It Works

Schoolwork is the child's job, and responsibility for it needs to rest firmly with the child. Requiring a parent signature on school tasks or practice logs sets up an unhealthy relationship between parent and child. The signature mind-set sends this message: "It's my parents' job to see I do my work." This leads to the next bad habit: "I will only work when someone [teacher/parent/boss] is watching." Or "I will only do my work when nagged." Parent educator Vicki Hoefle says parents need to question this role. She asks: "Do you want to become the homework police—and stay the homework police for the remainder of this child's academic career?"

The signature model strengthens external reward, not internal motivation. *If I don't get this signed, I don't get recess.* Or, conversely: *If I get this signed I get a prize on Friday.* Daniel Pink, author of *Drive*, and other researchers demonstrate that extrinsic motivation like this reduces internal motivation. And internal motivation—to read, to learn an instrument, to rise to a challenge—is what drives inner satisfaction and success. Outside punishment and rewards unwittingly steal motivational drive from the child. As Alfie Kohn, author of *Punished by Rewards*, writes: "Rewards for learning undermine intrinsic motivation." For families trying to raise kids based on internal rewards, insisting on a signature shows distrust and disrespect for family culture.

Daniel Goleman's work on emotional intelligence suggests that children learn best when they are calm and not anxious about threats or punishment. When the focus is on how much trouble they'll get in if they don't collect a signature, learning is put in the background.

Requiring a signature for every twenty minutes of reading or fifteen minutes of music practice has the effect of reducing learning to minimum results. Instead of reading for pleasure, the focus becomes: Meet the minimum minute guidelines, get the signature, be done.

Finally, some schools rely on signatures to solve complex social problems such as bullying. At Samantha's school, all students and all parents were required to sign an "anti-bullying pledge" at the start of each school year. Without more substance behind it, a behavior pledge becomes just one more signature. A real commitment to reduce bullying demands much more: conflict mediation skills, a positive school culture, and social courage. All of these take training, mistakes, and practice.

Some families are naturally engaged in their child's schooling and well-being, already supporting their child according to their own beliefs and styles. In other households, there's a chasm between school learning and home life. Huge social and economic issues are at play here, including financial stress, mental health, and addiction. The goal may be an involved, engaged family, but a signature line—signed or not—can't change the fundamental situation.

Take Off Your Adult Lenses

The signature system removes responsibility from the child and transfers it to adult overseers. It may be the child's reading or music lesson, but the parent must sign. This puts parents in an unwanted spot of being a patrol cop and a nag. *Did you do your math? Where's your reading log so I can sign it?* The ever-present signature requirement sends a clear message: We don't trust you. Parents don't. Teachers don't. We don't think you'll learn without constant surveillance.

Restore partnerships of trust. Give kids power over their own learning.

Parent-Child-School Communicator

A planner, or school communicator folder, typically involves a daily signature and is a growing practice in U.S. schools. A planner sums up the school day and tries to avoid conversations like this:

"How was school?"

"Fine."

"What'd you do in class today?"

"Nothing."

"Tell me about your day."

"Can I have a snack?"

With a planner in hand, it's easier to say, "Oh, I see you looked at caterpillars today."

"Yeah! That was cool. We got six painted lady caterpillars for our class and we fed them sugar water and . . ."

A planner has the potential to stir up good conversations between children and their families. However, most school planners require a daily parent signature. This turns a conservation starter into a checklist. Sharing is a natural and joyful activity. Getting credit for it is not.

The request for the parent signature on student planners is partly to instill student responsibility and partly to ensure parents are at least minimally involved in their child's school day. As one teacher explained, "It's the kids' responsibility to bring it to parents and talk about what happened in the day."

A child may want to talk about what they learned about caterpillars and planetary systems, or she may want to talk about what happened at lunch when Sonja took her milk and wouldn't give it back. The family is a place to support a child's well-being, including the emotional, social, and physical side. In our family, we share thoughts and news during an after-school snack. This is when we hear the most pressing news, such as, "I felt so stupid at recess today. This is what happened. . . ."

When I ask teachers why signatures are important to them, it typically comes down to their earnest desire to bridge the gap between home and classroom learning.

What teachers seek:

Communication between home and school

Assurance that the child has completed assignments

Parent understanding of what goes on in the classroom
The chance for parents to support and enhance classroom
    learning

These goals make sense. But a daily check mark on a piece of paper can also weaken the connection. The parent becomes a signature dispenser. The child may gladly share tidbits about his day, but knowing that he'll miss recess if he doesn't get that coveted parent signature, he's forced to stay locked in conversation until the parent declares, "I'm satisfied; you've shared enough."

Whose Signature?

If a signature is important, choose the right person. In terms of schoolwork, the right person is the child. "You can write your own initials if you like. You're the one who did it."

I'll admit it's tempting to say to your child: "Just sign my name." But that leads to other mixed messages. A child who is given permission to sign her parent's signature at a young age may see no difference in writing her parent's signature on later documents that matter.

Sarah's mother used this approach for her daughter's reading contract. It stated: "I do solemnly agree to read a minimum of 3 books every quarter." The contract included a reading log for every day of the week with lines for three signatures: child, parent, and teacher. Sarah's mother wrote in the margins: "I trust Sarah to handle this. No need for my signature."

What happened? It worked out for everyone. Teachers are usually open to different family styles as long as the child is learning. The year before, Sarah's mother tried out the "no signing for me" philosophy for the first time on her daughter's fifth-grade teacher. "After the initial shock wore off, he said, 'All right, then, I guess we'll give it a try.'"

Sarah signed her own name all year. One time she didn't, though. When her teacher asked her why, she replied, "Well, I forgot to do my reading last night."

This is student honesty, student self-reliance, student integrity, and student ownership of learning.

Homework Is Not for Parents

Ask kids and they'll tell you: "It's not fair for kids to get in trouble for when their parents don't do something."

Being blamed for parent behavior riles up kids' keen sense of injustice. The punishment for not bringing back parent signatures, or enough parent signatures, can be severe, including missing recess (see Rule 7: Recess Is a Right).

If your family decides to participate in homework, it should be the child's homework, not the parent's. Putting parent signatures on a child's work removes one of the few reasons adults use for supporting homework in the first place: child responsibility (see Rule 8: Ban Elementary Homework).

> When a practice is harmful or
> inappropriate, it's up to adults to talk.

Try This—Add to Your Toolbox

Be Proactive

Since it may not occur to you to expect parent signatures, it can be hard to be proactive (*You mean I have to sign his library book contract?*). Set up a meeting with your child's teacher as early as possible in the school year to explain your family's philosophy. You might want to start with a note. Wendy, a parent in Ohio, sent a short letter to her daughter's new fourth-grade teacher.

Dear Mr. _____:

We realize it is often expected for parents to sign a planner. However, our goal as parents is to raise a lifelong self-motivated learner and we believe signing a planner on a daily basis removes the responsibility from her and creates distrust at home. We are totally involved with her education, but would like to discuss an alternative method with you if this is a classroom expectation of yours.

Thanks in advance,

She signed the planner the first day and wrote, "See my note." When they met, the teacher was puzzled, but agreeable. Nora continued to share her planner with her mother as a way to talk with her about her day. No one signed it. That's the goal for many teachers anyway—to bridge the gap between home and school and make a school-parent connection.

Be an Advocate for Your Child

Bucking the system can be downright terrifying. It brings parenting to a new level, and can make us question our own deeply held beliefs. *This feels wrong. What do I know? The teacher thinks it works. Maybe I should just go along with it. I don't want to cause trouble. Teachers have hard enough jobs anyway.*

But "just going along with it" makes *your* job harder.

Your child's teacher has your son or daughter for one or two years. You and your child live together for approximately twenty years and are committed to a lifetime relationship. Taking the seemingly easy path can erode relationship lines of responsibility, trust, and internal motivation.

It's natural to feel qualms. It takes enormous courage to speak up when something bothers you. Relax. Remember, all you're doing is talking to one person—likely a very nice person, one who loves learning and already cares about your child.

What Will Happen?

You won't know until you try. Be respectful. Be honest. Let the teacher know you want to support your child's learning. Most teachers are delighted to know a child's family is involved and interested.

When one parent speaks up it can benefit the whole class. When Julie, the mother of a third-grader, spoke up about her concerns with parent signatures, the teacher rethought the policy and removed it for all her students.

Be prepared for some surprise, since these ideas may be new. You may be initiating a conversation the teacher never expected to have. So be kind. Say: "I know you may have been doing this for some time, but here are my concerns." Or: "We're trying to raise a self-reliant child. I feel this requirement conflicts with how we're raising Sophie and what we're trying to do as a family." If you think you'll muff it just speaking, write down your views, then ask to meet in person.

Simply talking politely to my son's teachers worked for us for several years in elementary school. "Trust me," I said, and explained our family values of trust and internal motivation. Myles continued to fill out a daily planner, and I read it, but no one at home signed it. The teachers knew I was involved. As they explained to me, the point was communication and involvement, and that was being met.

If the teacher is willing to try, be specific about what you both expect. For example: "I expect Sophie will learn her spelling words each week." "I expect Sophie will sign her own name, but not sign mine."

You might meet a teacher who strongly disagrees with your

view. Give it time. Whether you sign or not, it's OK to share your beliefs about student responsibility with both the teacher and the child. Modeling respectful disagreement is another life gift.

Speak up if signatures bother you. Yours might be the first voice, but it won't be the last. Sometimes we need to plant a seed that will grow.

Words to Say

DISCUSSING SIGNATURES

I trust you.

This is *your* reading log.

You're the one who knows if you did it or not.

You can't sign my name, but you can sign your name.

The idea is to help you learn. You're in charge of your
   learning.

What do you think? Is something worrying you?

SETTING ROLES AND MODELING DISAGREEMENT

Your job is to learn to spell.

My job is to talk to the teacher if I have a concern about
   what he asked me to do.

Don't worry. The signature part is between your teacher
   and me.

You can be there when we talk if you want.

I will let you know what happens.

Sometimes grown-ups disagree about things.

When I have a disagreement with your teacher, it's my job
   to let her know and listen to what she has to say.

We both want what's best for you.

Words to Avoid

How many minutes did you practice today?
Where's your planner? Where do I sign? OK, that's done.
That's so dumb you have to do that.
That's a worthless assignment.

Your Take

This may or may not be a battle you want to fight. Maybe lack of recess is more important. You may want to develop a deeper relationship with the teacher first, or simply take more time to gather your courage. No matter what you decide, be aware of the role signatures play in your parent-child relationship. Talk about it with your child, and let him know you trust him.

Section IV

MORE RIGHTS
at SCHOOL

The mind is not a vessel to be filled,
but a fire to be ignited.

—PLUTARCH

RULE
11

Reconfigure Kindergarten

Madelyn attended preschool four days a week, starting at age three. Her mother expected a seamless transition to kindergarten. After all, kindergarten was in the same school building, and the school day was the same: nine a.m. to four p.m. The first few weeks of kindergarten, Madelyn collapsed crying in the parking lot.

"It was total shock," said her mother. "She was ready to crash when I picked her up. At home she needed to vegetate. I know kindergarten is the new first grade, but I didn't think she wouldn't be able to handle it."

Renegade Reason

Kids deserve to thrive at age five. If kindergarten isn't a good match, there are lots of options. School learning belongs in first grade.

Kindergarteners show stress with their bodies. Jasmine, age four, slumped in her car seat, fast asleep by four thirty p.m. Five-year-old

Jack wet his pants. Casey cried every day before school, day after day after day.

What's happening here? It's Kindergarten Crash. When kids droop, drop, cry, scream, and dissolve into dervish mode, it's a sign something is seriously wrong. We need to listen.

My youngest was the first in our family to try out all-day, every-day kindergarten. Like the kids I've just described, Zach was a veteran of daycare. He was used to being away from home seven hours at a time in a group setting. But daycare moved at a child's pace. The daycare day was filled with play, naps, and plentiful outdoor time. When I picked up Zach after kindergarten, he fell on the sidewalk at the bus stop and shrieked. For months after starting kindergarten, he had no residual energy. I watched in amazement as this little jumping, yelling, pirate-loving child sat in a heap in the armchair, staring off into space. His toys lay untouched. He screamed at the slightest thing, and fell asleep for the night at five p.m.

Modern kindergarten is often at direct odds with what kindergarten-aged children actually need. Not every child struggles. Some kindergarten programs maintain enough play that children thrive. Kindergarten can be a good fit. But when it's not, we need to reconfigure kindergarten.

Renegade Blessings

Children deserve a chance to thrive at age five. Find an option that keeps her love of learning and play alive.

Learning is fun!
I like to run and play.
I have time to explore my own ideas.
I feel good.
Next year I'll learn to read. I can't wait.

Why It Works

Why can young three- and four-year-olds cope with all-day daycare and preschool, yet fall to pieces when kindergarten comes?

As one mother said: "Less play, less food, less rest."

Kindergarten days are now filled with first-grade expectations: reading, writing, and arithmetic. It's typically a seven-hour school day spent sitting still, followed in many cases by homework worksheets. Although most adults know five-year-olds need time to play, relax, and release boisterous energy, there's not room in a typical kindergarten day. Nap time is often gone, along with half days in most areas. It's rare to find a sand table or dress-ups. Instead the rooms are filled with calendars, chairs, and calculations.

Another reason kindergarten kids can't cope? Academic demands before the brain is ready to receive them.

Modern kindergarten teaches what psychologist David Elkind calls "miseducation"—teaching the wrong things at the wrong times. Five-year-olds have so much they need to learn: how to practice handling conflict with peers, control their impulses, express boundless physical energy, investigate bugs, build sand forts, fall in love with books, tell stories, and engage their creative minds in dramatic play. When kindergarten doesn't meet these needs, it obstructs learning and stresses kids.

We've embarked on a grand experiment with our youngest children. It's time to acknowledge it's failing. The push to compete with other nations, improve test scores, and invest in the future workforce has led to overly academic kindergartens. Research shows it's not a good idea. Researchers from Duke University performed a comprehensive review of multiple research studies done on kindergarten. Their findings? Starting academics early didn't help children academically or behaviorally in the long haul. Though kids who went through full-day, academic kindergartens were somewhat ahead on reading and math at first, these gains wore off by third grade. What's more, the same study found these kids had worse attitudes toward learning, lower self-control, and worse social skills. Studies by the nonprofit RAND corporation found similar results.

Because of the rigorous academics expected, many families delay and send their children to kindergarten when they are six or even seven. This creates a new suite of issues. The kindergarten year needs to match kindergarten kids.

Take Off Your Adult Lenses

"Everyone goes to kindergarten," we say, and remember happy times from our own kindergarten days. The kindergarten from your childhood may have been mainly digging in the sandbox, singing songs, and selecting a nap mat next to your friend. Or you may have gone to a kindergarten that emphasized reading and writing, but only in the mornings. Even in the past three years, kindergarten has changed. Toys are out; desks are in. Brain research on child development tells us five-year-olds learn best in other ways. Get creative when it comes to the kindergarten year.

Long Hours

When we focus on what is "off" with modern kindergarten, it's important not to be distracted by the trend toward "all day, every day." Long hours contribute to exhaustion, but time well spent doesn't wipe out a child.

All day isn't the problem. Every day isn't the problem. According to the U.S. Census, 15 million young kids are in daycare of some sort, many of them full time. That's close to two thirds of all kids five and under. If the program is appropriate, children can thrive in good childcare.

Kindergarten can be a healthy place and a fantastic part of a child's life. It can be a gateway to twelve more happy years of school learning. However, it's getting harder to find a program that matches five-year-olds' developmental needs. Individual teachers may make the difference in some schools. However, even seasoned kindergarten teachers who understand child development have a hard time keeping kindergarten age-appropriate. They have to follow new state curriculum requirements that expect kindergarten children to be reading, ready or not.

> Today's kindergarten rarely offers what kindergarten-aged children need.

Ready or Not

Four-year-old Sydney was ready. There was no question about it. The little girl was already reading, socially mature, and excited by academics. After a full day of kindergarten, she skipped off to piano lessons, bubbling with enthusiasm.

Ben needed more time to run and play. He started kindergarten at age six, but came home so angry he knocked furniture over. His parents quickly pulled him out of school and gave him another year in a daycare playgroup. Ben learned to read happily at age seven.

Development is not synchronous in young children. Some read before age three. Some take much longer, no matter what age reading instruction starts. As Denise Pope, a senior lecturer at Stanford, says, we know it's developmentally appropriate for some kids not to be fluent readers until age seven or eight. I was one of the late ones, so I wasn't concerned when Zach took his time before becoming interested in reading.

In some schools, there is no leeway. Kindergarteners may be expected to repeat a grade or go to mandatory literacy camps. A child is ready when her brain is ready. Years of premature forcing don't help. Appropriate literacy for this age includes story time, songs, rhymes, finger chants, dictated stories, and words integrated into play. Yet kids' time is being taken up by academics at younger and younger ages.

Mini-School in Pre-K

"Our four-year-olds are disappearing," lamented Hope, the director of a Connecticut nursery school. Chris, a parent from a California cooperative preschool, agreed. "Parents are pulling their four- and five-year-olds out to place them in transitional kindergarten. Enrollment in play-based preschools is down. They're all going to Young Fives."

Until the 1960s and '70s, it was rare for young children even to attend nursery programs. Now besides college prep, there's kindergarten prep. These transitional programs go by names such as KinderPrep, Ready "Four" School, and Young Fives. They're usually located in elementary school buildings, and start with kids as young as two and a half. That means kids even younger than kindergarten age are spending more time away from play. Kindergarten-prep programs tend to be miniaturized versions of the elementary curriculum.

Kids this age have lots to learn. If we take up their time with adult agendas, children miss developing in healthy ways. Doing double kindergarten years (for example, kindergarten prep and kindergarten) may not be the best recipe for youngsters just entering school. Children need their present needs met, not two years in age-inappropriate programs.

The National Association for the Education of Young Children (NAEYC) is the U.S. clearinghouse for early childhood. NAEYC knows child development and shares research on what kids really need. Among NAEYC's ten tips for finding quality programs for children ages three to six are these:

- Children are not expected to sit quietly for long periods of time.
- Children should not all be doing the same thing at the same time.
- Children should have long periods of time to play and explore.
- Worksheets are rarely used, if at all.
- Building blocks, art materials, and props for pretend play are available.
- Outdoor play is never sacrificed for instructional time.
- Children and their parents look forward to school. Children are happy to attend. They do not cry regularly or complain of feeling sick.

This checklist includes the needs of five-year-olds, the traditional kindergarten age. How many kindergarten or even pre-kindergarten classrooms meet these basic standards today?

As my kindergartener told me: "I don't want to go to school. I want to play and snuggle with Blankie. At school they don't let you do that. They keep you busy, busy every minute." In this case, research agrees with the child.

Finding a Good Preschool or Kindergarten

OBSERVE IN PERSON

Many schools describe their programs as "play based," but in reality play gets short shrift. Even classrooms filled with blocks and toys can be deceptive. Teachers may have toys on the shelves, but no time to break away from the academic curriculum. Ask to sit in on a whole school day.

CHECK THE SCHEDULE

Science, social studies, math, music, lunch, gym, Spanish, library . . . A cluttered schedule typically means there's an emphasis on academics over play-based learning.

Too many transitions are disruptive. Young children need blocks of time (one- or two-hour blocks) to play and explore their own ideas. Transitions can disrupt kids' ability to focus and experience deep learning.

ARE DRESS-UPS WELCOME?

Do you see firefighter hats, tiger suits, princess dresses, and capes? Kids of all ages like dressing up, but for kids seven and under, this play is especially important because it's part of how they learn. "Let's pretend" games are social and imaginative and can lead to deeply focused learning.

IS THERE BIG MUSCLE SPACE?

Play cannot be confined to quiet rooms, tables, and chairs. Not only do young kids need to move, at times they need to be fast, big, and loud. If the classroom is small, is there a nearby space where this level of action is welcome?

DO YOU SEE CARDBOARD BOXES?

Giant boxes can become anything and lead to endless creativity, social interaction, and joyous learning. Teachers who welcome large cardboard boxes understand the nature of true play.

IS THE ARTWORK IDENTICAL?

If you see rows of snowmen, all with the same top hat and smile, or displays of the same paper plate lion, watch out. Art is for expression and imagination. A program that understands child development promotes original creations.

SEEK DICTATED STORIES

Look for a classroom that values pre-literacy and emergent literacy. This is a joyful stage of songs, rhymes, books being read aloud, and stories that children dictate to adults.

WATCH THE PEOPLE

It all comes down to the people. Watch interactions between teachers and children. Look for signs of respect, genuine interest, trust, and joy between adult and child.

Kids Who Can Cope

Children who trot off to kindergarten without complaint don't alarm us. But if the program is overly academic, we need to be concerned about these kids, too.

Just because a child *can* cope doesn't mean his needs are being met. Five-year-olds can learn to deal with unrealistic expectations in kindergarten, but it doesn't mean they should. A fifteen-year-old can get pregnant, but that doesn't mean it's a good idea.

"Kindergarten is the new first grade" is a common refrain. If that's the case, it's a bad fit for nearly every child. Kindergarteners aren't ready for first grade. They are ready for age-appropriate play and instruction.

Reconfiguring Kindergarten

1. Kindergarten needs to acknowledge and follow child development stages.
2. Preschool and other pre-K and Young Fives programs should be unique to the ages they serve, not a simplified kindergarten curriculum.
3. Today's five-year-olds need a new program. This age group needs a place similar to the "old kindergarten," where they can thrive being five.

Redshirting a Generation

If their kids need more time before facing a rigorous kindergarten program, parents do their best to accommodate. Emily's mother delayed her daughter's kindergarten year.

"I wanted her to be the oldest in her class," she said. "Then she'll be able to do the work easily." Emily was eight for most of her first-grade year. She'll be nearly twenty when she graduates from high school.

"Redshirting" is the practice of delaying school entry to gain maturity. It's gaining widespread traction, especially among affluent families. These kids enter grade school a year older than their peers. The numbers keep rising, but approximately 7 to 12 percent of children are redshirted nationally, and the 2008 U.S. census shows that 17 percent of kids were six or older when they started kindergarten. Redshirting can be wonderful for individual cases, but it's also a cause for concern, for both the redshirted kids and their classmates.

Here's why. Most five-year-olds who can't handle a sitting-still-all-day, academic kindergarten curriculum *can* cope with first grade a year later if given the opportunity to be five now. These kids don't need delayed entry to kindergarten. They need a chance to act their age. In kindergarten they need to play, but by first grade they're ready to read. Redshirted kids, however, remain among younger, less skilled classmates, and teachers have to cope with increasing disparity among students. Sam Wang, a professor of neuroscience at Princeton, says children learn best when they are close to the limits of their abilities. Redshirted kids perform better than their younger peers academically, but only at first. By the end of elementary school that advantage is gone.

Boys are twice as likely to be redshirted as girls. Their emotional and social maturity is typically slower, and young boys use their bodies more vigorously, something most schools can't handle. But boys catch up.

When your child is five, it seems impossible to imagine he'll someday be a 150-pound high schooler, but it's important to look at the other end of the parenting spectrum. Redshirting has consequences for older kids and teens.

"I'm on the other end of things," said one mother. "I see that keeping my kids back for an extra year of preschool resulted in twelfth-grade boys who were 'overripe.' These kids really needed to have graduated sooner."

When parents tell me they plan to redshirt a bright child who's emotionally young, I'm conflicted. Play is good learning for five-year-olds, but these same kids will likely shoot ahead academically. As the oldest in the class, redshirted kids tend to grow bored and their behavior suffers.

As they grow, redshirted kids often display an increasing lack of interest and motivation in school. Elizabeth Graue, a professor at the University of Wisconsin–Madison, and James DiPerna, of Lehigh University, conducted research that indicates older, redshirted children showed more behavior problems, and pediatrician Robert Byrd's research says behavior problems tend to become even worse with teenagers. As teens, many redshirted kids are less motivated and perform worse than their younger peers. Why? These older, "over-ripe" high school students are itching for the next stage of life.

Instead of redshirting, consider giving kindergarten a complete skip. It may not be worth waiting for at any age.

Skip Kindergarten

Here's a little-known secret: *You don't have to send your child to kinder-garten.* Kindergarten is not mandatory in the United States. Many people assume the law says you have to send children to school, but in reality most state laws require schools to "offer" programs for five-year-olds, but do not require enrollment—not in homeschool, not in any school.

State law sets a school starting age. For most, that's six or seven. In two states, it's even age eight. When a child starts, she can begin in either first grade or kindergarten. Children do not have to gradu-ate from kindergarten in order to attend first grade. Even if you live in one of the few states with "mandatory" kindergarten, that means your family has to file paperwork, but you don't have to school your five-year-old child. You can bypass kindergarten.

I never went to kindergarten. Neither did my brother. He spent most of his kindergarten year in the sandbox. I stayed an extra year at preschool, since my mother decided I was emotionally immature as a five-year-old. By the time I was six the next July, she reevaluated and realized I'd grown up so much that I was ready to go directly to first grade.

You can still do that. When my first five-year-old was "ready" for kindergarten we gave official kindergarten a skip and cobbled together our own version: half days at Young Fives plus extended-day childcare (playtime) after school because we both worked. That added up to a play-filled four-and-a-half hour school day.

Friends were concerned when we said we'd skip kindergarten for

Myles. "But won't he fall behind?" they asked. I wasn't concerned about falling behind. I was concerned about pressing ahead in the wrong direction.

"Oh, but you can't skip kindergarten!" teachers protest. "There's so much we cover. Kindergarten's simply essential these days."

A child who can read can easily skip kindergarten. Even kids who don't read yet can do well in first grade. Ben couldn't read on entering first grade. He caught up by November. Lucas didn't know the sight words his first-grade teacher expected. "She wanted him to know all these words, but he was fine in first grade," said his mother. A child may be asked to take a first-grade readiness test. "I had to find a licensed teacher to evaluate Ben and say he was ready for first grade," explained his mother. It's quite possible to create an alternative kindergarten year (see tools on page 198), then go directly to first grade.

Even though kindergarten is optional, the rules change if you sign up. If your family chooses to participate, then attendance is required as part of compulsory school attendance laws. If you enroll, you have to go.

Go Directly to First Grade

Children in first grade practice reading and writing skills and basic math. Fresh first-graders are likely to catch on quickly, since their brains have matured. Unlike peers who may have endured two or three years of pre-K and kindergarten, these kids don't associate school with being bored and restless. First grade becomes an eager time. Learning to read is powerful. Kids love to feel that power when their brains are ready.

At age five, my son Zach was a blur of motion, constant action, and dramatic play. As a first-grader, his mind and body seem to have shifted. He still leaps and plays police officer and pirate, but there's a new maturity about him, a readiness.

Around age seven, children's brains undergo a seismic shift. This age has long been called the "age of reason." As documented by psychiatrists Theodore Shapiro and Richard Perry, it varies by child, and is called the "age of seven, plus or minus one." Armed with this new reason, kids are suddenly ready for abstract cognitive thinking and can quickly gain skills such as reading.

But will this work? Won't the go-directly-to-first-grade students be at a disadvantage? Not if we guide the five-year-old year wisely. Kids who spend their kindergarten year in a developmentally appropriate place will be better at coping with emotions and have more impulse control, social skills, conflict mediation, and self-awareness. Their pre-literacy foundation will be robust. Their brains will be stronger from an extra year of physical action. Successful grade placement is individual, but when a child's needs as a five-year-old are met, he's fully ready for the next step.

Try This—Add to Your Toolbox

We're not all lucky enough to have a good play-based kindergarten program nearby. We're not all able to swing another year of daycare bills or stay home with our kindergarten-aged child. There are plenty of alternatives to straight kindergarten. You can create a solution that works for you.

Reconfiguring Kindergarten for Your Child

1. Stay at Preschool or Daycare
   If you've discovered a wonderful play-based preschool or daycare, stay there. Most preschools will accept children who are five or six and haven't yet gone to formal kindergarten. Use this welcoming environment as the kinder-

garten year. This option can be expensive, however, so read on.

2. Find a Half-Day Program

   Some schools still offer half-day kindergarten, even if it's not at your local school. Look around. Maybe the Montessori school allows half days, or the charter school. Then, even if academics dominate the kindergarten day, it's only a short time, and you can add balance to the rest of the day.

3. Shorten the Week

   If your child is showing kindergarten stress, pull her out one day a week or arrange to pick her up midday.

   When Myles, age five, declared, "I hate school," I began to pull him out every Monday and hired a Monday sitter so I could work. Some schools and principals are open to half-day pickups or day-off schedules. Schools may be concerned about legal implications, including losing government funding. These are legitimate concerns, but you should still be able to work together at the local level. Zach survived his kindergarten year thanks to a reduced schedule. It helped the school that I had a pediatrician's note that said: "This child would benefit from rest."

4. Homeschool the Kindergarten Year

   Wait. Before you dismiss homeschooling on grounds you have to work, consider this. Even households with every adult working full-time can homeschool. How? By designating a trusted teacher or daycare person as your homeschool provider. Rules differ by state, but you should be able to send your child to a trusted caregiver and call it kindergarten.

"Where I live, anyone with a college degree can teach your child," says Jennifer. "I had a friend who ran an after-kindergarten program, so I filed the paperwork and put him in that. She was basically doing kindergarten better than our school district."

5. Try Young Fives

Young Fives is a lot like kindergarten, since it's free, but the school day is usually shorter and the academics somewhat less rigorous. These programs vary by state, but many schools offer some version of a free pre-kindergarten or "young five" year. Young Fives programs were originally set up for children with late birthdays, but they increasingly include children who are not emotionally ready for formal school. Most families who sign up for Young Fives are seeking a quasi-kindergarten program that's more manageable for a five-year-old.

Each pre-K program's appropriateness will vary greatly by teacher. Keep in mind that the curriculum is still kindergarten prep—what's inappropriate for kindergarteners is even less appropriate for emotionally young five-year-olds—but it might be a decent fit for your child.

Graduates of these programs are expected to go on to kindergarten the following year. If you select a pre-K or Young Fives year for your family, keep your options open and evaluate things at the end of the year. First grade might be the right place to go instead.

6. Declare Random Rest Days

The year my son attended kindergarten we had a severe winter with twelve snow days. The gift of the snow days gave him extra rest and playtime. If winter isn't cooperating or coming your way, take rest days when needed. Let your child recharge.

"I know kids," said Teresa, a mother of four. "When Eva was looking tired in kindergarten, I just pulled her out for a week. That did her a world of good."

"Mental health days are important," said Sarah, an elementary school office assistant whose job included tracking attendance. "Sometimes kids just need the rest."

7. Work with the School

Daniel was four when he started kindergarten—young, but still eligible for kindergarten based on state law. His mother knew kindergarten would be too much, but sent him anyway.

"We had to. There was no way we could afford to have me out of work another year," she said. "And the price of paying for preschool was beyond our reach."

Daniel approached kindergarten with the full force of his four-year-old, active boy energy. His behavior was entirely age appropriate, but it wasn't working for the school. The principal called. "Look, we think he'd be better off in preschool for this year." Like many elementary schools, Daniel's school had a paying preschool as part of it. They shifted him into the preschool class for free.

Arrangements like this can work. Educators deeply care about kids, and sometimes you'll meet allies who can find a way to be flexible within the system.

8. Look for Multigrade Classes

Mixed-grade classrooms can be a blessing. In a mixed-grade class, children are naturally expected to be at different stages and a teacher is used to meeting children with varying needs and academic abilities. A child who isn't reading by the end of kindergarten, for example, can be more seamlessly incorporated into first grade in a mixed-grade setting.

9. Go Directly to First Grade

If you take an alternative kindergarten year, be sure to read aloud regularly and give your child a strong foundation in the pre-literacy world of songs, rhymes, and stories. Your child probably knows kindergarten math concepts of "more" and "less" from daily situations ("He has more candy than I do!"), but before first grade, introduce symbols such as > and <. Check curriculum requirements. Some states may require an evaluation to test first-grade readiness.

Understand the specific rules and family rights in your state. Most areas have excellent resources through homeschooling websites.

Reconfiguring Kindergarten for Your Community

There is a desperate need to create a welcoming place for five- and six-year-olds, the children we used to call kindergarteners. This can be done within existing programs and by setting up a new program for five-year-olds.

1. Rally for Half-Day Options

Even for families who need full-day daycare, half a day of academics may be all a child can take. Petition your school board to retain or reinstate half-day kindergarten as an option.

2. Start Your Own Play School

That's what Danielle Cassetta did. A mother of two youngsters, she and her husband decided to set up their own play-based cooperative preschool in their home and backyard in Ann Arbor, Michigan. They researched play environments and philosophies and got their new school rolling with twenty children after seven months of planning. If you think you have the entrepreneurial spirit, the world needs you, and it certainly needs new play schools for children ages three to seven.

3. Reconfigure Current Kindergarten
Changing mismatched curriculum requirements is difficult work that requires many allies. When children's needs clash with adult expectations, those expectations need to change. Good kindergarten needs to include: movement and action, imaginative pretend play, dictated storytelling, pre-literacy, and plentiful outdoor time. Pursuing this option needs political support and deep understanding of child development.

Words to Say

What's the kindergarten schedule like?
If I don't enroll her this year, can she enter first grade
    directly next year?
How does that work?

He's not feeling well today.
I'm keeping him home to rest.
He's exhausted and can't function.

I'm concerned about Nathan. Can we talk?
Here's what I'm seeing at home: [describe stressed
    behaviors].
What are you seeing at school?
This isn't working for us.
Anna needs more rest.

Here's a note from her doctor. Would that help?

I need to pull him out for shorter days. What would
  work best?

Would you be open to half days on Tuesdays and
  Thursdays?

Let's try it for three months and stay in touch.

Words to Avoid

Everybody goes to kindergarten.

You'll like it.

Kindergarten is fun.

I remember loving kindergarten.

It's only kindergarten. Wait until you get to *real* school.

Your Take

Is your child ready for kindergarten? A better question: Is kindergarten ready for your child? Look at your local options. If kindergarten is not a good developmental fit, consider modifying the kindergarten year. The long-term answer is to develop more child-appropriate programs, but today's five-year-olds can't wait.

RULE

12 Banish Calendars at Circle Time

I loved circle time as a four-year-old. We sang songs and read books—all wonderful things. Once a magician came, and his tricks were so amazing the awe still lingers with me today.

The reason I loved circle time was because my teachers got it. Group time, which we called "rug time," was short, fun, and child appropriate. It involved noise, movement, and new delights. We didn't sit down all the time. We weren't asked to be quiet all the time. We never studied the calendar, talked about the weather, or counted to one hundred.

Circle time for kids five and under should not look like mini-school.

Renegade Reason

Group circle time needs to be short and meaningful. Don't take up time with calendars until children's brains are ready. It interrupts a young child's learning.

Circle time is that universal gather-on-the-rug-all-together time in front of the teacher. Done right, it boosts community and brings new ideas and joy. Dragged out—thirty, forty, forty-five minutes—circle time often bores kids and interrupts meaningful learning they could be doing. Usually the best circle times are short and sweet.

Today the calendar has crept in. If you peek in most classrooms for three- to six-year-olds, there it is, a giant calendar taking center stage. The trouble is, most young kids can't grasp the abstract meaning of time until mid-elementary school, despite daily drills.

It's time to question habits that aren't meaningful to children. Chuck the calendars. Tuck away the weather charts. Ideas of September, Monday, and twelve o'clock come easily when brains mature. There's no need to impose our ordered rows of time on them now.

Renegade Blessings

Give children what they need today, in the present, and you will also prepare them for the future. Kids gain most when expectations are age appropriate. What they will learn:

> I love coming together every day.
> I know how to be part of a group.
> Everyone has ideas to contribute.
> I'm smart. I can do what the teacher asks.
> There are times to be quiet in a group. I can do that when
>   it's not too long.
> I'm OK as who I am.

Clocks, Charts, and Calendars: Who Cares if It's Monday?

Calendars and clocks are useful tools for adults to make schedules. They help us meet together, work together, and arrange classes, celebrations, and appointments. For young kids, defined in this chapter as five and under, time is a vague notion of before and after, or first this, then that.

Grasping the days of the week is not hard, but it takes some growing up for it to be relevant. I've never known an adult who doesn't know what Monday is. Or a fourth-grader, for that matter.

Using a poster-sized wall calendar is a deeply entrenched routine in most early-childhood programs, but it's a time stealer. "The kids were all over the floor when we did the calendar, so it was clear they were not interested," said Cheryl, an early-childcare provider. "I took my big calendar down several months ago."

Along with calendars, it's become tradition in many classrooms to chart the weather. Is today sunny? Was yesterday rainy? Since weather tends to change every day, kids can learn about the length of time called a "day" by charting weather. I've watched countless classrooms of children asked to stare out the window to try to assess the weather. Weather is only relevant to children when they are outside in it.

Watch what the children are telling you. Are they fascinated? Is it meaningful? If not, shorten or change circle time. Reclaim the children's day.

Why It Works

"We need to play at Olivia's house soon," said my five-year-old, Zach. "Maybe tomorrow or yesterday?"

Time is a slippery notion for children. They toss around time vocabulary words such as "I'm baking this cake for two weeks." "I'm just reading this book for a short time. Maybe six years." Or "My spaghetti stew needs to cook for a hundred hours!" Children learn that certain words have to do with time long before their brains can grasp what time is.

William Friedman, a psychologist whose specialty is human concepts of time, studied children's understanding of big time spans—weeks and months—and discovered that calendar study for most children younger than first grade had *no meaning*. According to Friedman, children simply don't have the ability to judge calendar year time until between ages seven and ten. First-graders are often expected to begin to function with calendar time, and some of them can, but time clicks in at different stages.

Children learn sequence first. It's much more difficult for them to judge the time between things. *How long is five minutes? The birthday party is Saturday. How soon will Saturday come? Grandma's coming tomorrow. Why isn't she here?* Judging relative time—how long is a minute compared to an hour, or how long is a day compared to a month—is an abstract notion.

Early-childhood educators, such as Lilian Katz and Sallee Beneke, say children can follow time well through pictures and story, because they have a strong understanding of narrative story. Kids can follow you when you say, "First we have lunch, then we read a book." This works visually, too, since they can follow pictures of sequential events lined up like a story.

In an article published in the National Association for the Education of Young Children's journal, *Young Children*, Katz and fellow authors call calendar time "Good Intentions Gone Awry" and suggest teachers abandon this popular practice. Calendars and weather charts waste young children's time.

Don't expect too much of the kids. They're doing the best they can, at their own developmental pace. Besides, it's not just kids. In 1752 adults believed their lives were being shortened by eleven days when England switched from the Julian to the Gregorian calendar.

Take Off Your Adult Lenses

It's hard to give up something that's "always been done." We tend to rely on comforting traditions, like calendars, and believe that since the practice is so widespread, so many people can't be wrong. Banishing the calendar is not banishing it completely—it's just waiting three years or so. Children's brains need to mature first. We can drill, but we can't force comprehension. Trust the children. The day will come when they are ready.

Impacts on Children

When circle time takes up a big portion of the morning, kids lose out on other learning time. It takes time to check the weather, invite Keesha to put the Velcro sun on the weather chart, and have Ben point the star wand to Wednesday, October 22. It takes more time when these activities bore children until they grow restless and disruptive, prompting the teacher to focus on getting the class to sit still. This is true whether the circle time is teacher talk, calendar talk, or prolonged show-and-tell. It's a simple matter of opportunity cost.

What should children be doing instead? Going outdoors. Encountering peer conflict and sorting it out. Coping with their big emotions. Telling dictated stories. Playing following their own ideas. Listening to books and looking at books. Given how circle time is typically done, child educator Bev Bos says, "Circle time is the least learning time of the day."

When their brains aren't ready, it's frustrating for children to try and please adults and repeatedly fail. They can catch on to the routine of chanting calendar days, but the meaning behind it stays a mystery. This can have serious impacts on kids' self-confidence and attitudes toward school. It doesn't feel good to feel inadequate day after day. For children who experience the calendar routine every day for two to three years (and still don't understand it), this cumulative impact can cause real distress.

Circle time itself is precious. It feels good to be part of a human community, to sing together and gather for a puppet show or story. There's not time enough to read all the remarkable picture books available for young children. Children will grow old before we have time to get to them all. Save the best group activities—those that spark young minds—for the group. Let the rest go.

Try This—Add to Your Toolbox

Decide what you truly believe is important about group time. What do you hope to achieve? Why is it good to come together? Brainstorm a list. Maybe it's music, sharing news, welcoming people, solving community problems, or playing movement games. If you're ready to think beyond the calendar, here are some ideas.

Make It Short

"Ten minutes, tops." That's how long teachers at the School for Young Children suggest circle time should be. Circle time mostly imposes an adult agenda. What would happen if you cut it in half? Maybe one big circle time could be divided into two shorter ones to begin and close the day.

Time is just one guideline. Some days the topic is so intriguing that kids prolong circle time by asking questions and getting involved. Maybe you're doing a puppet show about mad feelings and kids are so caught up in brainstorming they don't want to stop.

Make It Meaningful

Circle time done right is marvelous. Kids love to belong to the group and participate in their own way. We call that community.

"I know a lot of teachers have forgone circle time in the name of giving children 'choice,'" writes Tom Hobson, known by blog readers and parents as Teacher Tom. "Not me; not us." Hobson, the leader of Woodland Park Cooperative School, loves circle time, but he makes group time child led, or as he calls it, "community led."

Teacher Tom's circle times are reminiscent of the ones I had as a child—times when it was fun to be all together, sharing ideas, singing, and building group cohesion. Sometimes Teacher Tom's circles go on for nearly half an hour. If you have rapt attention and child involvement, then circle time is where children want to be. Group time can be age appropriate and meaningful.

Make It Optional

Some childcare programs make circle time optional. Invite children, but if they are more engaged in other play, let that continue. If adults create an interesting enough circle time, children will want to come.

Maybe you will decide everyone has to be in the same room, but not necessarily sitting on the rug. Matthew, for example, was a three-year-old who had to be on the move. He jumped around during story time, but would retell it to his mom at home. Matthew's teacher recognized his need to move and still be part of the group (see Rule 13: Don't Force Participation).

Notice Everyday Counting and Math

Some teachers gravitate toward the calendar because it has the potential to introduce math concepts as well as time. There's counting, of course, and number recognition, plus patterns and sequence and other basic math ideas. Young kids gain better math thinking through hands-on play. Counting is naturally integrated in many children's songs and stories, such as "Five Little Ducks Went Out One Day" and "Five Little Monkeys Jumping on the Bed." Kids learn about sequence throughout the day, from daily schedules to waiting for their turn with a toy. They make patterns from blocks, beads, or simply lining up toy trucks. The building blocks for math are already filling their day.

Make Weather Relevant

Go outside. Weather is only relevant to young kids when they are outside in it.

Trust young children. Time will settle down in their minds soon enough. Meanwhile, embrace circle time for the wonderful community time it can be.

Words to Say

Let's read this book together.

Does anyone know this song?

It's circle time now. You don't have to sit, but you have to be in the room.

Looks like it's raining. Here are some extra boots.

Is it cold today? Let's go see.

Words to Avoid

(Especially for young children ages 1–5)

Today is Monday, October 20.

Let's count together: one, two, three . . .

Who will be my star today and use the pointer for the calendar?

What is the weather like today?

Micah, put a cloud next to the word *Monday*.

Your Take

As a parent, you may rush to your child's preschool or kindergarten and suddenly worry about the calendar on the wall. Chances are it's there, but no need to panic. So much of good circle time depends on the teacher. Ask if you can observe circle time. Track how long it is, and whether children seem engaged. Perhaps share this chapter with the teacher. If you're choosing a program, seek a place that doesn't make calendar lessons a prominent part of each day. If you're a teacher, be a calendar challenger. See what happens when you banish the calendar and let time take its own course.

RULE
13
Don't Force Participation

Kids spend much of their young lives herded into groups. Now we'll sing, now we'll march in a circle, now everybody clap your hands. Group songs and activities can be wonderful fun for children. What good is a giant parachute unless you have twenty other people to hoist it high? How can you make a "rainstorm" by snapping and clapping without a crowd? Group life suits most kids most of the time.

But there are always times a child doesn't feel like participating. What then? Relax. It's OK. Whether you're the teacher, group leader, or anxious parent on the sideline wondering why, of all the kids, *your* kid is the only one who shakes his head and hides, don't fret about 100 percent participation. Kids have a right not to participate in a group—what's more, sitting out may meet their needs best.

Renegade Reason

Kids have valid reasons for not joining in. Don't force participation in group activities. It's OK for kids to sit out, as long as their actions don't disrupt the group.

It's hard for us to watch a child who doesn't do what the rest do. To an adult, the nonconformist's behavior can feel disrespectful to the group leader and to the group. We feel a loss of control and worry that her actions will upset the group dynamic. A child who doesn't fit in pains us. *Oh, she's being excluded. She's not going to learn what the rest of the kids are learning. She won't be able to catch up. He's too sensitive. He's got to learn to get along with others. He's not special—we can't make exceptions. She has to learn to cooperate and be part of the whole class. He needs to get over it.*

Caleb wouldn't budge when his name was called. It was his turn for show-and-tell, but he didn't stand up.

At a music for tots class, Sophie didn't join the circle of singing children and parents. The rest of her class sang a wiggle worm song, but Sophie hovered ten feet away at the edge of the room and just watched.

Tyler's teacher put on marching music. "We're going to march around the circle," she announced. "Everybody stand up!" Everybody stood up except for Tyler and Brayden. The teacher hauled them to their feet. "You have to stand up," she said. "Everybody has to stand up now."

All behavior has meaning, so trust that there's a good reason why a child isn't joining the group action. Some children learn best through observation. Some need to build trust first before being ready to join in. Others may have a fear or concern about the activity or people involved. Forcing a child to participate so he "won't miss anything important" misses the point. No one can learn well when he's not feeling safe.

Renegade Blessings

When kids feel ready to join a group, they will. Here are some benefits of letting the child determine when that time is right:

I can learn in my own way. Sometimes I learn from
    watching those around me.
Not everyone is the same. I'm OK the way I am.
My needs are important, but so are the other kids'. I can't
    do things to hurt their learning or fun.
My parents and teachers respect me.
When I'm scared about something, I can tell adults, even if
    it seems silly.
I can trust my fears and feelings.
I can change my mind and take a risk when I'm ready.
If it takes time for me to feel comfortable, that's all right.
Just because "everyone's doing it" doesn't mean I have to.
I feel included and welcomed. I can always take on a
    bigger role.

Social expectations for group participation are strong. We often follow a mind-set of "Everyone has to do it. No exceptions," especially after kids hit school. Ryan's kindergarten teacher labeled him "extremely defiant" for not standing up and introducing himself on his first day of class. His mother was called in to see the teacher after class. "Does he frequently display this type of defiant behavior?" the teacher asked. Ryan, age five, was facing a brand-new school, new classmates, new teacher, and new classroom. No wonder he was overwhelmed.

At a preschool holiday concert, a crowd of thirty parents sat in folding chairs expectantly as twenty-eight children lined up wearing Santa hats. In the middle of his classmates, four-year-old Hunter burst into tears and tried to leave the choir. His teacher didn't let him. "You're OK. There's nothing wrong," she said, bringing him back to the bleachers. "You're fine. Now just stand there with everyone else and smile." Hunter didn't smile, didn't sing, and looked miserable through the performance.

Consider what the child forced to join the crowd can feel:

I'm scared. And nobody cares.

You have to conform and be like the rest—no matter what.

I can't concentrate on what's going on. I can't learn this
way.

I don't like this. I don't know how to stop.

It's noisy and crowded. Too many people bothers me.

Why It Works

Kids don't join in for a variety of reasons. Sometimes they're worried. Sometimes they have a need for control at that instant. A child
may be absorbed deeply in something and can't bring her focus
away. Kids sometimes can't take all the action. Groups can simply be
too much.

It's typical for children to have fears about new activities, groups,
and social situations. It could be the activity scares them (the whoosh
of the parachute, unwelcome sound effects on a music recording).
The group leader could be unfamiliar, have a raspy or loud voice, or
a manner that scares them. Then there's fear of other children. It may
simply be navigating space among so many bodies. There may be a
particular child who's viewed as a threat. Kids think: *Is the teacher
mean? Is that other kid going to punch me? Those noises sound scary. Will I
be safe?*

Developmentally, a crowd can be overstimulating. There's too
much going on to process. Children are still getting used to processing a variety of sensory information, sorting out what's important,
and learning to focus. The "focus" part of the brain, the frontal lobe,
is still developing in young children. A child's natural reaction to
overstimulation is to pull back. Sometimes they just can't take it.

Some children are not ready to be noticed in group settings. Introducing yourself can seem simple to adults, but kids may not be
ready to say their names out loud or participate in group "sharing"

exercises. Kids are newly discovering their sense of self and gaining social skills. This process moves more quickly for some kids than others. Sensitive kids may need more time, says Mary Sheedy Kurcinka. She has an excellent understanding of kids who don't enter groups easily, and devotes a chapter to it in her book *Raising Your Spirited Child*. These children need patience, practice, and understanding adults.

All young children learn through observation, and for some kids, this is their chief method of gaining new skills and information. Visual learners learn by seeing how it's done. They may choose to watch from the sidelines as observers, taking everything in but not directly participating. Some kids learn by listening (aural learning). Even if a child is doing something else nearby, chances are he's listening, and that could be the way he learns best. Of course, for the wandering, restless, on-the-go kid, movement may be the only way this kinesthetic learner can focus.

When kids join in indirectly, it's called parallel participation. Being off to the side helps all children at times. For children with sensory processing challenges, including kids with autism, it can be essential. Being in the same room or area but not directly involved can reduce anxiety and overstimulation, letting kids be the ones to decide when they are ready to join the group. It's a mark of respect. Children move forward when they are ready.

Children need to learn to trust their feelings, especially their fears. If something's making them uncomfortable, that's a vital gut reaction. As Gavin de Becker points out in his book *Protecting the Gift: Keeping Children and Teenagers Safe (and Parents Sane)*, safety begins with cultivating that inner voice and heeding it. As we guide children to independence, we need to respect the fears they feel. This is all part of establishing a sense of appropriate risk and safety (see more in Rule 4: It's OK to Talk to Strangers).

Groups aren't for everyone. Some kids (and adults) don't like big groups. Adults who dislike a crowd can choose to be alone. A child can't get away. Being part of a group may be a fact of life at times, but children need time to build coping skills when a social environment is uncomfortable. Give them time, understanding, and coping tools.

Take Off Your Adult Lenses

It can be tempting to push a child so he "won't miss out." But forced participation doesn't mean the child is learning. No one can learn well when he's not feeling safe. If a child doesn't follow the group plan, don't worry. As long as his actions don't disrupt the activity for others, it's fine to opt out. Respect the child enough to listen to his feelings and fears. Making exceptions does not make one child overly "special." What's fair is meeting everyone's needs. People are individuals and it's fair to treat them that way.

Protect the Child, Protect the Group

Insisting on group participation is about fear—*our* fear. It helps to examine what we're afraid of:

> She's missing out on learning.
> If *he* doesn't do it, they'll all want to quit.
> I need to maintain control. It's too hard if different kids
>   do different things.
> Making exceptions sends the message she's better than
>   the others.
> She'll never get over her fears.

Kids will be ready in their own way and time. Meanwhile, it's fine to let a child opt out. Kids have a right not to participate in a group. If he doesn't want to do what the group is doing, that's fine *as long as his actions don't disrupt the activity for others*. Set limits to protect both the group and the individual.

> Set limits to protect both the
> group *and* the individual.

If a child is standing up during library story time, respect the group and the individual. You can start by offering information and pointing out the impact on others: "I know a lot of kids want to see the pictures. When you stand up it's hard for kids to see." Some kids might think, *Oh!* and sit down at this point. Others have a continued need to stand or move. "Looks like you want to stand to hear the story. Move your body to the back of the room. That's a good place to stand."

Perhaps the group activity is active rather than quiet. "We're dancing right now. You don't have to dance, but you can't sit in the middle of the room. You might get bumped. Sit by the window if you don't want to dance."

A child shouldn't have to mimic the group, but she shouldn't be allowed to disrupt the group either.

She's Missing Out

Kaitlyn didn't play at preschool. Her mother despaired as she saw the other children busily engaged in painting, sand, blocks, and dress-up clothes. At school Kaitlyn quietly watched birds and observed other children. When she got home, however, she could report great details of what she'd seen.

In the early years, there is so much to observe. Some kids plunge in; others learn best through extensive observation. Liam, for example, observed other four-year-olds holding dance parties every day. He sat nearby and watched their moves and listened to the music. On the last day he joined the dancers and danced like crazy. It was time. He was ready.

"We often see kids who won't sing in a group," my mother, a preschool teacher for forty years, told me. "They'll just sit there. But when they go home, the children suddenly sing and know all the words to the songs."

Learning styles vary by child, and by mood of the child. A child sitting out is not missing out; she's simply attending to her needs at the time.

Check Your Own Feelings

If you're a parent and have just shelled out a hundred dollars on a music class, it can be agonizing when your child merely sits there and refuses to engage. *Come on*, you think, *I'm paying for this. Do something!* These feelings can be strong. Remember that every day is different and every child learns differently. Many times a child who "just watches" is learning at her optimal level. A child who wanders around the room may be absorbing everything. Expect this behavior, rather than expecting your child to dive into everything fully.

In class she may look blank, but trust that she's soaking up life in her own style. She may come home and sing the songs.

It's Not About You as a Leader

Whether you're a parent running a birthday party or a preschool teacher leading a finger chant, we all take turns being a group leader from time to time. If a particular child doesn't engage in an activity you planned, shrug it off. It's not about you. Furthermore, it's not a sign of disrespect when a child doesn't follow your plan. Children have many developmental tasks, and she may be working on a different one than you had in mind that day.

> Invite kids in, but don't make group
> conformity the goal.

Do your best not to take it personally. You can still feel competent; you're not a failure. Give up your need to control the situation. You can control how you protect the group, but you can't control how each individual will react. Instead of pouncing, find out what the real issue may be. Be ready to trust that the child may be right.

He's Old Enough

Of course, at some age, it's time to transition to the next level of group participation. A four-year-old may be legitimately scared of a group leader with a funny hat or a loud voice, but a fourth-grader should be able to handle it, and might be shirking to get out of a class exercise. When does the shift occur, and when can we reasonably expect a child to participate? A general rule of thumb is the same as when basic manners can be expected, around age seven. Most kids seven and older should be able to cope with group dynamics most of the time. They will have met enough people to not be as worried about the looks, actions, and personalities of people around them. Even so, moods change, days are different, and sometimes an older child chooses to opt out.

No matter what their age, individuals have valid reasons. If an older child is hesitant, try this:

Explain expectations clearly.
Ask her if she has any concerns.
Let her know she can tell you later.
Be aware that bullying or peer coercion may be involved.
Be open to the idea that she may be right.

> All behavior has meaning.

Just as a younger child may have valid developmental reasons why he can't participate, an older child may have equally valid social, emotional, learning style, or neurological processing reasons. If the activity is appropriate and engaging for the age, a child who backs out usually has good reason, even if she can't articulate it. Remember, all behavior has meaning.

The right age is as individual as each child.

Value of Nonconformity

Group dynamics by nature encourage conformity. What the group does, the individual tends to do. We can send the message that you need to follow the group at all costs, or we can support kids who feel uncomfortable and let them know they don't have to follow the crowd if it feels wrong. Peer pressure intensifies as children grow, and they need practice listening to themselves and saying no.

"It's critically important if we want to raise kids who will resist peer pressure," says early-childhood educator Emily Plank. "We have such a deep fear of our children being corrupted by peer pressure or bullying, yet we pressure them into participating in large groups against their will."

These kids aren't missing out; they're off to a good start.

Try This—Add to Your Toolbox

Balancing the needs of one with the needs of many can be baffling. Here are some ideas to help parents and group leaders.

Find a Space

If a child doesn't want to do the group activity, find a space where she can be. Observers are happy to watch from the sidelines, so find a place where they get full view of the action. Sometimes this means sitting quietly off to the side. For a child who wants to stand when everyone else is sitting, it might mean moving to the back or side of the room. If a child is needing to talk, there may be a space where talking is OK. "It seems you really want to talk right now. You can't talk to me because I'm reading the story. You can talk to Ms. Stephanie; she's by the table." Define the boundary, but allow kids freedom within it: "You have to be in this room, but you don't have to watch the puppet show if you don't want to." Or: "When you run it's distracting. You can join us with what we're doing, or go in the hall if you need to run."

Some adults who frequently lead groups of children set up a "centering area" ahead of time. This is a designated safe spot—perhaps under a table, behind a chair, in a nook—for taking a break. Children know they are free to go there anytime if the group becomes too much. If noise and overstimulation are a problem with children you work with, you might also stock the area with noise-canceling earmuffs.

Watch Faces

Is your child content? Does he seem OK or does he look worried? Before you urge full participation, take a moment to read children's facial expressions. Say: "Your face looks worried. Is there something you don't like?" A content-looking child may be a sign you have an observer on your hands. "Seems as if you just want to watch right now."

Invite and Include

Leave the door open. Let kids know they can always change their minds. This face-saving message is important, since a child who firmly declares, "I won't do it! You can't make me," may feel too sheepish to join in later. When battle lines of control are drawn, it's hard for a child to back down gracefully. Give children an out. Just say, "That's OK. You don't want to do it now. I know kids can change their minds." Check in and invite them back in periodically.

Individual Needs

Whether kids have diagnosable special needs or not, meeting individual needs helps kids feel comfortable and gain trust and focus. Addie walked in circles during group story time. Her family found walking and holding something in her hand helped her focus and she enjoyed the story more. Kids with sensory processing issues may benefit from a variety of touch.

Acknowledge Bad Fits

Michelle signed her kids up for a Mommy and Me class. Every week the teacher brought out a parachute to play games with. "It scared the crap out of them," said Michelle. "They would go nowhere near it and would only sit on my lap." Some groups aren't right for your child right now.

Make a Change

It's one thing if a child occasionally wanders off, disengaged for the moment, or if an observer watches from the sidelines, but if the whole group seems to be restless and bored, that could be a sign the group activity is an ill fit. Look for clues. The prime culprits: 1) group time is too long; 2) group time is not age appropriate (see Rule 12: Banish Calendars at Circle Time).

As a parent, evaluate group dynamics when choosing a school or class. Kids don't need practice sitting and listening to adults. Young kids do most of their learning by doing, so look for a program with a teacher who understands that. As a teacher, pay attention to signals the group sends you. The book you chose might be boring, or the activity might not catch their interest. That's OK. "If it keeps happening, then I know I'm doing something wrong," says one preschool teacher. Stop and think. You might be forcing an adult agenda.

Good groups respect individual needs and feelings. A child who opts out of the action may need a legitimate break from group time.

Words to Say

FINDING FEARS

Is there something you're worried about?
Is there something you don't like?
Are you worried someone's going to hurt you?
This is a noisy room. You can cover your ears.

ACCEPTING NONPARTICIPATION

Tessa isn't ready to dance right now.
I know kids take their time sometimes.
I know sometimes kids aren't in the mood.
You don't have to do it, but this is what we're going to do.
You don't want to do it now. I know kids can change their
    minds.
You can come back if you're feeling different later.
It's OK to change your mind.

PROTECTING THE GROUP

You can sit and watch, or you can read a book quietly.

Move to the window so you won't get bumped.

If you want to stand, stand in the back so other kids can see
the pictures.

I can't be with you right now. I'm busy with the other kids.

You're not ready to listen to the story right now.

You don't have to be here. If you want to be here, sit down.

It seems you really want to talk right now. Go to the
next room.

You don't have to sing, but you can't make noises that hurt
the song.

That's distracting when we're reading together.

You can't talk to Riley right now. She wants to listen to
the story.

You can whisper to Ms. Stephanie.

What can you do instead?

INVITING AND INCLUDING

Would you like to join us now?

Do you want to hold my hand?

I can stand next to you, if you like.

Do you want to sit with me?

And hello to Max, who's watching our song from the table.

Do you like singing?

You can join us anytime you're ready.

Words to Avoid

Everybody has to.
Don't say no to me!
You don't have a choice.
Martin! I see someone who's not cooperative.
I don't care. You still have to do it.
Don't be ridiculous. She can't hurt you.
There's nothing to be scared of.
All the other kids are doing it.
He's noncompliant.
She's defiant.
Your son won't follow directions. He may have a learning
    disability.

Your Take

Some of us naturally favor the group, and others the individual. It's possible to respect both. As a parent, think about ways you can support your child and still respect the group.

If you find yourself in the position of being a teacher or group leader, consider your own biases as you weigh the needs of both the group and the individuals in it. You may long for quiet and order, and favor sedate group activities such as story time. Some group leaders find themselves leaning instead toward the needs of kids who are boisterous and love action, but forget that many children love group songs and stories. Groups and individuals of all temperaments should be welcome. Community is created, not forced.

Section V

SORROW, EMPATHY, and DISASTER

Education is simply the soul of a society as it passes from one generation to another.

—G. K. CHESTERTON

RULE
14
Don't Remove Ogres from Books

My son recently brought home what I consider a "junk" book. I don't mind the cheap stapled binding—just what's inside. This one was supposedly the story of Chicken Little. Except it wasn't.

The age-old story of Chicken Little deals with a foolish chicken who gets plunked on the head by an acorn. Chicken Little jumps to the conclusion that the sky is falling, and rushes off to tell the king. Along the way, he convinces other birds to join him and encounters a much savvier fox, who tricks them all. The ending is apt: The fox has a tasty dinner.

The version my son clutched had a false ending. Not only did Chicken Little live, but he and the fox and all their bird friends sat down and shared dinner. The story had been completely sterilized.

When I told Zach the traditional ending, he loved it. Good stories satisfy the reader. The ending—happy or sad—is *fitting*. That's the essence of human storytelling.

Renegade Reason |||||||||||||||||||||||||||||||||||||||||||||||||||||||||||||||||||||||||||||||||||||||||||||

Share sad stories with kids. They need stories that resonate with a full range of feelings, not just happily ever after.

||||||||||||||||||||||||||||||||||||||||||||||||||||||||||||||||||||||||||||||||||||||||||||||||||||||||||||||||||||

When I was five, my aunt sent me a letter along with a postcard of a young girl's tomb. "Now I'm going to tell you the story of little Penelope Boothby," she wrote. "Poor little Penelope was only five years old when she died . . ." She described Penelope's life and ended by saying: "Isn't that a sad story?" I spent hours gazing at the forlorn form of Penelope, who'd died two hundred years ago, chiseled on her gravestone. I felt trusted and respected to receive such a letter. Most of all I was intrigued because the story didn't have a happy ending.

Many of the best stories don't. In children's classics such as *Charlotte's Web*, *The Red Balloon*, and *The Little Match Girl*, the title character dies. In a child's mind, it doesn't matter if the character is a spider, a balloon, or a person; that character is alive and loved and its loss is profound. These stories touch our hearts.

Sad stories have their place in children's lives. So do scary stories. A sad ending touches feelings of compassion and sorrow, and scary figures such as ogres and trolls give our heroes a worthy adversary. Where would the thrill and "what comes next" be without a fascinating bad guy? Most of the time, the hero should prevail. But if the story demands it, sometimes the wily fox must win.

Most stories for kids end happily ever after. But sometimes the richer story shares sad topics or has a sad ending. Kids need both.

Renegade Blessings ||||||||||||||||||||||||||||||||||||||||||||||||||||||||||||||||||||||||||||||||||||||

Books are a safe place for children to learn about the world and their own tough emotions. When stories reflect the range of human experience, kids feel wonder, empathy, and relief.

> Reading is fun!
> I love books and stories. I can't wait to see what
>   happens next.
> This character knows just how I feel.
> Wow, that was such a sad story. I guess not everything
>   works out in life.
> There can be big trouble if you do foolish things.
> Carnivores eat other animals.
> Bad things can still happen to good people.
> Sometimes people and animals die, even ones you love.
> This story is like something that happened to me. It's
>   comforting to know I'm not alone.
> Kids with sad stories can still prevail. I can find the same
>   courage.

Why It Works

What do kids want? "They love being spooked," wrote children's author Roald Dahl. "They love ghosts. They love the finding of treasure. They love chocolates and toys and money. They love magic. They love being made to giggle. They love seeing the villain meet a grisly death. They love a hero and they love the hero to be a winner."

Dahl knew that children care deeply about justice. Mean giants should live in a pit and eat snozzcumbers. Trolls should turn to stone or die. It's *not fair* if the ungrateful and lazy animals get to share the Little Red Hen's loaf of bread.

Young kids view the world in black and white, and their allegiance to fellow children against unfair or scary opponents is legendary. Jean Piaget and others explain stages of moral development, starting with this black-and-white outlook. We should save the nuances of the troll's tortured soul for a teenage or adult audience. Children's minds and hearts have different needs.

The stories we read in the early years must hook kids into a love of books. Psychologists know that human brains are hardwired to respond to stories. It's our job to share good stories—tales that fascinate, spook, elicit giggles, create wonder, share new ideas, add awe, and connect with deep emotions. Steven Pinker, a Harvard evolutionary psychologist, says stories help people learn and develop relationships in a social group. If stories are all happy or idealized, it truncates children's life learning. Stories literally transport us: Regions in our brain react to emotions in the story the way our brains react to experiences. Psychologists call this "narrative transport." When kids hear a range of stories it helps them learn about the range of human experience.

As author Mary Howarth points out in her defense of fairy tales: "We are often afraid to recognize that a child's life is made up of both light and dark feelings, which she also needs to name and utilize. How can she know that humankind has experienced all these same feelings for millennia?"

Stories for younger kids are getting happier these days. Picture books are removing conflict, changing endings, and letting the foolish, unkind, and truly bad guys go free. The Gingerbread Boy doesn't always get eaten by the fox anymore—sometimes he just gets wet in the river. The Little Red Hen now shares her hard-earned loaf of bread with the animals who rudely refused to help her. And in one of the many updated versions of *The Three Billy Goats Gruff*, the troll changes into a flower.

At the same time we've sanitized books, we're intensifying children's movies with graphic visuals and violence. That's the opposite of what we need to do. Reading a book—or telling it aloud—lets kids explore ideas from a place of safety. "Children picture what they can handle," says Susan Roscigno, a codirector at the School for Young Children. "They picture a scary spider, but not one as big as a movie shows." A movie moves fast. It flashes intense visual images and is unpredictable. The child is not in control; she is not the one turning the pages.

On the other hand, a book doesn't move. It's read at a human pace. A trusted adult is usually there to read and guide the story. You can stop and talk. If things get scary, adult readers can modify their voice to suit the child, or close the book.

Many sad stories for children deal with death. In *Charlotte's Web*, Charlotte the beloved spider dies. In *Goodbye Mousie*, a child's pet mouse dies. Psychiatrist Robert Coles, whose research focuses on the moral lives of children, reminds us that children need to investigate the powerful topic of death. Sorrowful stories about death give children information about mortality and the life cycle, and they fascinate children as young as three and four.

Sad stories come in different stripes. Some end happily, but deal with difficult topics, such as divorce or death of a parent, poverty, alcohol use, or child abuse. Children's author and linguist Donna Jo Napoli, of Swarthmore College, says all children need these difficult stories, but for different reasons. The privileged child with the happy childhood needs to peek into the lives of others. "In a book you crawl inside the skin of someone else," she says. "You gain empathy. Empathy is the cornerstone of civilization. . . . There is no safer way for a child to learn empathy than through a book." What about other children?

Books can be lifelines. Children enduring tough lives—poverty, abuse, loss, alcoholic parents—connect with characters in sad books. It can be life changing for these children to find out they're not alone.

> "Writers for children cannot afford to traffic in happy endings."
> –Richard Peck, Newbery Medal winner

Take Off Your Adult Lenses

We all want our children to be happy. But no one can "be happy" all the time. As humans, we feel a range of emotions every day. Our job as parents is to give kids tools to cope with the full range of human emotion. Books and stories are some of those tools, and they can do wonders to help children develop empathy and cope with fear and difficulty. It's tempting to share visions of an ideal world where everyone's a friend, but children need stories that grip the mind and heart, even if the story doesn't end happily ever after. Kids need sad. They need a bit of scary. They need stories in which things don't work out. Stories of tragedy, struggle, and foolish characters all have a place in a child's world.

Ending Sadly Ever After

Happiness is a relatively easy emotion to cope with. What about sorrow? Stories give us another opportunity—and a much safer one—to deal with sad feelings. The little mermaid dies and turns into ocean spray, but it's not happening to the child directly. It's on a different level from a lost blankie or a friend who hurts his feelings. Sad endings give children a safe way to experience sorrow.

"Happy endings are an adult agenda," says Jan Waters, past director at the School for Young Children. "We don't want bad feelings. That involves risk and emotion."

Children are particularly attuned to tales of other children. My son Zach heard me tell a true story about a little boy who died. "Tell me again about the boy whose lips turned blue," he said one day at dinner. He's thinking deeply about this little boy he never met, and the story is making him a bit more thoughtful and compassionate.

Katherine grew up knowing about her "angel brother," Samson, who died of leukemia before she was born. Samson was part of their family, and part of their family story. Her parents made sure to balance sad stories like Samson's with a range of other stories full of hope, joy, and silliness.

Stories are tales of the human heart. We want our children to be happy, but children need more than that. We respect children when we have the courage to share sad stories with them, too.

Justice Seeking

Children need optimism, hope, and happiness, but it shouldn't be their sole diet.

Especially for children with stable, happy lives, insight into others' lives offers perspective and compassion. Stories can also awaken a child's innate sense of justice. A child who first hears Hans Christian Andersen's *The Little Match Girl* might think: *Oh, some people don't have shoes. I would hate to sell matches like that. I can't believe nobody helped her. If I met her, I would help her.*

Sad stories like this frequently spark outrage and the desire to change the world. These are powerful tools to give our children (see Rule 16: Share Unfair History).

I never liked Shel Silverstein's *The Giving Tree* as a kid, but I read it over and over because it puzzled me. This is the fable's strength. Sad stories bother us and we seek to understand the causes. We want to shake the boy; it's hard to realize that some people take until old age to see the error in their ways, and yes, some people (parents, perhaps?) act like the Giving Tree, constantly giving too much of themselves in a lopsided relationship. Sad stories can awaken critical thinking in children. A sad story can point out a problem (an overly giving tree; a shortsighted boy) and stir up a desire to change it.

Like many children, I'm sure, I used to rewrite the boy's actions so he was nicer to the tree, so he appreciated her, and I wanted the tree to stand up for herself. It's fine for a child to rewrite a sad ending. This is all part of children's moral development.

> Sad stories can offer comfort and awaken compassion.

False Friendship

Stories are often cleaned up to create illusions of universal friendship. From the fox not eating the Gingerbread Boy to the Little Red Hen happily sharing her hard-earned bread with the lazy animals around her, these endings meet adult desires for everyone "just getting along and being nice."

False scenes of friendship like this do not fool kids. They simply lose interest. A good story touches something deeply human in us, whether it's laughter, surprise, or sorrow. A good story satisfies.

Foolish characters expose the consequences of thoughtless acts and gullible trust. Think about Beatrix Potter's Jemima Puddle-Duck and Peter Rabbit. Unlike some heroes, they don't get eaten by a sly and hungry fox, but Jemima's eggs do get gobbled up and Peter Rabbit loses his coat, shoes, and buttons.

Not every story should end with the hero dying, of course, but those that do are particularly powerful. When the fox snaps up the Gingerbread Boy, it's fascinating to kids. And realistic. The natural behavior of a fox is to eat its prey. The story doesn't shield kids from the consequences of foolishness.

Scary Stories

At Halloween, I checked out a copy of *The Legend of Sleepy Hollow* from the library. My kids didn't know the story, and I was eager to share this American classic with them, since the spooky Headless Horseman is so captivating.

On the way home, I told the story aloud as my kids looked at the pictures. Midway through the story I stopped. How did this version end? When the sinister Horseman hurls the pumpkin, does Ichabod Crane still die? The original story I remembered had a dire end: All that's left is poor Ichabod's hat. Did this picture book version change things to protect kids and "pretty up" the ending? Thankfully it stayed true to the original.

Trolls, ogres, and headless horsemen persist in stories because they have a rightful place. First, storybook monsters make the story exciting—hugely important for kids to gain a love of reading. The spooky villain churns up suspense so kids ask, "What comes next?"

Villains also present a powerful obstacle. The troll under the bridge in *The Three Billy Goats Gruff* is a worthy adversary. Kids learn that tough, fearsome trolls may bar the way, but even trolls can be overcome with perseverance and cleverness. Trickster stories, like *Anansi the Spider, Brer Rabbit, Robin Hood,* and many fairy tales, celebrate the clever underdog.

Four-year-old Ava was a timid child. She avoided noise and boisterous play and was easily scared. When she listened to the narrated story of *Peter and the Wolf* she covered her ears. But still, she wanted to listen. Peter's story fascinated her. For weeks afterward, Ava incorporated ideas from *Peter and the Wolf* into her play. She set traps for the wolf, digging holes and stringing rope. Playing out the story and "catching the wolf" was her way of dealing with her own big fears and feelings.

Stories are a safe way for kids to grapple with fear, build resilience, and experience courage. Children have all sorts of monsters to face in real life—from shadows in the closet and thunderstorms outside to social fears as they grow. These fears are legitimate and intensely real. Telling stories involving fear can help children confront their own fears and begin to manage them.

Most children love to be spooked, if it's just at the right level. Scary stories offer a risk, and many kids crave that jolt of energy and newfound courage. Adults tend to pull out the scary books at Halloween, but kids seek that thrill year-round.

Try This—Add to Your Toolbox

Look for Fairy Tales and Folktales

Many sad and scary stories for children come from folktales. Whether it's Baba Yaga from Russian lore, Anansi from West Indian and West African tales, or the demon king Ravanna from Asia, children gain a bit of cultural awareness at the same time they are treated to a rollicking good story. You may prefer to modify some stories to sidestep racist or sexist language, but fairy tales and folktales endure because they are stories worth telling.

Read Different Versions

Present different versions of the same story to your child. If the book you have of *The Three Little Pigs* has the pigs befriending the wolf in the end, go ahead and read it, but seek out the versions in which the wolf falls in the fire and dies and those in which the wolf splashes in the stewpot and singes his tail. Ask which ending your child likes best. You may be surprised.

Whatever your own family background, try versions of popular stories from different perspectives, such as *The Three Little Javelinas*, a Hispanic version of *The Three Little Pigs*; or *Catskinella*, an African-

American telling of the ancient Cinderella story. These stories cross cultures with universal themes.

Remove Scary Pictures

Three-year-old Charlotte hated her family's fairy tale book. The pictures terrified her. Even when her mother tucked it away in the closet, that wasn't good enough. The pictures still frightened her and she wanted the book physically out of the house.

Pictures are powerful. Even if your child likes a scary story once in a while, the illustrations may be too much. Exposing kids to scary pictures or movies can make fears worse because visual images are so intense. A child who fears a movie version usually enjoys the book. Telling a story aloud (instead of reading a book) puts the scary parts even more at a distance and can make the child feel safer.

Focus on Feelings

If you'd like to share a sad or scary story, warn your audience. "This is a sad story. Do you want to hear it?" "This story is a little bit scary, but I know it's OK in the end," or "Some kids think this book is scary. It's one of my favorites, but we can always stop if you don't like it."

As storyteller, you are the live link to your audience. It's up to you how you pitch your voice. You can read sad parts in a matter-of-fact tone of voice, or you can let the emotion make your voice crack. You can read text in a big, scary voice, or you can modulate the tension and ratchet it down.

No matter how you read it, pay attention to children's feelings. These feelings are real, even if the characters are made up.

My six-year-old sobbed for more than an hour after Charlotte died in *Charlotte's Web*. I held him in my arms and rocked him. "Why did Charlotte have to die?" he wailed. I answered his question, but not immediately. Sometimes a why question is simply an expression of sorrow. When his extreme anguish was over, we talked about Charlotte and sad feelings. "It's OK to be sad," I told him. "Everyone feels sad sometimes. People take care of each other when they're sad. I will take care of you." Then we talked about how spiders have shorter life cycles than pigs, and pigs have shorter life cycles than people. We also talked about what people do when they're feeling sad: cry, snuggle close to people they love, get cozy with blankets, share thoughts and stories, and eat warm food. As we cuddled and ate bagels, I felt grateful to E. B. White. Not only did he touch my child's soul, but he gave him an opportunity to practice how to cope when overwhelmingly sad feelings arrive.

Know Your Audience

If your child is highly sensitive or prone to nightmares, go gently. Some kids can't handle uncomfortable stories at all. Others like them in small doses, but not at bedtime. Choose a time in the middle of the day when there's plenty of daylight left to process feelings.

Don't force stories or pictures. Sensitive kids may have different needs. Know your child's temperament and help her feel comfortable.

Words to Say

Yes, it's sad, isn't it?
What a sad story.
Sometimes stories in books are sad.
Sometimes real-life stories are sad.
I wish she didn't die, too.
I wonder how that story might have ended.

This story is a little bit scary.
Do you want the scary version or the not-so-scary version?

You can cover your ears if you want.
Let's cover up this picture.
What part bothers you?
This book is too scary. Let's put it away.

Words to Avoid

There's nothing to be frightened of.
That's not scary!
Of course you'll like it.
Don't be silly. It's just a picture; it can't hurt you.
I can't believe you're scared of that.
Be a big boy.
You shouldn't think about that.
Don't talk about sad things like that.
I'll never let that happen to you.
Don't worry.

Your Take

What stories we share comes down to personal judgment. You know your child best, and what his current needs and fears are. Be open to sharing a range of story types at every age, but some stories are best held until a child is more mature. Trust yourself.

Deal with News Disasters

Jay, age three, prepared his toy airplane for another attack. It was just after September 11, and Jay was in the living room stacking block towers and knocking them down. *Zoom, zoom!* Jay's toy airplanes struck the block tower again and sent it crashing to the carpet. This scene took place in countless homes and schools across the nation.

Chances are, your child won't notice most of what floods adult news. That's good. But every once in a while a disaster strikes that's so big even the very young notice. Offer safety by talking about feelings.

Renegade Reason

Even young children are aware of many major news events. Kids feel safer when we acknowledge disasters and talk about feelings.

Daniel Striped Tiger is worried. Daniel, a puppet on the television show *Mister Rogers' Neighborhood*, asks his friend Lady Aberlin a question.

"What does assassination mean?"

Lady Aberlin doesn't answer right away. Instead, she asks the little tiger what he knows. "Have you heard that word a lot today?"

"Yes, and I didn't know what it meant," says Daniel.

"Well, it means somebody getting killed, in a sort of surprise way."

"That's what happened, you know!" exclaims Daniel in agitation. "That man killed that other man."

It was 1968, and Fred Rogers had created a special prime-time program to address children's fears soon after Robert Kennedy's assassination.

Fred Rogers understood children so well that he wasn't afraid of their deepest fears and feelings. Feeling scared was OK. Feeling confused and mad was OK, too.

You can offer safety by talking about feelings. Children don't need to know about each disaster the world suffers, but when a disaster dominates adult attention—through talk, thoughts, and feelings—your child already knows something is wrong. Respect her by clearing up confusion and helping her sort through tough-to-handle feelings.

It's important to keep in mind:

Children can tell when grown-ups are sad and scared.
Children, even very young ones, often know more than
    we think.
Children are often aware when major news events happen.
Children may hide sad or scared feelings, thinking they
    are bad.
Children have fears and questions. It's best to bring these
    out in the open.
Tragic events can promote closeness, empathy, and
    compassionate action.

When I was in elementary school, the Three Mile Island nuclear disaster transfixed the nation. I was nine. My teacher stopped the lesson plan for the day and calmly explained what had happened. She drew chalk diagrams on the board and answered every question. I don't remember the details, but I do remember how I felt: grateful. I was grateful someone had taken the time to explain it. My teacher didn't have all the answers, but that wasn't what was most important. An adult seemed to be in charge. It was enough to know people were working to fix it and make sure it didn't happen again. Her presence made me feel safe; she was a buffer from the world.

What does a child need from you when a disaster strikes? You don't have to have all the answers.

- You need to be the stable, caring person he knows.
- You need to offer honest, simple information.
- You need to accept all feelings.
- You need to be present. Take time to be together.
- You need to demonstrate kindness and ways to help.

Renegade Blessings

We may wish disasters and tragedies would never happen, but they are part of reality for each generation. Even a terrible event can bring blessings for our children:

I can handle fear, even big fear.
I can talk to my family about absolutely anything.
It isn't my fault.
I feel mixed up. That's OK; mixed-up feelings are normal.
It's better to deal with conflicts directly; I can solve my problems without violence.
I wish it hadn't happened, but it feels good to help people.
I can be one of the world's helpers.

Why It Works

When the U.S. sent bombers to the Persian Gulf, Max, Seth, and Kieran, all age four, spread their arms like airplanes and flew about the room dropping pretend bombs. "What do you think about the Gulf War?" their teacher asked. "We like it! We like airplanes. We like the stealth bombers," they cried.

Kids' reactions may not mirror ours. That's OK. Show your own emotions, but don't judge theirs. As psychologist Lawrence Shapiro says, elementary-aged children may not seem to care. Kids this age and younger are emotionally immature. Even if they know the basics of what's going on, they don't really understand. Don't try to change kids' play. Instead, open the topic for conversation and clear up misinformation. The same three boys appeared equally as happy when the war ended. "The war's over! Good! War's bad because people get killed."

Young kids may also be interested but have limited attention. After a tornado hit the Midwest, Megan did a puppet show about tornadoes with her two grandsons and they all went down to the basement. They liked it for a bit, then Nick said, "My dog eats grass." That's a signal he'd had enough and was ready to move on.

Children who regularly see violence in movies or video games may be desensitized to real violence. They may not "get" the significance of events, especially the fact that real people were killed. "Don't overprotect," advises Shapiro. "Let them know it's real. Sadness and concern are appropriate reactions. Model that. Don't let them be uncaring." Let them witness some of your caring, sadness, and anger.

Part of emotional intelligence is being able to cope with stress and difficult situations, says Daniel Goleman, author of *Emotional Intelligence*. When terrible events happen, our desire is to shield children. We like to think disasters are adult business. That's true to an extent, but the trouble is most children understand when a major disaster happens. They hear. They overhear. Even if your family keeps the TV turned off, children pick up information and misinformation from peers. In other words, your child may know more than you think he does. What's worrying, then, is your silence and your non-reaction.

But it's too scary! we say. *My son will have nightmares. My daughter will think all men are bad. . . .* "The truth is not scary," says Shapiro. Kids can adapt to stress. They may get upset, but not by the truth. The important thing is to reflect the feelings involved and tell the story with simple facts. "There was a horrible bus crash. It was very sad." As Fred Rogers reminds us, "Whatever is mentionable is manageable."

Kids may also harbor fears unique to children. The most common ones are: "Who will take care of me?" and "Is it my fault this bad thing happened?" You may think your child isn't even aware of the day's disaster, but she may be thinking that she caused it by spilling her milk. Better to get feelings and fears out in the open.

The advice to "focus on the helpers," from Mr. Rogers, has become standard for comforting children in the face of disaster. Pointing out the helpers builds hope and optimism—qualities kids need to be resilient. Find the helpers. Model your own sadness and concern, and take action to join the helpers. That's the most powerful comfort of all.

Take Off Your Adult Lenses

You might think she's too young, but chances are even a three-year-old has heard about a major news event. Don't dodge the topic. Ask: What do you know? Your child gains peace and safety from having her fears addressed. She will absorb what her mind can handle. Disasters often mean adults are confused and conflicted too. It's hard to explain events that defy explanation, so don't worry if you don't know all the answers. That's not what your child needs most from you. Focus on facts and feelings. By allowing difficult questions to be aired and space for angry, sad, and scared feelings, you are giving your child the best comfort.

Feeling Safe Versus Being Safe

"Mama, are you going to die?"

When my grandmother answered that question, she often said, "Yes, dear, but probably not tonight."

It's tempting to hush a child's worries with "Don't worry, honey, nothing like that will ever happen to you. You're safe. I'll never let anyone hurt you. I'll always be here to take care of you." Words like that smooth over big unanswered questions and may open up new fears. Young kids are savvy enough to realize that even grown-ups sometimes can't stop a bad thing from happening.

You can't offer complete safety from random events, so don't give false assurances. Besides, she doesn't need it. The trick is to balance direct honesty with a *feeling* of safety. A child feels safe when she feels listened to, when she's given real answers, and when she has space to express her feelings (see more about safety and risk in Rule 1: Safety Second).

Kids thrive when they feel safe. They also need the truth. We are mortal creatures, and no matter how much we might wish it, we cannot guarantee our child's complete safety or our own safety, but we can create a safe and trusting environment. Safety comes from feeling safe. We can help children feel safe while still telling the sometimes bitter truth.

Safety comes from feeling safe.

Technology Heightens Impact

Be judicious about which disasters to share and how to share them. Visual images are particularly vivid, so consider limiting children's exposure to visual media, especially TV and videos. It can be hard for children to get a visual image out of their mind. A better approach is to talk about a disturbing event. When kids hear about a disaster, rather than seeing it, they imagine the event in a way they can handle, in a way that's meaningful to them.

Technology has sped things up. More children are exposed to images they can't grasp, whether it's at home or on the school bus. Filter the world. Limit what you can, and check in with your children from time to time to see what might be worrying them.

Current Events

As with tough history, approach current events by connecting the news with a child (see Rule 16: Share Unfair History).

When I was nine, my dad showed me a *Newsweek* feature about the Cambodian genocide going on across the world from where I lived. To this day, I can see the face of an eight-year-old boy staring back at me from among the portraits of adult refugees. I identified with him immediately. Not only was he a child, but he wore glasses, as I did. The Khmer army was killing anybody who wore glasses because it was routing out intellectuals. This little boy lived in fear of someone spotting the nose-pad imprints on his face. I wanted to help and was glad he was safe. Compassion grows with connection.

Today's news is filled with unrest in the Middle East. Be a news filter for history in the making. If you are going to share current events, focus on the children and emphasize empathy and safety.

"This child lives in a country where there is a war going on. Her family ran away from their home to a new country because they want to stay safe."

When current events impact a child more directly—taking place in her own state or country—be sure to find out her fears and answer questions. News about police violence targeting nonwhites, for example, can awaken personal fears and spark children's outcry of "That's not fair!" Remember, if she's old enough to ask, she's old enough to get an honest answer.

Be selective. What you share will likely make a big impact. It often feels scarier for a child to learn about current events than to learn about injustices in history. As Kim John Payne says in his book *Simplicity Parenting*, we can reduce stress in children by "filtering out the adult world."

School Shootings

"The Talk" is not only about sex these days. There are many talks, and one of them is about school shootings.

School shootings are still rare. Statistically, one will *never* happen to your child or your community. However, school tragedies deserve to be singled out because, unlike other disasters, even the youngest toddler knows school is a place for children. These disasters are rare, but relevant to children's lives.

When talking about a tragedy that happened at school—a place your child goes every day—be sure to put things in perspective for your child: It's rare, like being struck by lightning. Sometimes people do get struck by lightning. It doesn't mean we should never go outside. We go outside, but we take steps to be safe.

Most adults agree we shouldn't frighten young kids about school shootings. The reality is that children as young as three and four go to schools that have lockdown drills. Like a tornado drill or a fire drill, these can be scary to young kids and bring up fears and worries. Here's how you might talk about it:

> We practice fire drills in case there's a fire. We leave the
> building and go outside.
> We practice a lockdown drill (or shelter drill) in case there's
> other kinds of trouble.
> If a dangerous person is nearby, we can do a lockdown to
> stay safe.
> In a lockdown drill, we lock the doors. We hide in our
> shelter and stay quiet.

The purpose of a lockdown or shelter drill is to practice moving people to safe places. There is no need to terrify children and strip away their sense of security in the process. Find out if your school conducts any unannounced drills and what their procedure is.

After a new tragedy, I see Internet posts filled with anxious parents wondering how to keep their kids safe. What's the right strategy? Duck and cover? Run? There's no way to completely prepare. Instead, focus on feelings. Feelings about the news. Feelings about drills.

Remind your child and yourself: It's OK to go to school. I wouldn't let you go if I thought it was dangerous.

Natural Disasters: Earthquakes, Tsunamis, Tornadoes, and More

When a hurricane strikes or a tornado rips through a town, there is inevitable sorrow, but it is also simpler to explain. There is no evil in a hurricane. There is simply geography and weather.

Explain to your child which natural disasters occur in your area and which ones are far away—ones they don't have to worry about personally. Together you can talk about how to be safe living where you live. Explain how helpers send emergency signals, such as tornado sirens. Come up with a family plan and practice these drills. Knowing what to do—and more especially, that *adults* know what to do—can give kids a sense of calm.

Take this time to be amazed by the awesome power of nature. Be impressed. Be respectful. Get out books about geology or climate and learn about our planet. Even though a natural disaster causes great destruction, its sheer power is impressive. The more we can engage children in a sense of wonder and respect for nature, the more they can understand that life is marvelous. A sense of awe and optimism helps develop resiliency.

> Avoid false assurances. Say, "I'll do everything
> I can to keep you safe."

Resilience

Although we hope with all our might that terrible events will not happen, here are some benefits that come when they do.

Benefits of Being Open About Disasters

Come together more closely as a family or community
Generate compassion and empathy
Become active helpers
Practice handling fears
Practice dealing with negative emotions
Gain opportunity to talk about mortality and death
Renew focus on conflict mediation work
Develop resiliency and ability to cope with stress

Disasters come to every generation. Mr. Rogers was thirteen when Pearl Harbor was bombed; he came of age during the horrors of World War II. We do not know what will happen next. Ours is not the worst age—terrible things have happened throughout human history. Ours is not the perfect age—from time to time, disasters do happen.

What doesn't change is what children need from us in times of disaster.

Disasters help us focus on one of the most fundamental questions: What can I do every day to prepare my child for life's inevitable problems and tragedies? A resilient child is one who is fueled by optimism and can handle difficult emotions. You support this already by teaching these three elements: 1) daily support for the full range of human emotions and their expression, 2) guidance for conflict resolution, and 3) helping others as part of daily life.

Together we can cope because the world is filled with good.

Try This—Add to Your Toolbox

Children are expert eavesdroppers. In our desire to shelter kids, we may assume they are too young to know what's going on, but they overhear media talk and adult conversations. Though they may not pick up details and reasons, children do understand serious and worried tones of voice.

Invite Kids In—Ask What They Know

Start from where kids are. Ask: "What have you heard?" or "What do you know about that?" This gives you a chance to assess the child's level of understanding, both factual and emotional. It's common for kids to be confused and have odd information, so clear up what's wrong. If the child hasn't heard anything or doesn't seem interested, then drop the topic. The key is to *invite* the child into the conversation; don't force it.

Go to the Feelings

Tell kids it's OK to feel sad, scared, or angry. These big feelings are natural and normal for people. You can say, "I feel that way, too. I wish it hadn't happened." Accept the range of negative feelings, and find an outlet to express them. If revenge pops up, say, "You sound really mad. The best thing we can do is to help people."

Answer Questions Truthfully

Keep words age appropriate, but tell the truth when talking about difficult subjects. A good rule to follow if you're wondering if your child can handle it: If a child is old enough to ask, she's old enough to get an honest answer.

Ask: "What do you want to know?" then answer the question honestly. "A man did a very bad thing. He hurt a lot of people and some of them died." There's no need to give too much information (you might introduce new fears), but be sure you've answered their burning questions. Check in and make sure before you move on: "Did I answer your question?"

Let Them Play It Out

After the 2011 earthquake in Japan, Nate and Caleb, both five, played Earthquake. They constructed a bridge from blocks, placed cars on it, then violently shook the bridge so all the cars fell off.

Play is how children process life. Offer abundant time for free play, especially in the wake of a disaster. Don't worry if the child is re-creating the disaster or playing the part of the bad guy. Don't judge the child's play or try to change it. You might discover new fears a child has by watching or asking questions, though. Let the play unfold.

Limit Video and Turn Off News Media

When a scene replays, young children may think the disaster is still happening or happening over and over again. Repetition can heighten fear and delay healthy coping. Turn off news media, especially TV and video, when children are in the vicinity.

Create Room for Emotional Release

Take time for hugs, walks together, drawing pictures or creating other art, pounding play-dough, throwing rocks at streams, running fast, or other ways to allow big feelings to be expressed. Kids may need more time for loud action, such as running, banging, or yelling, which brings emotional release. Just by being there, your steady presence offers emotional support.

Look for the Helpers

Point out the people who are helping to make the disaster better. Focus on the firefighters, doctors, police, and strangers who donate food or open their homes. This naturally leads to the next item.

Take Action

You can't change what happened, but you can change how you respond. Respond with care and compassionate action. We tend to feel most angry when we feel helpless, so reassert control. Take some action to help. Let your child see you help, and ideally include your child in the action.

Disasters are part of the world. Children can learn that bad things and sad things sometimes happen, but there are always people to help make the world better.

> Loud action—such as running, yelling, and pounding—helps bring emotional release.

WAYS YOUR CHILD MIGHT REACT

Lots of questions and intense interest
Loud, fast, and big action
Incorporating the disaster into play or stories
Whiny or clingy behavior
Potty accidents, separation fears, or sleep troubles
Bad dreams
No difference

WAYS YOUR CHILD MIGHT HELP

Draw a picture or write a card.
Share piggy bank money.
Help deliver a box of supplies.
Write a note and send money to a nonprofit.
Attend a vigil or ceremony.
Dictate a letter to a news editor about what should
    change.
Be part of family actions to help.

Words to Say

INVITATION TO TALK

Have you been hearing people talk about that?

What do you know about it?

What do you want to know?

Do you know what that word means?

How does it make you feel?

RESPONDING

It's OK to feel scared and mad.

It's natural to feel that way [sad, scared, angry].

A lot of people feel that way.

Sometimes really bad things happen.

I don't know why.

It makes me sad, too.

This is what happened.

A dangerous person tried to hurt people and three
people died.

It's a scary problem and people are working to fix it.

How would you like the story to end?

Me too. I wish the storm hadn't hurt people.

WORDS YOU MAY HEAR

Will it happen to me? Will I be hurt?

Will Mom, Dad, and other caregivers be OK?

Did I make it happen?

Will a tornado hit our house?

Will a shooter come to my school?

Is Uncle Joe's airplane safe?

HELPING YOUR CHILD FEEL SAFE

I'll do everything I can to keep you safe.

I will take care of you.

I don't know when I will die. But I will do everything
I can to stay safe so I can be with you.

I do know thousands and thousands of people are working
to keep everyone safe.

My job is to take care of you and keep you safe.

At school, teachers take care of you. They know what
to do.

RESILIENCY

When I feel scared it helps to _____.

Look—the firefighters and neighbors are all helping.

The world is a good place, even if some people do very
bad things.

People show they care by helping.

Let's do something to help.

This is what I'm doing to help. Would you like to help, too?

It makes people feel good when they get cards and pictures.

RESPONSES TO SCHOOL TRAGEDIES

It's normal to feel scared.

It's in the news right now, but it hardly ever happens.

Bad things sometimes happen in this world, even to
children.

It's OK to go to school.

Mostly these things don't happen.

I know your school practices how to keep kids safe
with drills.

School is one of the very safest places you can be. It's even
    safer than the car.
I wouldn't let you go if I thought it was dangerous.

Words to Avoid

Don't worry.
It'll be all right.
This will never happen to you.
You'll always be safe.
I will never let anyone hurt you.
I'll always be here for you.
That could never happen here.
We're not going to talk about that until you're older.

Your Take

How much to share and how much to shelter is extremely personal.
You know your child and her temperament. Be aware that news
leaks out, even to young children's ears. When in doubt, ask what
she knows. You can open the conversation in a general way: "Is there
anything you've been hearing people talk about that worries you? I
can answer questions." Remember every reaction is normal for a
child—from active interest to disinterest. You don't need to have all
the answers to respond to a child's questions; just be prepared to accept the range of feelings.

RULE

16   Share Unfair History

"There's a game we play at recess," said eight-year-old Gabe to his mother. "It's called Slave."

It turns out Slave was a game the kids had made up that focused on freeing people. His third-grade teacher had been reading the book *Trouble Don't Last*, the story of a boy and the Underground Railroad. Inventing the game Slave was the kids' way of processing this heavy information. A mix of white and African-American kids played the game. Some days white girls were the "slaves" and other days kids randomly changed roles.

Slavery. War. Genocide. Terrorism. Can these possibly be topics for preschool and elementary kids? Maybe you're thinking: *This can wait for middle or high school.* But children encounter ideas about race, war, and difference long before. Be gentle but direct. Kids understand "fair" and "not fair," and need you as a guide. Caring adults offer hope, context, and emotional support.

Renegade Reason ||||||||||||||||||||||||||||||||||||||||||||||||||||||||||||||||||||||||||||||||||||||||||||||||||||||

Kids have a deep sense of fairness and readily understand injustice. Start young. Children need to make sense of the world and their place in it.

||||||||||||||||||||||||||||||||||||||||||||||||||||||||||||||||||||||||||||||||||||||||||||||||||||||||||||||||||||||||||||||

Ellen was terrified that Hitler was hiding under her bed or in the toilet. At age three, she knew a lot about Hitler. Her parents had made it a point to share the atrocities of the Holocaust because some of their distant relatives had died in concentration camps. By age four, Ellen had been to a Holocaust museum and seen graphic pictures of concentration camp prisoners. It was all too much.

Chloe, age six, lay awake upset by stories from World War II. Her older sister, age nine, had been learning about the war at school, and hearing about it upset Chloe. President Obama and his wife started teaching their daughters about African-American history when they were "very young." Tom Joyner, a blogger on Black-AmericaWeb, says kids need to start learning about slavery "from the womb."

When is the right age to teach about mass injustices and how they relate to children today? How early is too early? No good comes from terrorizing a child. Young children (approximately three to six) need only simple stories, an introduction to different cultures and reassurance that the world is filled with good people of all types. Older elementary kids can begin to take on tougher topics, but they need you beside them as a guide.

Learning human history is emotionally charged work. We can't relegate it to history class. At some age—individual for each child—kids *should* be upset by upsetting history. Mixed-up feelings of anger, horror, sorrow, remorse, and guilt are natural reactions. We can't change unpleasant history, but we can guide children to develop compassion.

Enormous topics such as race, genocide, slavery, war, and human trafficking need to be talked about. Kids deserve to come to terms with these parts of humanity gradually, at their own pace and emotional capacity. History can be a safe place to start, since current events can be scarier to children (see Rule 15: Deal with News Disasters).

Be selective. Be child centered. Begin now. Add complexity as your child grows.

Renegade Blessings

Children gain positive self-identity, compassion, empathy, and even feelings of safety and relief when we talk about problems and history that baffle adults. Don't be afraid to be honest.

> My family is great. I come from kind and strong people.
> The world is a wonderful place.
> Most people are good.
> When something's unfair, people try to fix it.
> Some people have really been treated badly. That's not fair.
> I felt sad and mad hearing that child's story.
> I'm not going to be like that. I'm going to be nice to
>   people.
> I wonder what it's like to be someone else.
> The world is filled with differences. Differences aren't bad.
> Families who are different from mine are just regular
>   families.
> Things change. Countries that used to fight wars are now
>   friends.
> I can talk to my family about anything, even scary or bad
>   topics.
> I feel better knowing what it was all about.

|||||||||||||||||||||||||||||||||||||||||||||||||||||||||||||||||||||||||||||||||||||||||||||||||||||||||||||||||||||

Take Off Your Adult Lenses

"But he's too young. . . ." We all have a desire to protect our kids, but it's more important to protect them from being insensitive and intolerant. Bringing up injustice will not poison innocent young minds. Studies suggest that staying silent on big topics often confuses kids and inadvertently makes them leap to the wrong conclusions. Kids are good at seeing what's fair and what's not fair. They also long to make sense of the world they find. It can start gently. It can start with child-based stories. Learning about life's biggest issues is a lifelong process.

|||||||||||||||||||||||||||||||||||||||||||||||||||||||||||||||||||||||||||||||||||||||||||||||||||||||||||||||||||||

Young Kids, Big Topics

Seven-year-old Cayden loved reading *I Survived the Sinking of the Titanic, 1912* and *I Survived the Bombing of Pearl Harbor, 1941.* His mother hid the I Survived book about September 11 that came with the set until he was a year older, but by second grade Cayden devoured that one, too.

The topics of death and destruction may seem gruesome, but children want to know. We worry about keeping kids safe, but they feel safer when they understand their world.

Children today were born after the attacks of September 11. Major world events such as World War II are receding into deeper generational history. Kids hear snatches of this and that, but they need tough stories explained to them. As Lauren Tarshis, author of the I Survived series, says in her author's note: "I have received more than a thousand emails from kids asking me to write about this topic. At school visits, there are always kids who raise their hands and ask, 'Will you be writing about 9/11?' . . . I was shocked that you would be so curious about that terrible day." Kids, librarians, and teachers convinced her to write an easy-reader chapter book about September 11. She realized why children have a deep need to know: Major world events, even ones with unspeakable horrors, shape the world children are born into. Kids have an urge to know.

Our reasons for not talking are well meaning and legitimate. They include:

I don't know what to say. I might get it wrong.

I don't want to upset him. He's such a happy guy.

If I don't mention racial difference, my daughter won't notice.

Children should stay innocent as long as possible. It's important to protect childhood.

They'll get that in school history class. The teachers can handle it.

Go ahead and give yourself permission to make mistakes sometimes. The biggest mistake may be not talking about it at all.

> When kids learn stories that make them say, "That's not fair," it helps them understand the world and connect with justice and compassion.

Why It Works

Preschool and early elementary years are an excellent time for children to encounter stories of fairness and unfairness in human events. Even if kids individually slip up (snagging the biggest cookie for themselves), they have a keen sense of justice and will holler, "That's not fair!" to history and to real life. Ann Pelo, coauthor of *That's Not Fair!*, says kids are ready to learn about social justice topics when they notice other people's feelings, observe differences, and express indignation about fairness.

Morality is rapidly emerging in these years. Psychologist Lawrence Kohlberg and others have described children's stages of moral development, including developing empathy. Sharing selective stories from history can awaken that sense of empathy and moral outrage. "Why wouldn't they let girls go to school? That's not fair." "Why wouldn't they let Chinese-American people own houses? That's not fair."

Getting a grasp on history and current society is intertwined with self-identity. *Who am I and how do I fit in?* Developing identity is major work throughout childhood, beginning in the preschool years.

Kids shouldn't have to be scared of real-life bad guys under the bed, though. Give just enough information to young children. For the early years, focus on your family, other families, and understanding different points of view. By the time they hit the "age of reason," around age seven or eight, children are ready to hear a little more about the world they live in, especially through safe places such as books.

The young years are just right for instilling a lifelong passion for justice and caring, when we tap into kids' innate love of fairness.

> ### Kids feel safer when they understand their world.

Start Young

As with discussions about sex, death, and other sensitive topics, starting young gives kids the emotional support they need, sets a pattern for open communication, and establishes you as a go-to person for tough topics. "Think about how important the topic is to you," suggests Deb Baillieul, who teaches sensitive topics such as sex ed and diversity to children. "If you want to be the first place they hear it, then you need to start early."

Around age four or five can be a good time to start. That's when most children can truly see things from another's perspective. Daniela O'Neill and Rebecca Shultis, researchers from the University of Waterloo, in Ontario, found most three-year-olds hadn't developed the ability for story comprehension yet. But older preschoolers could follow a story from inside a character's mind. Seeing things from another person's perspective is vital to developing empathy.

Many early-childhood programs use anti-bias education in preschools. Anti-bias education, developed by Louise Derman-Sparks, has four parts:

1. **Positive self-identity.** Feeling a sense of pride about who I am and where I come from.
2. **Community.** Appreciating people from diverse backgrounds around me.
3. **Critical thinking.** Noticing and naming injustice.
4. **Action.** Ability to stand up for myself or others.

Is the topic too much? "Children usually take in what they can," says Jan Waters, from the School for Young Children. "They imagine what they can cope with and change the topic if they're done."

What age you start and which topics you share may vary depending on your family. You might start talking about family differences and physical differences in preschool but wait until mid-elementary school to talk about genocide.

History Helps

History is a safe place to learn about human injustice. Although it brings up sad stories, it's a good starting point for kids to under-stand the world and eventually connect with justice and compassion today.

History is emotional and social learning, and topics such as slav-ery and war are bigger than the classroom. "How could people do this?" children want to know. "Why?" Kids need space to process emotional reactions with their families.

You may need to filter history for children under age twelve, but don't ignore it completely. Besides, kids are already soaking up more than we think. Stories of history surround us from birth. Whether it's watching *The Sound of Music*, singing freedom songs from church, or witnessing life around them, history is already shaping our chil-dren's lives.

Families of All Colors

Race and ethnicity inevitably come up when we explore history, and that leads to talking about bias today.

Depending on your family background, you've either already jumped into these discussions, or you're hesitant. Good parenting for most families of color includes teaching children about racism and helping them thrive despite it. Good parenting for most white fami-lies has come to mean being "color-blind" and not mentioning it.

"We teach children from birth to identify and categorize by color—the blue ball, the red bicycle," says Emily Plank, an early-childhood educator, "and then we're somehow surprised to find chil-dren notice people whose skin color is different from their own."

The research says: You gotta talk. Erin Winkler, professor of Africology at the University of Wisconsin–Milwaukee, says white parents worry that bringing up race will poison children's minds and implant ideas of difference and inequality. But infants can distinguish skin color and children already form strong ideas about race by five. Young kids are natural categorizers and favor groups they're part of. In families that don't talk about race, kids jump to their own conclusions, including ideas like: *My parents don't like people like that.* Children soak up messages about how society works from media, peers, and the world around them. If white culture is the high-status culture, kids of all backgrounds absorb that message.

Young children are interested in power and sorting out power relationships. Louise Derman-Sparks, early-childhood educator and coauthor of *Anti-Bias Education for Young Children and Ourselves*, says white children and children of color both need help sorting out prejudice, but the messages are different. White children internalize white superiority as early as preschool and need help valuing others. Nonwhite children need help resisting negative messages about themselves and forming a strong identity.

It's OK to point out differences—children already notice them. "Why is that man's skin like that?" "Why are that girl's eyes funny?" When we shush children, they get the message that some topics are taboo. Kids notice taboos, too.

Try This—Add to Your Toolbox

On a visit to Ghana, six-year-old Nan came face-to-face with what her mom called "difficult history." They arrived on the Gold Coast, an epicenter for the transatlantic slave trade where historical holding cells for slaves still stand. Her parents answered questions and talked candidly about slavery.

Whether you're visiting historic sites in person, talking about family history, or reading a book, there are plentiful teaching opportunities for these conversations. Talking about tough universal topics is everybody's job and starts with each family.

Make It Gradual

Add layers of information as the child grows. It's not one big "talk." Like honest and age-appropriate talks about sex and death, these discussions are ongoing and organic. It's the spiral method of learning, revisiting the same topics year by year as your child grows. Share during teachable moments. "Dad, why is that man lying there in the street?" "Why does she have that thing on her head?" Preschoolers begin to ask questions and can understand basics about sameness and difference, fairness and unfairness. Give little bits here, little bits there. You are beginning a lifelong conversation, and hopefully a lifelong engagement to make the world a fairer place.

Spell It Out

If you read a book such as Dr. Seuss's *The Sneetches*, don't expect children will make the leap to equality for everyone. Young children are literalists. After reading the book, they're likely to feel friendly toward all Sneetches, but not get the book's metaphorical meaning.

You can use a book to jump into a talk about differences in people's looks, but remember to spell it out. "You and Keyvan are like the Sneetches. You don't have stars, but you look different. His skin color is lighter than yours. Should you be treated differently? I bet you both like marshmallows." Or: "We go to a mosque. Some families go to a church or a synagogue instead. Families have different ways of trying to be good people." Acknowledge the differences and normalize them: You're different in this way, but you're the same in this way.

Adults often rely on vague phrases such as "everybody's equal" or "we're all the same" to do the work of teaching acceptance and diversity. Kids need things spelled out more clearly.

Family History

Share stories from your own family history. Children deeply need these stories even if they can't grasp the full meaning for years.

If your family history includes being on the victims' side, add balance and strength. For instance, Doreen Rappaport grew up Jewish, hearing that the "Jews went like lambs to the slaughter" in the Holocaust. As an adult, she researched Jewish resistance and realized how incredibly strong and far-reaching the resistance was, writing about it in a book for young people, *Beyond Courage*.

If your family history includes participating in oppressing other people, share your own view. "White people used to take Native children away from their parents and make them go to boarding schools. I don't think that's fair."

Share the facts, but tell stories that emphasize strength, kindness, and courage wherever you find them.

Children Identify with Children

Children identify with other children. When talking about differences and stories of injustice, share those stories through children's eyes. Find books with child characters. Tell family stories about grown-ups when they were young. If the story comes from a child's perspective, a child can handle it.

Befriend Books

The elementary years are rich years for understanding history and global diversity through child-based stories. Preschool picture books focus more on different types of families and cultures. Children's literature for ages eight and up can delve into complex topics.

1. Kids Need to See Themselves
   Ninety-two percent of children's books published in the

U.S. still feature white children. The Cooperative Children's Book Center, in Madison, Wisconsin, has been tracking this figure for years. The ratio remains unchanged for the past twenty years, despite the fact that less than half of the nation's schoolchildren are now white. All children need to see themselves in public culture. Seek out books with a range of stories and images.

2. Kids Need to See Others

The flip side of kids seeing images of themselves, of course, is seeing others. Books are a marvelous way for them to do that. Even if your child's neighborhood or classroom is a mix of races, it's not usually enough. Stories have a unique way of entering the soul.

The key is to make it normal. Chinese or Latino tales shouldn't always be immigration stories. Native American stories shouldn't always be creation legends. Non-Native children often say, "There aren't any Indians anymore," so broaden their view by reading books about contemporary Native people.

Normalizing other lives means telling universal stories with a variety of main characters. Books such as Ezra Jack Keats's *Peter's Chair* or *The Snowy Day* are good examples of normalizing. The stories are about other topics—a new baby sister, a day of freshly fallen snow—but the pictures show an African-American family (mother, father, brother) engaged in daily life. The story of five sisters, *All of a Kind Family*, published in 1951, was the first U.S. children's book normalizing Jewish family life, and there have been many more since. When we think of different types of families going on picnics, making friends at school, wishing for a puppy, having sad days, and loving their grandparents, then we humanize them and each other.

We can never read enough normalizing books to children. This is where compassion flourishes.

3. Go Beyond History

Nigerian novelist Chimamanda Ngozi Adichie warns of the danger of hearing only a single story about any one group of people. "Show a people as one thing over and over again, and that is what they become," says Adichie in a TED talk. "They make one story become the only story."

Kids need books that explain major parts of history (books such as *Chains*, *Number the Stars*, *Hiroshima*, and many others do that beautifully), but discrimination, oppression, and war can't be the whole story. Tell tales of escaping to freedom, but remember to balance it. Enslavement, civil rights, and discrimination can't be the whole African-American story. War and genocide can't be the whole Native American story. Tell those stories, but tell others.

4. Tell Many Sides

Talking about history includes choosing which story to tell. Ideally, tell many sides.

My son Zach loved *Sam the Minuteman* when he was five. In a companion book, the author tells the story of the same battles in Lexington and Concord from the point of view of the "enemy"—a British drummer boy. Turn history on its head as often as you can. Read about the invasion of America and the discovery of America. Read about the Vietnam War and the same war from a Vietnamese perspective: the American War.

The more we can share multiple perspectives about the same history, the more humanity we add.

Tips for Talking About Tough Topics

Frame it as fairness
   Tap into a child's innate sense of fair and not fair.
Humanize
   Tell stories with child characters.
   Tell stories from many sides.
Normalize
   Share stories about people in which the story's main point is not race or difference.
   Tell stories that aren't exclusively about one point in history.
Spell it out
   Use specific words. Be overly clear.
   Kids are literal. Don't rely on metaphors to make your point.
   Mention what's the same and what's different.
   Make "different" a description, not a value.
Be age appropriate
   If a child's old enough to ask, she's old enough for an honest answer.
   Preschool: Talk openly about differences; read stories about families.
   Elementary school: Read books to build empathy and a sense of history.
Give kids time to process
   Learning about injustice in history needs emotional support.
   Let kids play it out.
Share without paralyzing
   Share just enough.
   Help kids feel safe.
   Point out fairness in everyday life.
   Connect kids to stories of hope, change, and progress.
   Connect kids to action.
Keep the goal in mind: knowledgeable, compassionate world citizens.

Your Tears Are Good Teachers

Kids can't take in history's full implications. Their emotional awareness is still developing. Don't be surprised if they seem somewhat
callous in the face of raw facts. But go ahead and share your own
emotion. Even if kids can't comprehend, they notice our values and
reactions.

When my fourth-grade class studied the Civil War and slavery,
what I remember most vividly was my teacher's viewpoint. After she
told us some of the horrors, her voice cracked and she said, "The
worst part was that families were sold apart from each other. Parents
got sold away from their children." I was surprised. As a nine-year-
old, I thought the worst thing must be being whipped; that's what
my child's mind was afraid of. I paid attention to my teacher's strong
reaction, though, and filed it away. If it made her cry, it must be bad.
Children pick up values from the adults around them.

Children learn from books and media, but they learn most deeply
from our reactions. Be there with them. Let your voice crack and
your tears flow. We teach children best heart-to-heart, even if the
true meaning comes later.

Engage with "That's Not Fair"

When children cry "fair" and "not fair," it's easy to dismiss it. "She
got more! Her piece is bigger than mine. That's not fair." "How
come he gets to stay up and I don't? That's not fair." According to
Emily Plank, we often correct kids, adjust for equality, or discount
their words, but it's better not to. What we tend to say:

Yes, it is fair. See? You each have three berries. (correcting)
Here. If I give you this one, then you can each have three.
    (adjusting for equality)
Life's not fair. Get used to it. (discounting)

The concept of fairness is something we want to cultivate, so don't dismiss it. Instead, connect with kids about fairness. "Sounds as if you're still hungry." Or "You wish you could stay up late tonight." As you discuss fairness with kids, give them tools. This might include knowing they can ask for more food or take a nap to stay up later. Being fair does not mean giving in or treating everyone the same, however. "You go to bed at seven thirty because your body needs more sleep. When Jack was four, his body needed more sleep, too. That's why bedtimes are fair."

"It's not fair!" is a sign that kids are ready to tackle topics of injustice. This can be done in small ways when kids are young. When they notice ramps or curb cuts, explain that makes the city more fair so people using wheelchairs and strollers can get around. When kids notice a basket of food at the grocery store entrance, explain some people don't have enough to eat, and that's not fair, so people donate food to help.

Offer Optimism and Change

Remember, every tough topic can be paralyzing. Balance the serious side with hope.

I grew up in the 1970s, the era when children were first bombarded with messages about environmental destruction on a large scale. From "Give a hoot, don't pollute" to facts about animal extinction, I grew up convinced the planet I lived on was doomed and there was nothing I could do about it.

Share stories of change and progress. Talk about new laws for fairness. Kids should grow up knowing they can all be "good guys" and helpers of humankind. Then take some action together. Donate money. Learn more about conflict mediation. As Martin Luther King Jr. said: "The arc of the moral universe is long, but it bends toward justice."

Resources

Unsure what to say? Consult Teaching Tolerance, the educational arm of the Southern Poverty Law Center. This nonprofit creates quality teaching materials for all ages. Visit a children's museum with diversity exhibits geared for young children. Search "multicultural children's literature" on the Internet for plentiful lists of titles, or better yet, talk to a children's librarian. Good librarians offer a wealth of knowledge for sharing child-centered stories about diversity and history.

Words to Say

There are all kinds of families.
Some families are small. Sasha's family has two people.
Tala's father uses a wheelchair.
The people in your school have mostly white skin, but most
    people in the world have brown skin.
In some places, girls can't go to school.
No, it's not fair.
There were people on both sides who helped.

Now we're friends, but at one time England and the U.S.
    were at war.
It used to be against the law to _____. That wasn't fair, so
    people worked to change it.
People used to think women weren't as smart as men, so
    they didn't let them vote.
People used to think _____, so they made bad laws.
There are still people who think that.
Sometimes people are scared of things that are different.
Grown-ups make bad mistakes sometimes.
What do you think?

Words to Avoid

Everybody's equal. (vague)
We're all the same.
I didn't notice he was black.
Shh! That's not nice to say.
We don't talk about that.

Your Take

What's right for your family is highly personal. It's based on your background, beliefs, and life experience, as well as your particular children. We all do our best to give our kids "roots and wings"—pride and understanding of family heritage mixed with tools to take on the life they were meant to lead. As you guide your child, think of the other mothers and fathers in the world guiding their precious children, and how best we can do the job together.

Section VI

MEAN WORDS and PRINCESS POWER

A person's a person, no matter how small.

—DR. SEUSS

RULE
17 Princesses Are Powerful

Layla loved princess pink. Her barrettes were pink, her mermaid shirt was pink, and she read fairy books with glitter on the covers.

"All the tiaras and such are annoying," said Janice, mother of a purple-loving daughter. "I worry she might just swallow the princess formula completely."

Renegade Reason

Girls can be strong and still play princess. Keep media at bay, but let kids experience princess power.

Princess pressure can be intense. I know. My children also caught the princess bug. Our dress-up box was (and is) stuffed with gauzy tulle skirts, veils, and dresses decorated with ribbons and flowers. At age four, my youngest child begged for "sparkly shoes," so we added a pair of glitter flats. When birthday time came, this is what I heard: "A princess cake! A princess cake with turrets and with a princess coming out!"

Both my children are boys. The allure of princess play is even stronger for girls. Princess culture surrounds young kids, and as Peggy Orenstein, author of *Cinderella Ate My Daughter*, says, it can swallow them up.

Here's what we worry about as adults:

Our children will never ditch the princess phase.
They will be thralls to media images of helpless princesses
who need a man to rescue them.
Our kids will become overly focused on physical looks and
beauty.
Girly-girl culture doesn't offer positive role models.
Obsessions like this just aren't healthy.

The Great Princess Debate is raging in this country. In the anti-princess camp, parents and psychologists warn against limited options for girls, body image dissatisfaction, commercialization of play, and sexualization of childhood. The pro-princess fans point out the rise of strong female role models in the media and real life, and celebrate the enormous freedoms girls have today to do almost anything and be almost anything they want. If what girls want is to play princess, then so what? As the senior editor from *Slate* said in the blogosphere: "What is it with you moms of girls? I have never met a single one of you who isn't tortured about pink and princesses."

Moms, dads, princess haters, and princess lovers, we all care about the same result: We want to raise girls who will be strong, confident women in the future, girls who will have good childhoods today.

On the whole, we can relax. Just because a child plays princess today doesn't mean she's going to be a helpless princess type when she grows up. In fact, true princess play gives girls power. Princess play can help our children, just as princess pressure can hurt them. The key is to know the difference.

Renegade Blessings ||||||||||||||||||||||||||||||||||||||||||||||||||||||||||||||||||||||||||||||||||||||||

Girl or boy, your child has a right to play princess. Limit exposure to scripted plots (watching the same movie over and over again) but allow the play to run its course. There's a reason kids gravitate toward this play. Here's what your child can learn:

> I can be someone powerful.
> Imagination is powerful. I love playing what I dream up.
> My parents and teachers respect my ideas and interests.
> Stories are exciting. I love books, movies, singing, and acting out stories.
> Dressing up is fun. It feels good to explore and try out different parts of myself.
> Friendships feel good; I feel close to my friends when we share our dreams.
> In some ways girls are different from boys.
> It's great to be a girl. It's who I am and what I want to be.
> *For boys:* Maybe this is what it feels like to be a girl. I've always wondered.

Take Off Your Adult Lenses

Kids have compelling reasons to explore princess play. We may see old-fashioned and unwanted gender roles appearing, but to kids, princess play is about finding power. This power includes being proud of being a girl (confirming gender identity) plus having fun ordering people about, living in a castle, wearing fancy clothes, and being special. Princess play usually peaks between ages three and seven, then drops off. Provide a range of other experiences to your little princess to offer a balanced life. If you're worried princess play has gotten out of hand, examine your *own* actions and attitudes. Maybe it's time to cut media exposure, stop buying the next toy, and set limits on movie viewing.

> Princess play can help children.
> Princess pressure can hurt them.
> The key is to know the difference.

Why It Works

Princess power reaches its peak in preschool and early elementary school. A child's interest in pink princess culture is mainly a mix between natural child development and strong media messages, but it's also influenced by family actions and a child's own personality. To understand whether this play is healthy or worrisome, you need to unpack the mix.

First, child development plays a huge role. Preschool-aged children are busy sorting out who's a boy and who's a girl and what it means to be male and female in their culture. To solidify their own gender identity, it's typical for children to go to extremes with gender roles for a while. What could be more "girl" than a frilly princess? This extreme interest is one way girls shout to the world, "I'm a girl! That's who I am!" Young children dress up in extreme girl wear because they believe external factors can change who they are. Psychologist Lawrence Kohlberg said children need to develop a sense of gender constancy. *If I wear pants and don't have ribbons in my hair, people won't know I'm a girl and I won't be a girl.* In the case of a boy interested in princess dresses, the ideas are much the same: *I wonder what it feels like to be a girl. I can become a girl by wearing this dress. Hey, people think I'm a girl! Now I'm a girl.*

Dress is one way children express this developmental stage. They also change whom they play with. As Karen, the mother of four-year-old Anita, said, "My daughter played with the boys all the time, but now she'll only play with girls." Siding with same-sex playmates is another way kids figure out who they are and who they're not.

Psychologist Michael Thompson, author of *Raising Cain* and other books on gender differences, says it's typical for kids to split apart and play with only one gender from ages three to eleven. Identity is often expressed through gender in the early years. By later elementary school, kids are more likely to form identity around abilities and interests, such as "I'm a musician" or "I'm an athlete," and these new identities also give them power.

As children divide into gender camps, peers also reinforce the boundary between girls and boys. "My daughter wore Buzz Lightyear shoes until kindergarten," says Rebecca. "Then she was told: 'You can't like Buzz. You have to like Jessie, because she's the only girl.'" As parents, we often bemoan this gender policing. It's fine to add outside information to balance peer mandates, such as "I know girls can like Buzz Lightyear, too. I like Buzz Lightyear," but keep it in perspective. Kids typically have to go to extremes before they can find a balance. Planting seeds about a more equal world is worthwhile, but don't be surprised if young kids don't seem to hear you. At least not yet. This need to sort boy from girl is so strong that a four-year-old like Benjy, whose mother was a doctor, announced: "Only boys can be doctors."

Of course, marketers are fully aware of this developmental stage. The trouble comes when they exploit it and when parents and other adults go overboard in trying to support their child's interest.

"Pink princess marketing is so forceful, backed by so many billions of dollars, that it's not really a *choice* anymore," writes Rebecca Hains, media studies professor at Salem State University and author of *The Princess Problem*. "It's proscriptive, it's coercive." Hains and others are right in pointing out the industrial bankrolling of pink princess merchandise. A girl who is already inclined to love princesses and all things glittery can easily be overwhelmed.

That's where limits come in. Your daughter does not have the money to buy all those princess toys and related backpacks and pajamas. Adults buy them for her. Maybe it's you or your partner; maybe it's doting friends or grandparents. Neither can she take herself to the movie theater, rent a DVD, or subscribe to Netflix or cable TV.

Media influence on kids is huge, but be aware of the media's influence on you. Parenting the pink means adopting strong family limits on technology and commercials (see Rule 5: Embrace Amish iPads). Adults need to provide just enough props (dress-ups and other multiuse toys) so play can unfold, but be a force to protect the kids against too many outside ideas imposed.

"If your child's being swallowed by Cinderella, take a look at how much access she has," says Susan Roscigno, codirector at the School for Young Children. How many times did she watch the movie? How many branded books and toys does she have? It's OK to say no.

Accept the powerful play of princess make-believe, but keep back the outside pressure. It's too much for a five-year-old to handle.

> **Don't take away a child's interest. Add balance.**

Power Play

In the wake of the Disney movie *Frozen*, three-year-olds in Heidi's preschool class all wanted to be Elsa. Although Anna was the movie's actual heroine, Elsa was more powerful. They were both princesses, but Elsa could zap bad guys with her hands and create cool magical ice castles.

Why do children play princesses? "It's all about power," says Jan Waters. "Princesses are likable and respectable. They're the female version of a good guy." Of course, not every girl finds power in princesses. Eight-year-old Hayley was greeted with "Hello, Princess!" at every turn when her family visited Disney World. As the day went on, Hayley burst into tears. "Tell them I'm not a princess!" she cried. "Tell them I'm a warrior!"

Kids of both sexes seek out power in their play. While boys tend to find power through weapon play or superhero play, other children find power by playing teacher, Mommy, bus driver, tiger, or princess. Power characters are in charge; they can be fierce or strict, but whatever they are, they elevate the child from her position of constantly being told what to do into one of magical control.

Princess play conveys social power. "I'm the princess," says Abigail, age four, who's playing with three friends. "You be the one who cooks the food, you be the dog, you be the baby." Girls are particularly interested in relationships and understanding power within those relationships. Princess play gives ample opportunity for this to unfold. "One of kids' favorite things to do is to tell people what to do," says Deb Baillieul, a long-term teacher at the School for Young Children, who's observed princess play for forty years.

Sometimes the power in princess play can be hard to see or even disturbing. Three-year-old Madelyn played princess by standing at the top of the climber and calling out, "Oh, save me! Will someone save me?" Then she waited for the boys to rescue her. There's still power here: Madelyn had the power to get other kids involved in her game. Still, this game certainly had its helpless side. Madelyn's teachers said, "See if another princess can rescue you," and "Sometimes princesses save themselves." Madelyn's play evolved from the I'm-helpless-please-rescue-me theme. She still liked playing Rescue the Princess, but now she played with either girls or boys, and added a sword along with her frilly princess dress. The look on her face when she brandished the sword summed it up: "I'm powerful."

In general, though, young girls have more freedom than boys and can try on different gender roles. Phoebe, age six, loved adventure stories. Sometimes she'd dress up in her princess dress and pretend to be Maid Marian. Other days she'd pretend to be Robin Hood. Girls need strong female role models, but they can also learn from male ones.

Fantasy Play

When I was eight, I wanted to live in the opulent Ohio Theatre, a restored baroque opera house filled with gilt carvings, plush carpets, multiple balconies, and chandeliers. My friend Maria would live at one end, and I would live on the other. We would both be princesses and come visit each other. Tapping into dream worlds is healthy work for childhood. It opens imagination and cements friendship. The only danger is when princess dreaming—or any fantasy play—becomes scripted.

Princess play is imaginative fantasy play—except when a child's original ideas have been co-opted by media. "If you see kids playing Cinderella only by the script, then it's a sign play is being limited. They're relying on someone else's imagination rather than their own," says Roscigno.

It's typical for children to start with a character they love. But watch what they do as play develops. Savannah, age four, loved playing Elsa, but in her hands, Elsa became the bad guy and had unique adventures that had nothing to do with the original movie.

Overly scripted play doesn't just afflict princess-crazy kids. Jeremy loved Ninja Turtles—he had to have Ninja Turtles in all his play, and he couldn't depart from the preprogrammed script. Kids need to be able to insert their own ideas, such as: "I'm a princess called Elsa. I'm feeding my tiger."

Even scripted play can be helpful for a time, however. Ethan and his friends, all preschoolers, reenacted the story of *The Lion King* over and over. The part they repeated was when Mufasa, the father, dies. This was a big topic, involving life and death, good and bad. Big topics attract kids' attention and need to be worked out in play.

Watch how long the repetition goes on for, and whether the kids move on after they've worked it out. In healthy play, kids tend to use movie characters as a starting point, then branch off with their own ideas.

Whose Passion?

For a parent who's dreamed of a sweet little girl, it's tempting to doll her up and indulge adorable girl fantasies. "It's easy to go overboard. It becomes as much your passion as theirs. Keep princesses the child's passion," says Roscigno. "Be open and alert to when your child is ready to move on."

If this might be you, remember your job is to expose your child to a broad range of interests and role models. Think to yourself, *Am I supporting this interest or pushing it?* Take time to understand your child's ideas and interests. She may not like what you like.

Princess Clothes—Looks and Limits

Princess clothes are beautiful and fanciful, but there's also a helplessness that comes from dressing like that. A princess who can't drop her princess heels for tennis shoes or who isn't willing to participate because her pretty dress might get messed up is missing out on active play. Then princess play isn't powerful anymore; the dress code becomes limiting.

Luckily, most kids figure this out on their own. When clothes stop them from doing what they want to do, kids modify their ways. Mara, for example, loved her green princess dress and her high-heeled satiny princess shoes. "I'm a princess and this is my castle and this is my baby," she'd say, and wore her princess outfit everywhere. But Mara also liked to run at the playground and climb on monkey bars. She discovered she couldn't do that in her princess shoes—they were too slippery—so Mara stopped wearing those shoes to the park.

We also need to watch our words as adults. Body image concerns can start young, especially if children hear us say repeatedly: "Oh, you look so cute in that!" "You're beautiful." "You look adorable."

The more girls hear people praise their looks, the more they naturally seek praise for their appearance, including their dress, hair, and body. Next time an adorable princess walks by you, simply make an observation ("You've got a princess dress on today") or praise an action ("Wow, that was a high jump!"). Girls need to be noticed primarily for their ideas and actions, not their looks.

Girly-Girls

Some kids are girly-girls by nature. That's simply who they are. How do you know which kid that will be from the lineup of preschool princesses? You don't yet. As long as you expose your child to a range of experiences, ideas, and yes, clothing, your child will show her (or his) true colors as she grows older. Some adults become fashion designers. Some make money as models. Some love to accessorize and read *Glamour* magazine. If that turns out to be your child, you can't stop it, even if this personality is extremely different from yours.

> You can't change the inner nature of a child.

Try This—Add to Your Toolbox

The bedspread, the pajamas, the wallpaper, the movies, the books, the lunch box, the toothbrush. Quick, take a look around. How much of it sports Dora, Elsa, Cinderella, Jasmine, Sleeping Beauty, or other commercially driven girl figures? The marketers know how to worm their way into every part of a child's life.

Princess marketing can creep up on you. If you feel overwhelmed, here are some sensible steps you can take to restore balance to your home.

Parent the Pink

When you first met your daughter, you knew you "had a girl," but you won't know who she really is for years. Neither will she. Expose kids to a wide range of experiences, places, characters, and possible interests.

Introduce a range of strong characters. Many shows offer only one token female character (think Wonder Woman among all the superheroes). If you don't know what to introduce, ask librarians for books and children's movies with strong girl characters. Kids will notice. Seven-year-old Addie turned to her mother excitedly after watching *Frozen* and said, "Mom, true love is not a boy! It's her sister! It's saving her sister!" If you're looking for role models, this movie is still based on white characters with skinny beauty, but not only is true love sisterly love, but the princess saves *herself*. As for the handsome prince, the princess throws him overboard.

Go ahead and read stories with old-fashioned gender roles, but discuss them. "Gosh, that was mean. They didn't even let her pick who she was going to marry. Can you believe that?" Or say, "This is a story from long ago. Back then they thought . . ." Seeing how life has changed can offer kids a sense of optimism and power.

Do an Inventory

Do you have books at home with commercial movie characters? Do you check out books like that from the library? What about T-shirts, backpacks, and water bottles? Are they all commercially licensed products? Do they attach to their own TV show? Brand licensing even extends to underwear, so take a good look around. Kids enjoy princess fantasy play, but brand images can limit it. For example, does she love Cinderella or princesses in general? *Star Wars* or outer space?

Limit Media Exposure

Sure, it's fine to show a Disney movie, but what happens when you own that movie and your child gets to watch it over and over? Set limits on how often your child watches a certain movie. To make it easier, rent or check items out at the library—items that must soon be returned. Movies are fun and sometimes help kids bond with friends, but too much media exposure imposes scripted plots and makes it harder for kids to create their own imaginative play.

Look for "Off the Script"

Ask yourself this: Can your child break loose from the prefabricated script, or is she stuck? If she insists on re-creating the same scenes from *Sleeping Beauty* or *Frozen* down to the dialogue, and the story and characters have to be "just like this," she could be overexposed to commercial media.

If a child is too scripted and seems "stuck," she may need help breaking out of it. What to do? The two best solutions are to 1) limit media exposure, and 2) wait a few years. Another option for kids who are stuck to a rigid script of a storyline is introduce new ideas. Say: "What would happen if . . . ?" Add a new prop or insert yourself into the game for a change (go easy on this; manipulating play can also ruin it). Help her be flexible in other parts of her day. A child who adheres to a rigid storyline may need practice to gain flexible thinking.

Avoid the Pink Aisle

Better yet, don't take young children into toy stores. Chances are, your children have too many toys already. Today's stores dramatically market certain colors and items to girls. The "Pink Aisle" is ablaze in pink cartons filled with mermaids, glitter, princesses, purses, dolls, and all things officially considered "girl." You won't find Legos, toy swords, or trains there. Excessive marketing like this limits children's range of choices, telling them, "This is what you should like. This is what you shouldn't like." If you must let kids choose a toy, head to the thrift store—aisles aren't pink-erized there.

Coping with Presents

Sarita received her first princess board book at age three months. Tala got a princess tiara, pink shoes, clothes, and a sparkly fairy wand at age two from her grandmother. Sometimes princess pressure comes in the form of presents from well-meaning friends and loved ones. What to do about a princess-doting grandma?

The relationship is more important than the presents. If it's an ongoing pattern, share your concerns, but sometimes the best thing to say is thank you. Instead of trying to limit Grandma's urge to bestow pink presents, set new expectations for toys that enter your house. Keep excess princess toys at Grandma's house. Put them in a special rainy day box and bring them out once in a while. Rotating toys declutters the child's world and opens room for imaginative play.

Take Princesses Outside

One element of princess play is that your child may be missing out on active play. Princess clothes make it hard to run around, and too much inside time limits outside play. If she insists on wearing a princess outfit when you go out, put pants underneath and add sturdy shoes, or bring them with you in a bag and let her know they're available.

Having a hard time avoiding commercialization? Ads and brands are everywhere—but luckily not in the mud and the woods. Bring your children to places free from all messages and watch their play bloom. Sticks, rocks, sand, and leaves are gender neutral.

Wait a Few Years

Most kids break out of their princess phase on their own. It's typical for this intense interest to taper off in mid-elementary school.

If you bring balance to their lives, girls will find their way. Mara lived in long princess gowns and shiny shoes from ages three to six, but grew up to be an athlete, invited to train at an Olympic center. Addie is now eight. She loved tiaras and tutus, especially from ages four to six, but decided pink was "too girly." The only princess she still likes is from *Star Wars*. Princess Leia is tough: She's Jedi material and shoots a blaster.

Words to Say

Oh, you're a princess.
I wonder what this princess is going to do.
I see you're wearing a fancy dress today.
You like that dress.
I see you put on a sparkly crown.
What do you like about it?

I know princess shoes can be hard to run in. Let's bring
   your tennis shoes, too.
A princess can also save herself.
You've got strong muscles.
Can princesses jump high?

That's how the movie goes. How does *your* story go?
I know you like Belle. You can still like her, but this is
   staying in the store.
We're not going to buy that movie, but we can check it out
   from the library sometimes.

You really want to watch the movie again, but we're taking
   a break from it.

I'm happy to read you a book.

You can wear your princess outfit, but we're going
   outside now.

Words to Avoid

You're beautiful/pretty/adorable.

You're so cute!

That's not how the story goes.

You shouldn't play princess all the time. Here, do this
   instead.

Nice girls don't do that.

A princess would never do that.

Boys/girls can't do that.

Your Take

It can be hard not to worry when children's play seems to dip back into old-fashioned gender stereotypes. Don't try to change your child's interests. Give it time. You may wish she'd have more variety, but some kids stick to favorite characters for a while. Princess play is an outlet for imaginative dress-up play in childhood. Your little princess will find ways to be powerful if you give her ample time for play.

RULE
18 Mean Words Matter

There's so much name-calling," said one mom. "What do you do with all that verbal aggression?"

"My girls don't hit," said another parent. "What I have trouble with is the teasing, verbal comments, and friend issues."

Teasing, threats, and name-calling are conflicts just as sure as pushing, hitting, and kicking are. And words can hurt just as much.

Renegade Reason

Mean words matter. Kids need tools to deal with social conflict.

"Abby's a big dummy."

"You're a baby."

"You always scribble. You always paint messy."

"I won't be your friend anymore and you can't come to my birthday party."

Mean words can start young. Some of it's innocent—a child may say, "That's ugly," and not mean to hurt anyone, or she may say,

"Moron brain," because she thinks it's funny. Other times kids are experimenting with power.

Cope with the conflict when mean words come up. Point out what hurts, and remind kids, "People are not for hurting. Not their bodies and not their feelings." Just like learning that it's not OK to hit your brother, kids need to learn what's acceptable when it comes to words. There's something else going on underneath the mean words. Uncover the problem and set limits. The Renegade Golden Rule applies here: It's OK if it's not hurting people or property. If a child kicks a playmate, it's easy to see the hurt. But "People are not for hurting" applies to feelings, too.

Renegade Blessings

Tough talk covers up big feelings. Pay attention to those feelings in kids, then help them set limits. Your child needs to learn that people are not for hurting—not their bodies or their feelings.

Words can hurt people, just like hitting.
I can be mad at my friend, but it's not OK to call her
    names.
My parents will listen to me even when I'm mad.
I can stand up for myself. I don't have to take it.
I know how to set limits on stuff I don't like.
I can stand up for my friends. I can help when my friend is
    teased.
I know what tattling means.
I know how to get out of a teasing situation. I can help
    stop it.
I can get help from a grown-up when I need it.

Why It Works

Even four-year-olds can make life miserable for each other. According to psychologist and mother Michelle Anthony, coauthor of the book *Little Girls Can Be Mean*, kindergartens are full of harsh verbal exchanges.

Of course, teasing is not only a girls' issue. But there are two reasons why preschool-aged girls are more apt to lash out with words that hurt. First, girls at this age are more verbal than boys. They naturally express themselves and their feelings through language. When young boys get riled up, scared, or uncomfortable, they tend to react physically. When girls have strong feelings, they tend to use words. Second, research by David Geary, William Pollack, and others shows that girls are more likely to focus on relationships than boys. Because they understand how powerful relationships are, girls attack relationships when they get upset. They also may use mean words to try to protect relationships ("Only Emily can sit next to me. You're ugly. I'm not your friend anymore."). From preschool age on, girls are more likely than boys to tease and attack each other with words and threats against relationships.

Many times teasing and other verbal attacks are about figuring out friendships: power in friendships, compromise in friendships, how to make friends, how to keep friends, and how to still be friends (or caring siblings) even if the other person doesn't agree with a play idea. It's natural that your child struggles with these skills—they're not easy. Deal with hurt feelings whenever you can and teach her better friendship skills.

Mean words mask deep emotions. "Let girls be angry," says Deb Baillieul. "Not always 'nice.' Accept the tough feelings, not the hurt."

Take Off Your Adult Lenses

Don't brush off teasing. It's not just words. Verbal attacks hurt—and often are intended to hurt—just like physical attacks. Mean words can escalate in the school years, so it helps to practice coping skills. Whether your child is the speaker, target, or an onlooker, let her know that stinging comments are not acceptable. To do so, focus on the feelings that caused the mean words. Mean words are a signal something's wrong.

Verbal Conflict

For years we offered kids just one defense against teasing: Ignore it. For generations, children have chanted the familiar phrase: "Sticks and stones may break my bones but words can never hurt me." But the truth is words *do* hurt. And children need stronger tools than a playground chant to help them cope with verbal conflict.

When Ada kicks Peyton, things seem straightforward. Break up the fight. Talk it out. Kicking a person isn't acceptable. But name-calling and other mean words seem especially hard to handle. When words get involved it all seems more complicated.

Words that hurt can certainly be harsh, but they're just like any conflict. Feelings are involved. Boundaries have been crossed. Ignore the particular insults for now and get to the root of the matter. What's going on here? You sound mad. What is she doing that you don't want her to do? What are you worried about? What do you think will happen?

Instead of a chant, give kids practice with conflict mediation. And let them know they can enlist adult help if they need to.

Power Words

My six-year-old, Zach, loves his teacher. To show how much he loves her, he bestows the three highest compliments a young child can give: "I want to marry her." "I wish she were my mother." "I want her to come to my birthday party." These are power phrases for a child.

On the flip side, kids have negative power phrases they pull out when they're super mad or simply trying to control power in a situation. The top two: "You're not my friend" and "You can't come to my birthday party!" Kids commonly experiment with power by using these words as threats. These words are signals. They tell us a child is mad or trying to get her way. Translate them, then offer tools to help kids find a better way. State feelings, ask questions, and offer information: "You sound mad. What's she doing that you don't like?" Often kids will use the birthday party line when another child won't do what they want. "Sounds as if you have different ideas about what to do. I know kids can have different ideas. Dominic is the boss of his body. He doesn't have to play that way if he doesn't want to."

Name-calling

"You dummy! Get away from me."

What happens when we hear this? Often we jump too fast. As adults, we focus on the words themselves. "That's not nice," we might say. "Don't say the word *dummy*." We worry about the obvious insult. "My first concern," one mother told me, "is that they understand it's unacceptable to insult someone."

Sure, words like *dummy*, *boogerhead*, *fartface*, and *stupid* are not nice. But when it comes to name-calling, the words themselves distract. It's important to deal with first things first.

> Disregard the word. Go directly
> to the feeling underneath it.

First, address emotions. Find out what's going on and sort out the conflict. Then talk about how harmful name-calling and teasing can be. In our sincere effort to stop kids from hurting each other's feelings, we sometimes trample right over *their* feelings. Until a child's emotions are acknowledged, she won't be able to listen.

In this case the child (let's call her Mikayla) is angry. To resolve the conflict, we need to get to the root of her anger. State the emotion you see—"Mikayla, you look mad"—and sort out the conflict using conflict mediation.

"She knocked my animals over!"

"Sophie, your body knocked Mikayla's animals over. That made Mikayla mad. She was playing with the animals and had them lined up in a special way."

"Well, she called me a dummy."

"Did you want to be called a dummy? No? Well, tell her how it made you feel."

All sorts of mean names may tumble out of kids' mouths, including racist and sexist slurs. Kids pick up social information wherever they are and try out words that seem powerful. They may repeat words they hear at home, on TV, or in their neighborhood. No matter how shocking it is, try to focus your attention on the underlying emotion first. Remember it's a verbal conflict, not just words to be outlawed.

Four-year-old Carson and Jayden were both at preschool. "Hey, black mutt!" Carson yelled.

Jayden didn't say anything, but the teacher did. She brought the two kids together. "You sounded angry," she said. "Are you worried Jayden is going to do something to you?"

"Yeah," said Carson.

"Do you think he's going to hurt you? Jayden, are you going to hurt Carson?"

"No."

"What do you think he might do to you?" she asked Carson.

"He's going to take my toys!" Carson shouted.

The feeling underneath was fear. After this fear was addressed, the teacher turned to talk about the racist name-calling. "I heard him call you a black mutt. Do you want to be called a black mutt?"

"No," said Jayden.

"Well, tell him," said the teacher. "Tell him you're *not* a black mutt and *don't* want to be called one!"

Both these kids had their feelings listened to and sorted out. They also learned a lot.

Here's what Carson learned:

Calling names hurts people.

I'm not worried about Jayden anymore.

I feel safe knowing he won't take my toys.

Even though I made a mistake, my views got listened to.

I can't get away with it; nobody puts up with mean words.

Here's what Jayden learned:

Being called a name like that really hurt.

I'm strong. There are steps I can take.

I can tell him what I don't like.

Adults will listen and help me. They know it's a big deal.

I feel safe knowing he won't call me names.

Even though being called a terrible name hurt, Jayden got practice asserting himself and setting limits on another child's behavior. "My name's Jayden. That's what I want to be called."

When a slur is involved, as in this case, investigate the source.

Where did this child pick up that mean word? There may be more going on. The child is certainly hearing it somewhere. Involve other adults to figure this out.

You can't stop kids from getting hurt, but you can give them the tools to cope. Conflict mediation is one tool. Books, such as *Desmond and the Very Mean Word*, written by Archbishop Desmond Tutu, are another. This story of forgiveness shows kids how to get out of the cycle of verbal insults.

> People are not for hurting.
> That includes bodies and feelings.

Teasing

"I have a pink hat and you don't."

"My cookie's bigger than yours." "No, it's not!" "Yes, it is." "No, it's not!"

Teasing can escalate quickly. For many kids, there's something peculiarly powerful and satisfying about getting a rise out of the other person. You can't stop all teasing, but you can teach kids how to get out of a teasing situation they don't like. When kids are going back and forth at each other, show them how to get out. Ask, "Is this fun for both of you?" Ask the picked-on child, "Do you like this? Or do you want to get out?" Help her learn how to extricate herself: 1) Stop talking, and 2) walk away. You can also coach kids to stand up against teasing—"I'm not going to play your game"—then stop talking and walk away. Kids need to know there's a way out.

Tattling

Two girls entered the store with their mother. As the mother talked to the clerk at the counter, Alaina and Jada sat down by a rack of cards.

"Mom! Jada's touching things!" yelled Alaina.

"No, I'm not!" Jada said, quickly putting the cards back.

"Mo-omm!" her sister yelled again.

Mom hauled Jada up to the front of the store. While her mother was distracted with Jada, Alaina sat quietly in the corner touching all the cards herself.

Tattling is about power and getting someone in trouble. We talk about ratting someone out, snitching, or being a tattletale, but when to tell is confusing to kids.

My son Zach came home one day excited about a book his class had read. "It's about a tattle tongue!" he said. He chanted a funny rhyme from the book, but missed its message.

"What's *tattle*?" he asked. "Do you know?"

"Yes, I do. Would you like to know what *tattle* means?" He nodded vigorously.

"Tattling is when you tell a grown-up to get someone else in trouble. It's not about trying to get help when you need it. Getting help could save someone from being hurt."

"Oh!"

Most kids get the difference right away. If kids forget in the heat of the moment, ask, "Are you trying to help Jada or get her in trouble?"

Other times kids "tattle" to show they understand the rules. For example, "Maya's not holding hands." Your response could be: "Sounds as if you know the rules." Sometimes kids need reassurance that they can relax—it's not their job to take on the adult's worries. "Are you worried Maya might get hurt? I'm here. I can see her."

We say, "Stop tattling," when we want kids to solve their own conflicts, but it's no surprise they're confused. Kids are used to structured time with an adult in charge. Kids tell on other kids partly because they don't know they can talk directly to a peer. If telling is a problem, reinforce conflict mediation skills.

Bullying

Bullying can be physical or verbal, but it's always about power and picking on someone. A common definition of bullying is repeated behavior meant to hurt another person.

Young bullies aren't usually bullies—at least not yet. Early bullying can often be about fear or anger. Four-year-old Levi, for example, walked in the door and shouted, "I'll kill you!" at John. John, also age four, looked frightened.

Levi yelled his threat again: "I'll kill you!"

"Does John do things you don't like?" asked the teacher.

"Yeah," said Levi. "Sometimes John knocks into me and hurts me or calls me stupid."

Even when four-year-olds threaten each other, underneath the bluster usually there's somebody who's scared or mad, or both. John and Levi sorted out their fears and each set limits on the other. Levi agreed not to say, "I'll kill you," again. And John agreed to watch out where he was walking and not call Levi stupid.

Kids at this age are experimenting with power. Young kids are attracted to power and like to test the strength of their bodies and the power of language. That's OK, but they need to learn what's acceptable and what's not. Show them where the boundaries are. When you take the time to teach kids social limits, many young "bullies" at age four or five will change their behavior.

But if bullying behavior pays off, kids will do it again and again. That goes for victims, too. Kids can fall into patterns that make them targets for bullying.

That's why conflict mediation is so important. When kids get practice asserting themselves they learn how to set limits on peers. This makes them less likely to become victims. They know how to speak up and when to get help from an adult. And bullies learn alternative ways to deal with their fear or anger. They learn how to cope with rejection and how to make friends.

What about social exclusion? Most experts say "you can't play with me" is a form of bullying. It can be. But young kids have plenty of reasons (often legitimate) for excluding playmates (see chapters on friendship and rejection in *It's OK Not to Share*). "She's mean!" is usually a cover for being rejected or another person not doing what the child wants.

Kate was an angry seven-year-old. Her parents had just divorced and she entered second grade frowning and pushing people. Most of her classmates were scared of her and said things like "You're not nice," "You're mean," and "I don't like you." When she tried to make friends with Zoe, things were different. Zoe had gone to a preschool that taught conflict mediation skills and she had practice setting limits on peers. She said, "If you don't make mad faces at me and don't jump on my back, I'll be your friend." The friendship helped Kate become a child many kids wanted to play with.

Young kids need help understanding friendships. It takes practice and savvy to set social limits. Saying "You can't play with me" isn't automatically bullying, but if it happens repeatedly, then watch out. Bullying is usually repeated behavior, targeting the same victim.

Modeling Insults

Children model what they see. When kids hear verbal barbs used around them, they are more likely to behave this way, too. This ranges from words we might say when we are trying to hustle them out the door ("You're so lazy—get a move on!") to insults overheard from older siblings and parents.

John Gottman's research shows that insulting behavior deeply impacts relationships. Gottman, a psychologist and national expert on family relationships, says divorce can be predicted for couples who routinely insult each other. When kids listen to parents using insults, they fall into this pattern, too. Children's TV is also full of insults. A study by psychologist Cynthia Scheibe found that nearly every children's show contained insults, even educational shows, and most insults were rewarded by canned laughter.

Try This—Add to Your Toolbox

It can get intimidating for adults when kids speak harshly to each other. Remember, they're still young kids; they're not monsters. Kids are looking for direction from us on how to behave and how to stop.

Point Out the Pain

It may seem obvious to you that being called "fat," "stupid," or "weirdo" might hurt someone's feelings, but sometimes kids need this basic information. "Saying that word could hurt her. Nobody likes to be called names. It hurts people's feelings." Speak up when you see kids hurting each other, even if it's accidental. When things go wrong between friends remind a child: "You can be mad at Jackie, but you can't hurt her. Saying things like that can hurt her feelings." Sometimes a child will stop just because she doesn't intend to hurt anybody. Other times there is real conflict, and you'll have to go deeper.

It's not unkind to tell people how you feel. "When you say _____ to me, it makes me feel _____." Also acknowledge hurt feelings. Just as you might say to a child with a skinned knee, "Ouch! I bet that hurt!" it helps to acknowledge how bad a put-down feels. You can say simply, "Ouch! I bet that hurt your feelings." Or "Gosh, I know it can feel really bad when someone says something like that. How do you feel about it?"

Allow the Word, Not the Hurt

If it's nothing deeper than the thrill of saying the word *dummy*, then treat the insult as a bad word and relegate it to another location. Example: "You can say *dummy* all you want, but not here where people can hear you. Saying *dummy* can hurt people's feelings. Go to your room and say it as much as you want." If two kids are giggling and having fun calling each other "spaghetti brain" and "weirdo head," treat it like a verbal wrestling game. "Is this still fun for both of you? Because I know those words can hurt."

> We stop a child when she
> hits someone in the face.
> We need to stop a child when she
> hurts someone in the heart.

Be Specific

"You're mean!" "That's not nice." "She's so mean. I never want to be her friend again." Vague words such as *mean* and *not nice* only give one piece of information: Somebody's upset. Help kids get specific. "What is she doing that you don't like?" "What is it about Stella that worries you?" In the preceding story, Zoe was able to set limits on Kate's "mean" behavior because she got specific: Don't jump on me and don't make mad faces. Setting limits means getting specific.

Help kids translate if they get stuck:

"Claire's mean."

"What's Claire doing that you don't like?"

"I don't know. She's just mean."

"I wonder if she's mean with her body, pushing you or pulling your clothes."

"No, it's not that. She always says mean things about my pictures. . . ."

Help All Sides

When words fly, many people can get involved. Pay attention to the speaker, the target, and the onlookers. Everyone plays a role in the hurt.

Help the speaker. Ask, "What are you worried about?" Find out what's going on. Is the child mad, hungry, tired, or scared? Is she modeling behavior she's seen? Trying out power? Does someone else have the best princess dress? Is she worried about keeping a friend or making her do what she wants her to do in a game?

Help the target. Of course, the "victim" may be a participant in the mayhem, but often one child is the main target. Ask her, "Do you like it when she calls you that? How does it make you feel?" First help her understand her feelings. Then help her take steps to feel powerful again. Ask her, "How can you feel strong?"

Help the onlookers. Kids who watch a friend get insulted (or watch a friend insult someone) often feel stuck and confused. They may feel guilty or mad and don't know what to do. These kids need attention, too. Ask them, "What can you do to help your friend?" Kids can learn to be kind to each other in group situations. The onlooker role is particularly important because bullying often stops when the group doesn't allow it.

All children need to feel safe and strong. Use the question "How can you feel strong?" with all sides, and show them what steps they can take to express their feelings appropriately.

Sorting Out Verbal Conflict

1. Take it seriously.

Hurt feelings matter. Both physical and verbal conflict need to be sorted out.

2. Focus on feelings.

Behind the mean words there are strong feelings on both sides. Pay attention to the feelings of the speaker and the victim.

3. Point out the hurt.

Young kids still have a lot to learn. Let them know these words can hurt. Ask the insulted child, "Did you like being called a baby [idiot, etc.]?"

Tell the other child, "That hurt her feelings. Saying words can hurt."

4. Give information.

Let kids know it's OK to feel mad, scared, or jealous, but it's not OK to hurt someone. Point out what *is* acceptable. "You can tell Sarah what you don't like. You can show us how mad you feel by jumping on this bubble wrap. . . ."

5. Be specific.

Get beyond vague words such as *mean*. Help kids get specific about what's really wrong. That's the first step toward finding a solution.

6. Set clear limits.

Help kids set limits on each other. Get a clear statement so each child feels safe and knows what the boundaries are. "My name is Grace. That's what I want to be called." "I won't call you stupid."

7. Show kids how to stop.

Teach them how to stop a teasing match from escalating. Show them how to stop talking and move away.

8. Help all sides.

"How can you feel strong?" Help everyone feel strong and gain new skills: the speaker, the target, and any onlookers. All the kids are learning.

Be Patient

You may have told your child multiple times that it's "not OK to hurt feelings," yet she still hurls insults at her sister. Young kids don't have well-developed impulse control. They *know* they shouldn't hit, they *know* they're not supposed to take candy from the jar, they may *know* they shouldn't call names, but still young kids can't always stop themselves. Keep repeating and modeling the message.

Words to Say

People are not for hurting. Not their bodies and not their
feelings.
When you call him "dummy" you hurt his feelings.
Is there something you're worried about?
What is she going to do that you don't like?
You look mad/scared.
Sounds as if you're mad.

I heard him call you a _____. Did you want to be called
that?
Tell her. I'll help you.
What do you want to be called?
Her name is Samantha and that's what she wants to
be called.
I can't let you keep hurting Samantha, and I won't let
anyone hurt you.
Can you stop saying those words?

Name-calling hurts people's feelings.
Nobody likes to be called names. It hurts.
I know some kids say that when they're mad.
I bet that hurt your feelings.

You didn't like those words.
Ouch. It's no fun when that happens.

How can you be strong?
What can you do?
I can help you talk to him.
What can you do to help your friend when that happens?
Is this fun for both of you?
Do you like this? Or do you want to get out?
Sounds as if you know the rules.

Words to Avoid

Don't say that word.
We don't call people dummies.
That's not nice. Say you're sorry!
He's just teasing. Don't worry about it.
Of course you're still friends. Anna's still coming to your
    birthday party.

I don't care what he said. You're in time-out.
I don't want to hear another word.
Quit acting like a baby!
That driver's an idiot.

Your Take

Most parents don't tolerate verbal put-downs, but not everyone goes
deeper. You may find the other parent says, "That's not nice. I won't
let you call Samantha names." If you can, add on to the prohibition.
Encourage kids to stick up for themselves and say what they like and
don't like. Add specifics and name the underlying emotions.

When you overhear rude comments at the store or walking down the sidewalk, it's fine to point out the emotions you witness and remind kids it hurts people. "Sounds as if that man was mad." "Looks as if they were having an argument. Grown-ups don't always agree with their friends, either."

RULE
19

Give Whiners
R-E-S-P-E-C-T

My first child was not a whiner, so I didn't understand why parenting polls show that whining is rated the Top Annoying Habit to aggravate adults. Boy, now I do.

Whining grates on the nerves and wears us down. With constant bellyaching squeals of "Moommmmy! Daaaaad," "I don't waaaaannnt to," or whatever the plea of the moment might be, whining has a peculiar way of deranging our brains. When the verbal bombardment starts we don't respond with optimal parenting skills. We just want the dreadful noise to stop.

Whining kids are actually trying hard to communicate. Don't close your ears.

Renegade Reason ||||||||||||||||||||||||||||||||||||||||||||||||||||||||||||||||||||||

Young kids don't understand what whining is, so they don't know how to stop. Listen to their emotions.

|||||||||||||||||||||||||||||||||||||||||||||||||||||||||||||||||||||||||||||||||||||||||||||||||

There is no cure-all for whiners, but there are tools that work. What *doesn't* work is to tell a child: "Stop whining!" Chances are, your child has no idea what you're talking about.

My voice must have whined as a kid, but I was never aware of it. I *do* clearly remember my dad ordering me to "Stop whining!" in an exasperated voice. Whenever he said it, I felt confused and misunderstood. I wasn't "whining" (whatever that was); I was just trying to talk to him about something very important to me. The more important and desperate my message, the more he heard a whine.

Renegade Blessings

When children feel listened to, your entire relationship blossoms. Kids can learn:

When I want my mom or dad's attention, I know what
  to do.
I know effective ways to ask for things.
My parents care about what I have to say. They help me
  express myself when I'm having trouble.

Why It Works

Sometimes I tried to wait out Zach when he whined. I wasn't in the mood to deal with it, so I tried to block out the infernal noise.

This always backfired.

Kids love repetition, and stubbornness is one of the few tools they know they've got. The longer I ignored Zach, the higher his pitch climbed. Psychologist Rene Hackney and many other child development specialists agree: The longer you let your child complain, the more determined she'll become.

Kids who whine have a message to share that needs translation. Laura Davis and Janis Keyser refer to it as "needing subtitles." It would be handy if our kids' cries came with subtitles (*I need a nap. I want to sit on your lap. You're not paying enough attention to me. I'm wor-*

ried about the new babysitter.). They say one of the best ways to put an end to whining is to pause, slow down, and be together with your child. A Swedish proverb says: "Love me when I least deserve it, because that's when I really need it."

Take Off Your Adult Lenses

Whining is annoying, but kids do it to communicate important messages and strong feelings. They don't do it to annoy. Take time to see the true message hiding beneath the whine. Often it's a call for attention. Sometimes whiners get caught in patterns of whining—break the emotional tension and help them out.

The Squeaky Voice

Don't give in; simply strive to understand. The crux of the matter is that your child badly wants to communicate and you can't concentrate on his message because of the excruciating way it's delivered. Enter the "Squeaky Voice." Tell him you're trying to listen, you *want* to understand, but he needs to use his regular voice. My mother and her fellow teachers tell kids all the time: "I can't understand you. You're using a squeaky voice. Tell me again using your regular voice."

It certainly reduced my aggravation when I remembered the squeaky voice. Zach wasn't whining; he was telling me something in a high-pitched, squeaky voice. You can even demonstrate what a whine sounds like to your child—though don't use this trick too often, or it loses its power.

Escape the Whine Trap

Whines are emotionally charged. Kids may whine from frustration, tiredness, or lack of attention, but the edge in their voice is an emotional call. Underneath, they might be feeling misunderstood, unloved, or ignored. When kids whine at you, they are directing this emotion at you, too.

Just like with any emotional issue, focus on the feeling beneath the behavior. Stop and validate the emotion. "You want another cookie now. It's so hard to wait until after supper." See if you can figure out what the underlying emotion is. Give it voice.

Focus on the feeling beneath the behavior.

Sometimes kids get locked into a whine trap with us. If you're stuck in a whine trap, it can help to bring in a new person. Deflect the emotion that's bogging down your child's message. Change parents, or bring in a new adult or older sibling. This alters the whine dynamic. Say: "Jason wants to tell me something, but it's hard for me to understand. Jason, can you tell Nana?" Often the child will speak clearly, amazingly politely, just by changing people. If there's no extra person around, don't worry. Borrow one of his teddy bears or other toys and jump into an imaginary conversation. "Hi Jason, what's wrong? You really want to tell your mom something. What is it?" A child like Jason can tell Brown Bear everything in a well-pitched, conversational voice. There's no emotional tension between the bear and the child. With the tension broken, you and your child can get back to talking directly again—with no whines.

Another time when deflecting the emotion works well is when two kids are in a tiff together. One child invariably whines: "Mooomm! He took my Legos again. He's always getting into my stuff!"

You can easily hear the grinding tone here: complaint mode. Many kids drop into an automatic whine when they complain about something. Change the habit by changing the complaint into dialogue using conflict resolution. Don't let kids complain to you. Step out of it. Say: "Tell Jacob what you don't like. Tell him what your rules are about your Legos." Whenever Myles whines to me in complaint, I ask him to face Zach himself and talk it out. Immediately, the pitch of his voice alters. No longer whining, he speaks carefully, in a measured voice. He's entered diplomatic relations with Zach, and somehow he understands that it's better to be calm and polite to get his message across. Time and again, I hear Myles pause, take a deep breath, and say, "Zach . . ." The whine is gone.

Older Whiners

Whining is most common in the preschool years, and some ideas—such as dialogue with teddy bears—work best at these ages. If your older child continues to use whining to get attention and emotional needs met, you may need to alter your tactics. Instead of signaling an intense emotional need, whining may have become a habit. A child of seven can typically tell the difference between a whiny voice and a regular one. It's not such a mystery. If your child is still whining at older ages, watch your own reactions. You may be giving in or encouraging whiny behavior. Then set clear limits—both on yourself and on your child—about what you expect and what you will respond to. Still, no matter what their age, tired, stressed kids may descend into whines from time to time. When they do, bypass the whine and go directly to the feelings inside.

Tips to Combat Whining

1. Remember food and rest.
   Often whining spikes when kids are tired, overwhelmed, or hungry. You may know this, but still lash out at your child for whining, even though *you* were the one who made him skip his nap.

2. Stop and slow down.

Whining also crops up when kids feel ignored, unnoticed, or misunderstood. Slow down. Stop and give your child some full attention. You're probably moving at a pace he can't tolerate. Maybe it's your phone? (See Rule 6: Discipline Your Phone.)

3. Talk to her—don't tune her out.

No matter how disagreeable, whining is about communication. Ignoring her only makes it worse, since your child badly wants to tell you something. Listen.

4. Ask for a regular voice.

Tell her you can't understand her squeaky voice. Ask her to try again using her regular voice. Reinforce that you really want to hear what she's saying.

5. Rephrase it.

Ask her to try again. Give her exact words to say ("Milk, please, Mama!") and demonstrate by putting a pleasant pitch to your voice.

6. Respond to the feeling.

Once you know what the matter is (a cookie, hard to wait to go outside), empathize with his feelings: "You don't want to wait." "You really want to go out now!" Simply having feelings acknowledged meets many of the child's needs.

7. Deflect the emotion—change the person.

Change people on him. If he's whining at you, bring in grandma and say, "Tell Nana what's wrong." Or grab his teddy bear and have him talk to the bear. Adding a new person changes the emotional dynamics. Often his whine will drop and his voice will moderate to a conciliatory pitch when explaining things to a new person or a toy.

8. Don't give in and reward whines.

If you buy a toy in the checkout line when your child whines for one, you are promoting whining. Kids will repeat whining if it works. Before you pour your whiner milk, or give her an extra cookie, make sure she's dropped the whine first.

Try This—Add to Your Toolbox

Kids will repeat what works. The key is to meet their needs without rewarding the whiny behavior.

Words to Say

> You're speaking in a squeaky voice. When you speak in a
>   squeaky voice I can't understand you.
> Can you say that in your regular voice?
> Your voice sounds like this: "eeee eeeee!" I can't
>   understand you.
> Gosh! I really want to understand what you're saying. Tell
>   me again.
> It's hard to hear your words when you're talking and crying
>   at the same time.
> Slow down.
>
> Sounds as if it's hard for you to wait.
> Sounds as if you have some strong feelings about that.
> Sounds as if that's really important to you.
> You're still feeling ___.
>
> Tell Brown Bear (Grandpa, Aunt Susie) what's wrong.
> Tell Emily what you don't like.
> Try again. Say: "Milk, please, Mama!"
> I'm glad to get you milk now. You asked just the right way.
> If you want me to listen, say: "Daddy, I need to talk to you."

Words to Avoid

Quit your whining!
Stop whining.
Don't use that baby voice!
Look, I told you already you can't have another cookie.
If you can't stop your grousing, you won't get anything.
Oh, all right. Here you go.

Your Take

When whines ratchet up in a public setting (candy at the checkout) it can be tempting to give in. We get embarrassed to be seen as the parent of such a whiny child. *Am I a bad parent? Why is no one else's child kicking up a fuss, only mine?* When it comes to whining, almost every parent has been in the same spot, so ignore your inner critic. Stick with what you know you should do and don't buy the candy bar. Validate her emotions ("You really want that. You wish you had that chocolate bar.") and repeat your firm answer ("We don't buy candy at the checkout." You might try using humor to stop a whine, especially out in public. "I wish we could eat candy bars for breakfast every day, don't you? I wish we could make a mountain out of candy bars . . . yum!" Then skedaddle home, where you can give your child the food, rest, and attention she needs.

Section VII

RENEGADE RULES IN THE REAL WORLD

Man's mind, once stretched by a new idea, never regains its original dimensions.

—OLIVER WENDELL HOLMES JR.

RULE
20

Families Are Not Entertainment Centers

I know free play is great," said one mother, "but I don't know what to do with my daughter. We're always going on outings because I don't know what else to do. One day I thought, *We'll try this play thing*, so I planned a free morning at home. Rachel didn't start playing. She just stood there in the middle of the room and looked at me. 'Where are we going, Mama? What are we going to do?' she said. So we went out."

Transitioning to playtime isn't always easy. For some families, play is second nature. For those who want to make a change, it can be hard to know how to begin.

Take heart. The transition to playtime is worth it. Your child will be learning at her highest level, and you will find more time in your day for *you*.

Renegade Reason ||||||||||||||||||||||||||||||||||||||||||||||||||||||||||||||||||||||||||||||||||||

Kids are not on earth to be entertained. They can entertain themselves. If your family's caught in the entertainment net, it's time to untangle it and transition to adult time and playtime.

When my first book came out, I was asked to write a guest blog piece about "entertaining the kids" for the summer. This was tricky, since I don't believe families are meant to entertain kids.

As soon as children are born, it's easy to fall into the role of Chief Entertainer. We think we must play with them. We think we must stimulate them. We think we must keep them happy at all times. So we play endless games of peekaboo, stack the blocks, and role-playing games we have no stomach for. We quiz them on their colors. We set them up with another video. Entertainment means outside ideas imposed on kids. It also tends to mean prescribed or prepackaged fun.

Respect a child's inner life enough to slow down. Constant entertainment means children have no time for thoughts of their own.

There are two issues here. One is helping kids transition to more open-ended free-play time. Although kids are wired to play, children who are accustomed to adult-led activities, outings, and media entertainment will need a period of transition to uncover their own play potential. The other issue is harder, especially for many parents who tend toward self-sacrifice rather than limit setting: establishing adult time as a parent.

Renegade Blessings ||||||||||||||||||||||||||||||||||||||||||||||||||||||||||||||||||||||||||||||

When your child learns to play on his own, you both gain wonderful blessings. As an adult, you reclaim adult time, a healthier relationship with your partner, and time to get things done.

YOUR CHILD LEARNS:

I'm an important part of this family. So is everyone else.

Sometimes I'm not the center of attention.

I can do a lot of things on my own. If I *really* need my
mom, she's here.

I have neat ideas.

I know the rules.

Adults need time by themselves. When I'm grown up, I'll
need that, too.

AND FOR YOU:

I enjoy my time more.

I get more done. My life is less pressured.

My child won't grow up too self-centered.

My relationship with my partner is healthier.

I still have a life. A different one, but it's liberating to have
balance.

Why It Works

A survey of one thousand parents in England conducted in 2014
found 80 percent of parents of young children felt a need to make
sure their children were always entertained. Not only that, but parents were worried they weren't doing more to stimulate their children. Back in the U.S., this resonates with many families. Author
Jennifer Senior described the situation in her book, *All Joy and No
Fun*. She showed how parents carry a host of expectations with them
into parenthood. Chief among them: They must play with their
young children. Over and over again.

Playing alone contentedly is a valuable skill for every child.

Twenty percent of U.S. children are only children, and many kids with siblings find themselves with time on their own also. David Whitebread, an early-childhood psychologist at Cambridge University, says children's emotional well-being and thinking skills are both enhanced by playing and following their own ideas. "Children often have purpose in their play when left alone," he says. It's fine for adults to play and interact with their children, but this type of play shouldn't dominate. Child-led play should take up the bulk of play each day.

Kids typically have highly scheduled lives, even by the early age of three. Nancy Darling, a psychologist and author of the blog *Thinking About Kids*, says children can become passive and not know how to rely on themselves when they are not given the chance to experience boredom.

"Have no fear of boredom," says Janet Lansbury, author and early-childhood educator. "Whatever children choose to do (or not do) will be 'enough.'" There's great value in playing alone. Even if the activity seems odd to us—flipping a lid back and forth, for example—it could be meeting the child's needs best at that moment. When kids are left to their own devices they get creative and play. Free play enhances imagination, problem solving, and persistence.

Overstimulation, on the other hand, tires them out. Children quickly lose interest in adult attempts to entertain them, and at the same time, they lose their own capacity to focus and follow their own interests. It may look as if children aren't "doing anything," but instead of jumping in, adults need to trust the growing process. Sometimes that means hearing the silent cry: "Leave me alone." "If you don't have a capacity for solitude you will always be lonely," says psychologist Sherry Turkle.

When adults play with children all day, it bores most adults and doesn't meet children's needs the best. You don't have to interact with, stimulate, and try to entertain your child for hours on end. That's a sure recipe for your brain to go mushy and your child to zone out. Children need us to be parents, not entertainers.

Take Off Your Adult Lenses

It's easy to worry about our children being bored. They'll make a mess if they're not kept busy. They'll bug us. They'll be deprived of enriching experiences. Many of us work hard to prevent it—we keep them busy precisely so we don't hear plaintive complaints: "Dad, I'm borrrred!" In a fast-paced modern culture, it can be hard to remember that children don't need constant stimulation. The most precious thing is what's inside each child. At times, "boredom" is one of the ingredients children need to discover their own ideas.

Families Aren't Entertainment Centers

It can help if you think about parenting outside of modern middle-class industrialized countries. How did women in the 1800s get all their chores done with babies and young kids in the house? How do others do it today? The first step is realizing that parents playing with children and entertaining them nearly full time is not a long human tradition. Most families have never lived that way. It's natural for families to interact, but interaction is not the same as entertainment. You can step out of this role.

Take confidence that this is what children are meant to do. It may take some transition time if you've trained your family to expect constant diversion and attention, but have faith in age-old skills: All children can play.

Try This—Add to Your Toolbox

When my two kids fall into a spontaneous game of make-believe, my job is to stay out of the way and offer supplies such as cardboard when needed. It may take some time before this scenario becomes common in your house. Take little steps as you transition.

Giving children the gift of free time may be the best gift you can give them. The ideas kids pursue when left to their own devices are typically the ones that most fascinate and inspire them. Other times, their play is simple, but restful. Don't worry if your child chooses to stare at patterns on the sofa or trace lines in floorboards. Life is stimulating enough. Kids need downtime and thoughtful times in their play, too.

Transitioning to Free Play

1. Announce the Change
   If free play is a big change for your family, say so. Talk about it with your kids and let them know you'll be making more free time for playing now. "We've been going places a lot, but now we'll mainly be home or playing at the park."

2. Offer Naturally Exciting Objects
   Rhonda wanted to encourage free play for her six grandchildren. When it came time for holiday gifts, she gave each family props to use for creative play: a folding card table and big blankets. "I wanted the kids to make blanket forts and houses," she said. "Kids love to be inside tiny spaces."

   Children engage the most with open-ended toys. These are objects that can turn into multiple props for play. You know the ones—the stick your son plays with instead of the brand-new birthday present, or a blanket.

   Here are some tried-and-true ingredients that naturally stimulate play:

   - Blankets and a card table for making tents, forts, and houses

- Big cardboard boxes
- Sand
- Water, stones, pine cones, sticks
- Rain boots
- Sturdy metal shovels
- Darkness—going outside in the dark, or playing in a dark space
- Marbles
- Lots of dominoes (or blocks)
- Wheeled toys plus a board for a ramp
- Capes, funny hats, other dress-ups
- Little figurines with movable parts
- Recycling items and tape

If you're struggling with how to get started, get some of these supplies. An empty cardboard box in the middle of a room is like a magnet for kids.

3. Reduce Your Role

When you play together, take a smaller role. "OK, so we're going to be pirates. What do pirates do? Where should I go?" Let your child direct you. Once most of the ideas are coming from your child, you should be able to step out more easily since she is not relying on you to keep the story going.

4. Co-Play Nearby at First

You may have to separate gradually. New habits take a while to establish. If the goal is to help your entertained child learn to play independently, try playing in parallel for a time. If your child is making something from play-dough, you can make something, too. If your child wants to be active, maybe you can be active in the yard. This co-play keeps you nearby, and gives your child reassurance. As she becomes used to this new way of doing things, your actions can diverge. You can garden while she builds a cardboard castle.

5. Help Everyone Feel Safe

Part of helping children unhook from your attention is allowing them to feel safe. Decide what you're going to do (read a book in the den, drink your coffee by yourself, work in the kitchen) and then tell your child: "I'm taking some quiet time on the porch now," or "If you need to find me, I'll be cooking in the kitchen." If you seem unsure about leaving your child alone, your child will pick that up and feel unsure and unsafe, too.

6. Notice the Environment and Make a List

Make suggestions by stating observations. "I see a box of trains." Or "There's clay in the cupboard." Brainstorm a list with your child. Write down what types of toys and play ideas she comes up with. The list can be in words and in pictures. She can refer to this list other days when she's stuck and doesn't know what to do. With time, she may not need a list to guide her.

7. Transition with a Timer

To help your child build up confidence and practice in independent play, try setting a timer for ten minutes. "Time for us to play together, then time for you to play by yourself and let Dad work." Gradually shift the balance toward more independent playtime.

8. Don't Be Afraid of "I'm Bored"

Trust your child. Say: "I know you'll find something to do when you're ready." Be patient and wait. Don't give in. She may not be used to it, but eventually she'll find some-

thing to do. Even if the "something" turns out to be gazing at ceiling cracks, that's OK. It's OK if she doesn't seem
to be doing anything at all. Times of nothingness and
quiet may be what she needs most to think, daydream, or
process a difficult day. "I'm bored" shouldn't become an
adult's problem. If a child is longing for attention, tell him
when you can be with him ("I can read you a book after
lunch"), then remind him, "It's OK to be bored."

9. Go on Open-ended Outings
   Find the local woods or an undeveloped park. Sticks,
   leaves, pebbles, sand, and water are guaranteed to open up
   free-play ideas.

10. Invite a Playmate
    Some kids bloom when a friend's around. Invite a friend
    over and your child often rediscovers the joy in his own
    toys. This also happens with babysitters, especially teen-
    agers who jump into play. Outside friends and sitters may
    introduce play ideas that carry on for your child after the
    visitor has gone home.

As your family gains joy and confidence in unstructured time
and child-led play, you may rely on this list less and less. The ultimate step is trust.

Reclaim Adult Time

Being a good parent does not mean being available all the time. Kids
can be demanding, but they also thrive when they understand house
rules for adult time. Establish times that are sacred for you. Mix this in
with time when you are engaged with your own tasks and kids are
playing on their own. Be around, not constantly at their beck and call.

1. Institute Quiet Time

   Designate a Quiet Time for your family. Typically this works best after lunch during the traditional nap time. Your child's body is ready to slow down, and you can schedule Quiet Time to coincide with nap time for younger siblings. During Quiet Time each child has to play quietly in her room or read on her bed (reading can mean looking at picture books). No questions or talking to you. Let your child know she can only summon you for emergencies (my nose is bleeding, the house is on fire, I threw up). Children preschool-aged and older can do Quiet Time of about an hour.

2. Offer Special Time—Not All Your Time

   Give each child exclusive, Special Time. Maybe it's once a day, or maybe a few times a week. During this time your phone is off, your other children are not intruding, and your full attention is devoted to one child at a time. Bonding with Special Time deepens your relationship more than hours of half attention: "Just let me check my e-mail. Yes, I'm coming. I hear you! Just a minute." (See Rule 6: Discipline Your Phone.)

   Special Time might be only twenty minutes. It will depend on your style, your work schedule, and the age of your child. Set parameters for Special Time, such as playing at home or in the yard (not watching screens or going places). Then let your child choose what to do and how to play. This combination of attention and control is a balm for children. Special Time, plus regular parent-child rituals such as bedtime and story time, give you both the regular dose of pure togetherness you need.

3. Stop Saying, "OK?"

   "We're going to the park, OK?" "I'm going to do something by myself for a few minutes, OK?" Few children in their right mind will reply, "OK." They want you; they want control. If you already know what you plan to do, don't ask permission. The dangling "OK?" tells the child he's in charge of you and the day's schedule. We say it to be nice, or possibly out of habit, but "OK?" sends the wrong message and deprives adults of their rightful role. Tell kids what's going to happen and help them deal with mad or frustrated emotions if they have any. Then do what you said you were going to do.

4. Trust

Jared couldn't say no when his three-year-old son asked to play with him. He agreed every time his child asked, no matter how rotten the timing was. "My own dad never played with me," said Jared. "I wanted to so much, but he was tired after work and turned me down. I remember that and feel terribly guilty when I say no." If you spend time with your child regularly, it's OK to say no to her request to play. True play is when both partners want to participate. Trust your child will still love you even if you say no right now. If you have time but don't want to play actively, then watch your child play. That attention can feel almost better to a child because she gets to direct the play ideas herself.

5. Start the Morning Ready

Decide when you are realistically "on duty" in the morning. Do you tend to your offspring the moment the first child peeps?

I love to see my kids, but not before six thirty. If they get up earlier, it's understood they can play quietly on their own. How do you do that when kids are too young to tell time? With a nightlight on a timer. This "morning light" comes on automatically in each child's bedroom. Children as young as one or two can grasp the concept. *I can wake up early, but I can't call for Mama or Papa until the morning light comes on.* Before I'm officially on duty, sometimes I sleep, or sometimes I'm up at dawn typing away at a book. In either case, it's "Mama time." Talking's OK, but not talking to me. I'm unavailable. When official morning time comes, I'm fully theirs and greet my kids with loving hugs.

As children reach elementary school, they don't need the cue of the morning light any longer. They have internalized that early morning is a time of quiet independence.

6. Reclaim Your Evening

Adults need adult space in the evening, at least some of it. This makes you a better parent the next day, rejuvenates you, and establishes adult relationships as important.

"I wish I'd focused more of my energy on my relationship with my husband," said Jennifer, a mother of teens. "I poured energy into my kids, but now that I'm on the other end of parenting, I realize that was a mistake." Kids need to realize the relationship between partners is central to the family. Watching you is the main way they understand what a marriage or parenting partnership is, and they will likely carry these unspoken expectations into their own future relationships. They also need to see that adults need adult time, whether you are single parenting or not. Show them these values.

7. Sleep

You know who you are.

"I didn't sleep a whole night for eight years," said one mother. "I haven't had enough sleep since Tyler was born.

He's six now," said another father. Modern parenting seems to be an experiment in who can lose the most sleep for the longest period of years.

Occasional sleep loss is part of parenting. At times we are called on active night duty, for sickness, nightmares, or nighttime potty learning. Regular sleep interruption is a choice. That's a hard truth to face, but once you decide it's truly bothering you, you're suddenly free to consult the many sleep resources out there.

Don't entertain your child on the night shift.

Words to Say

I know you'll find something to do when you're ready.

It's OK to feel bored sometimes.

I'll be on the porch.

I know you're mad. You really want to play with me now.

I'll read to you after lunch. Right now I'm cooking.

Right now I'm doing something. I'll come see you when I've finished.

Now I can come watch.

During Quiet Time you stay on your bed.

You don't have to sleep; just stay in your room.

You can read. You can play with something quietly.

I'm talking to Dad now. This is our time together.

Time to play outside.

Words to Avoid

I'll put something on while I'm busy. What do you want to watch?

We're going to the park, OK?

You're bored? What do you want to do? Do you want to go someplace?

Of course I will. I'll always play with you.

Your Take

Children are skilled at getting attention from the people around them. When we set limits we give kids the chance to feel the power of their own resources. This is a type of risk that's easy to incorporate into your home (see Rule 1: Safety Second).

The time to make a change is when something is bothering you. Maybe you'll decide that one Quiet Time after lunch is what's right for your family, or given the ages of your kids, a morning wake-up time is not a good fit for you until next year. What's right for your family could be dropping scheduled music or sports for children under seven. We all need time to be at peace. Take a step toward transitioning to free time and you will open up your day and your child's mind.

RULE
21 Relax

There's no one right way to raise a child. There's no one right way to educate a child. There are many right ways.

Renegade Reason

Don't try to do it all. Pick what's right for your family.

If the idea of tackling all these topics overwhelms you, relax. There's no need to feel you have to do it all. No one can. Find the style of renegade parenting that fits you and your child. Some ideas may grow on you. Other sections you may never like. As Walt Whitman says: "Reexamine all you have been told at school or church or in any book, dismiss whatever insults your soul."

Be kind to yourself. Not all of us are activists. Not all of us are good with words. You can be an advocate for your child in your own way. Look for the most urgent stress points in your family or classroom. Focus on relieving stress there. Make these your priorities, and take steps to restore balance as best you can. When we all do the best we can, as often as we can, it will be enough.

If you don't like certain policies or habits, but don't have time or energy to make meaningful change right now, acknowledge that and let it go. Do what you can instead: Begin the conversation. Share your ideas. Share research. Try alternatives. Listen to your partners.

May you and your children have confidence to go up the slide.

Appendix

Sample Letters

Recess Preventive Letter

Dear [teacher's name]:

We feel strongly that recess is an essential part of the school day for optimal learning. The American Academy of Pediatrics recommends that no child should be deprived of recess time for any reason (behavior, missing classwork, or any other). If you need to discipline [child's name], please do so in a way that does not compromise recess. We're happy to discuss this more with you at any time that's convenient. We'd like to do whatever we can to support you in the classroom.

Thank you for all you do for the children.

Best wishes,

Recess Advocacy Letter

(for principal or school board)

Dear [principal's name]:

As you know, recess is an essential part of the school day—not just for fun and blowing off steam, but for improved test scores, behavior, and overall academic learning. [School name] currently offers one fifteen-minute recess per day. Researchers are finding this is not enough recess time for optimal learning. Here's what recess can do:

Recess improves classroom behavior.
It helps kids academically.
It sharpens kids' executive function abilities including: attention, memory, learning, creativity, and problem solving.
More recess boosts test scores.
More recess helps kids with ADHD focus better and be less disruptive in the classroom.
The American Academy of Pediatrics (AAP) considers recess essential for all elementary-aged students.
The AAP also recommends that no child should be deprived of recess for any reason (behavior or school work).
Recess experts recommend two or three recess periods a day for all elementary grades.

As other school districts recognize this growing body of research, recess is being reinstated and expanded around the country. I would like to see students in [school name] at the leading edge of educational success. To do this, let's work together to explore expanding recess for K–6 students and create a recess policy that protects recess time for all elementary-aged children.

Enclosed is a sampling of articles and research that may be helpful to you. I'd be happy to meet to discuss your ideas and concerns regarding recess for [school name].

Thank you, on behalf of our children.

Sincerely,

No-Homework Letters

(Sample letter our family sent)

Dear [teacher's name]:

Can we talk? We'd like to support you in the classroom, and at this early stage I don't know your views on homework, but . . .

I don't believe in homework for children ages ten and under. A comprehensive review of research on homework backs this up and surprisingly shows there's no benefit to kids doing homework in elementary school. Homework becomes important in high school, with a year or two of "practice" homework in middle school. I know that's not how most of American education works right now.

As a parent, perhaps you understand. There is such a short amount of time in every day. School learning takes up most of the day, and when school is out kids need space and time for other things.

My son gets home around four p.m. He gets into pajamas around eight p.m. In those short four hours, he:

Has an after-school snack, talks, and unwinds from his day
Plays/pursues his own interests
Goes outside and climbs in tree forts
Giggles with his brother
Does family chores

Practices piano
Has a family supper
Reads his own book and listens to a bedtime story

These are all important uses of his time. My view is homework interrupts home learning. Homework tends to give school and learning a bad name and when it's given too young, kids learn to resent it instead of value it.

The only type of "homework" I value at this age is reading at home. In our family we already do this every day.

I realize this is not the prevailing view in education right now, and perhaps it flies in the face of the school's policies or your own ideas. Can we talk? I'd like to find something that's comfortable for everyone and make sure your goals are supported as well as ours.

Sincerely,

(Examples of letters sent by families)

Dear [teacher's name]:

I just wanted to touch base regarding homework.

*Please know that we support you and want to support your classroom routines. Our parenting philosophy on homework is _____.
We think unstructured time to play outside and to play at home is also valuable. This doesn't mean we don't talk about school or work with her in other ways educationally. She does her reading every night and we do discuss her vocabulary words throughout the week.*

Thank you,

Dear [teacher's name]:

If you have a few minutes in the next few days, could we talk about homework? I was a bit surprised at the amount Jo brought home yesterday. I really want to make school a positive experience and so would like to discuss options. Thanks.

Dear [teacher's name]:

I trust [child's name] to handle her own practice time [or reading time, spelling list, etc.]. Please know there's no need for my signature. I'm free to talk more anytime. Thank you.

Resources

Risk

Almon, Joan. *Adventure: The Value of Risk in Children's Play.* CreateSpace, 2013. See more at allianceforchildhood.org.

Mogel, Wendy. *The Blessing of a Skinned Knee.* New York: Simon & Schuster, 2001.

Schiller, Abbie, and Samantha Kurtzman-Counter. *Miles Is the Boss of His Body.* Los Angeles: Ruby's Studio, 2014.

Skenazy, Lenore. *Free-Range Kids.* San Francisco: Jossey-Bass, 2010. Also see the *Free-Range Kids* blog.

Tulley, Gever, and Julie Spiegler. *50 Dangerous Things (You Should Let Your Children Do).* New York: NAL Trade, 2011. Also see Gever Tulley's TED talks at www.ted.com/speakers/gever_tulley.

Technology

Bilton, Nick. "Steve Jobs Was a Low-Tech Parent." *New York Times*, September 10, 2014.

Carr, Nicholas. *The Shallows: What the Internet Is Doing to Our Brains.* New York: Norton, 2010.

Granic, Isabela, Adam Lobel, and Rutger C. M. E. Engels. "The Benefits of Playing Video Games." *American Psychologist* 69, no. 1 (2013): 66–78.

Gray, Peter. "The Many Benefits, for Kids, of Playing Video Games." PsychologyToday.com, January 7, 2012.

Guernsey, Lisa. *Screen Time: How Electronic Media—from Baby Videos to Educational Software—Affects Your Young Child.* New York: Basic Books, 2012.

Linn, Susan, Joan Almon, and Diane Levin. *Facing the Screen Dilemma: Young Children, Technology and Early Education.* Boston: Campaign for a Commercial-Free Childhood; New York: Alliance for Childhood, 2012.

Richtel, Matt. "A Silicon Valley School That Doesn't Compute." *New York Times,* October 22, 2011.

Sax, Leonard. *Boys Adrift: The Five Factors Driving the Growing Epidemic of Unmotivated Boys and Underachieving Young Men.* New York: Basic Books, 2007.

Steiner-Adair, Catherine, and Teresa H. Barker. *The Big Disconnect: Protecting Childhood and Family Relationships in the Digital Age.* New York: Harper, 2013.

Recess

American Academy of Pediatrics. "The Crucial Role of Recess in School." *Pediatrics* 131, no. 1 (2013): 183–88.

Bailey, Melissa. "Parents Call for More Recess." *New Haven Independent,* June 19, 2013.

Dornfeld, Ann. "Recess Shrinks at Seattle Schools; Poor Schools Fare Worst." KUOW News and Information, 2014.

Gallup. *The State of Play: Gallup Survey of Principals on School Recess.* Princeton, NJ: Robert Wood Johnson Foundation, 2010.

Jarrett, Olga. "A Research-Based Case for Recess." US Play Coalition, 2013.

National Association for the Education of Young Children. "Recess—It's Indispensable!" *Young Children* 64, no. 5 (2009): 66–69.

Nussbaum, Debra. "Before Children Ask: 'What's Recess?'" *New York Times,* December 10, 2006.

Ohanian, Susan. *What Happened to Recess and Why Are Our Children Struggling in Kindergarten?* New York: McGraw-Hill, 2002.

Parker-Pope, Tara. "The 3 R's? A Fourth Is Crucial, Too: Recess." *New York Times,* February 24, 2009.

Pellegrini, Anthony. *Recess: Its Role in Education and Development.* Mahwah, NJ: Erlbaum, 2005.

U.S. Department of Education, Institute of Education Sciences, What Works Clearinghouse. "WWC Review of the Report 'Findings from a Randomized Experiment of Playworks: Selected Results from Cohort 1.'" 2013.

More Recess Resources:

International Play Association USA (IPA/USA) American Association for the Child's Right to Play: Nonprofit devoted to preserving play, leading the recess cause with a full line of resources. Its excellent Recess Support

Network includes research links, the case for recess, advocacy tools, and recess contacts state by state.

Ranger Rick Restores Recess (National Wildlife Federation–sponsored campaign): Includes tools to conduct a recess audit on your school as well as a model recess policy.

Right to Recess Campaign by Peaceful Playgrounds: Peaceful Playgrounds provides structured recess to schools but also actively promotes recess. Its many worthwhile resources include the Right to Recess Advocacy Tool Kit, with a speaker's guide, webinar, sample letters, PowerPoint presentations, and links to research.

Homework

Abeles, Vicki, and Jessica Congdon. *The Race to Nowhere.* Lafayette, CA: Reel Link Films, 2010. The Race to Nowhere website includes a homework toolkit and Healthy Homework Pledges.

Bennett, Sara, and Nancy Kalish. *The Case Against Homework: How Homework Is Hurting Children and What Parents Can Do About It.* New York: Three Rivers Press, 2006. Excellent guide to combating inappropriate homework; includes framework for changing homework policies.

Cooper, Harris, James Lindsay, Barbara Nye, and Scott Greathouse. "Relationships Among Attitudes About Homework, Amount of Homework Assigned and Completed, and Student Achievement." *Journal of Educational Psychology* 90, no. 1 (1998): 70–83.

Cooper, Harris, Jorgianne Civey Robinson, and Erika A. Patall. "Does Homework Improve Academic Achievement? A Synthesis of Research, 1987–2003." *Review of Educational Research* 76, no. 1 (2006): 1–62.

Faber, Adele, and Elaine Mazlish. *How to Talk So Kids Can Learn: At Home and in School.* New York: Scribner, 1995.

Gray, Peter. *Free to Learn: Why Unleashing the Instinct to Play Will Make Our Children Happier, More Self-Reliant and Better Students for Life.* New York: Basic Books, 2013.

Kohn, Alfie. *The Homework Myth: Why Our Kids Get Too Much of a Bad Thing.* New York: Da Capo Press, 2006. For help deciphering what research really says about homework, see chapter 4: "Studies Show . . . or Do They?"

Kralovec, Etta, and John Buell. *The End of Homework: How Homework Disrupts Families, Overburdens Children, and Limits Learning.* Boston: Beacon Press, 2000.

"Stop Homework" groups on Facebook keep up with current trends. Also see reports from nonprofit groups such as the Alliance for Childhood and Common Sense Media.

Strauss, Valerie. "Homework: An Unnecessary Evil? Surprising Findings from New Research." *Washington Post*, November 26, 2012.

Kindergarten

Beneke, Sallee, Michaelene Ostrosky, and Lilan Katz. "Calendar Time for Young Children: Good Intentions Gone Awry." *Young Children* 63, no. 3 (2008): 12–16.

Cooper, Harris, Ashley Batts Allen, Erika Patall, and Amy Dent. "Effects of Full-Day Kindergarten on Academic Achievement and Social Development." *Review of Educational Research* 80, no.1 (2010): 34–70.

Elkind, David. *Miseducation: Preschoolers at Risk*. New York: Knopf, 1989.

Gurian, Michael with Kathy Stevens. *Boys and Girls Learn Differently* (revised 10th edition). San Francisco, CA: Jossey-Bass, 2010.

Le, Vi-Nhuan, Sheila Nataraj Kirby, Heather Barney, Claude Messan Setodji, and Daniel Gershwin. "School Readiness, Full-Day Kindergarten, and Student Achievement: An Empirical Investigation." Santa Monica, CA: RAND Corporation, 2006.

Leonhardt, David. "A Link Between Fidgety Boys and a Sputtering Economy." *New York Times*, April 29, 2014.

Miller, Edward, and Joan Almon. *Crisis in the Kindergarten: Why Children Need to Play in School*. College Park, MD: Alliance for Childhood, 2009.

Orenstein, Peggy. "Kindergarten Cram." *New York Times*, May 3, 2009.

Princesses, Empathy, and Other Topics

Derman-Sparks, Louise, and Julie Olsen Edwards. *Anti-Bias Education for Young Children and Ourselves*. Washington, DC: National Association for the Education of Young Children, 2010.

Hains, Rebecca. *The Princess Problem: Guiding Our Girls Through the Princess-Obsessed Years*. Naperville, IL: Sourcebooks, 2014.

Howarth, Mary. "Rediscovering the Power of Fairy Tales: They Help Children Understand Their Lives." *Young Children* 45, no. 1 (1989): 58–65.

Orenstein, Peggy. *Cinderella Ate My Daughter: Dispatches from the Front Lines of the New Girlie-Girl Culture*. New York: Harper, 2012.

Payne, Kim John. *Simplicity Parenting: Using the Extraordinary Power of Less to Raise Calmer, Happier, and More Secure Kids*. New York: Ballantine Books, 2009.

Pelo, Ann, and Fran Davidson. *That's Not Fair! A Teacher's Guide to Activism with Young Children*. Saint Paul, MN: Redleaf Press, 2000.

Tutu, Archbishop Desmond, and Douglas Carlton Abrams. *Desmond and the Very Mean Word*. Somerville, MA: Candlewick Press, 2013.

Acknowledgments

Thanks to Sara Carder, my editor, for her ongoing support of renegade parenting ideas. Grateful thanks to the entire team of professionals at Tarcher/Penguin, including the extraordinary copy editors. Thanks also to my agent, Joëlle Delbourgo.

Heartfelt thanks to my wonderful team of test readers. Once again, you took time from your busy lives with children to offer feedback on early chapters. Thanks go to Mary Haley, Vicki Hoefle, Stephanie Krause, Jennifer Nault, Emily Plank, Jennifer Finnegan Poole, Tanya Schlam, and to the ever-loyal team of SYC review readers: Julie Ballinger, Deb Baillieul, Gudrun Herzog, Angela LaMonte, Ann Rigney, Susan Roscigno, Stephanie Rottmayer, Amy Rudawsky, and Jan Waters.

Thanks to all the SYC family who contributed ideas to the making of this book, including: Jenifer Bojanowski, Ellen Cook, Joanne Frantz, Denise Jacobs, Sejal Kothari, Lisa Marquand, Maureen Moore, Dawn Nauman, Adele Stratton, and Patti Zahara.

To my writing group, the Powerfingers: Mardi Link, Cari Noga, Anne-Marie Oomen, and Teresa Scollon, special thanks for your ever-insightful improvements. You help me get to the heart of the matter.

Renegade Awards go to Susan, Emily, and Tanya, who guided me when I had gone astray and who found time to read yet another chapter. Special thanks to Kima Kraimer for her unique support in finding this writer a quiet space to write.

Many thanks to *It's OK Not to Share* readers everywhere who sent encouragement and ideas for this new book, and thank you to the many families who shared their stories in these pages. Your willingness to share some of your most tender moments helps us all grow.

And to my own family, thank you for being by my side through another book.

Index

If you enjoyed this book, visit

www.tarcherbooks.com

and sign up for Tarcher's e-newsletter to receive
special offers, giveaway promotions, and
information on hot upcoming releases.

Great Lives Begin with Great Ideas

Connect with the Tarcher Community

· · ·

Stay in touch with favorite authors!
Enter weekly contests!
Read exclusive excerpts!
Voice your opinions!

Follow us

 Tarcher Books

 @TarcherBooks

If you would like to place a bulk order
of this book, call 1-800-847-5515.

Also from TarcherPerigee: